W.E.B. DU BOIS

**Recent Titles in
Greenwood Biographies**

W.E.B. DU BOIS

A Biography

Gerald Horne

GREENWOOD BIOGRAPHIES

GREENWOOD PRESS
An Imprint of ABC-CLIO, LLC

A B C 🌐 C L I O

Santa Barbara, California • Denver, Colorado • Oxford, England

Library of Congress Cataloging-in-Publication Data

Horne, Gerald.
   W.E.B. Du Bois : a biography / Gerald Horne.
      p. cm. — (Greenwood biographies)
   Includes bibliographical references and index.
   ISBN 978-0-313-34979-9 (hard copy : acid-free paper)—
ISBN 978-0-313-34980-5 (ebook)   1. Du Bois, W.E.B. (William Edward
Burghardt), 1868–1963.   2. African Americans—Biography.   3. African
American authors—Biography.   4. African American intellectuals—Biography.
5. African American civil rights workers—Biography.   6. Intellectuals—United
States—Biography.   7. Civil rights workers—United States—Biography.
8. African Americans—Civil rights—History.   9. Pan-Africanism—
History.   I. Title.
   E185.97.D73H68   2009
   303.48'4092—dc22   2009031618
   [B]

14 13   12   11   10   1   2   3   4   5

This book is also available on the World Wide Web as an eBook.
Visit www.abc-clio.com for details.

Greenwood Press
An Imprint of ABC-CLIO, LLC

ABC-CLIO, LLC
130 Cremona Drive, P.O. Box 1911
Santa Barbara, California 93116-1911

This book is printed on acid-free paper ∞
Manufactured in the United States of America

CONTENTS

CONTENTS

Photo essay follows page 98

SERIES FOREWORD

In response to high school and public library needs, Greenwood developed this distinguished series of full-length biographies specifically for student use. Prepared by field experts and professionals, these engaging biographies are tailored for high school students who need challenging yet accessible biographies. Ideal for secondary school assignments, the length, format and subject areas are designed to meet educators' requirements and students' interests.

Greenwood offers an extensive selection of biographies spanning all curriculum-related subject areas including social studies, the sciences, literature and the arts, history and politics, as well as popular culture, covering public figures and famous personalities from all time periods and backgrounds, both historic and contemporary, who have made an impact on American and/or world culture. Greenwood biographies were chosen based on comprehensive feedback from librarians and educators. Consideration was given to both curriculum relevance and inherent interest. The result is an intriguing mix of the well known and the unexpected, the saints and sinners from long-ago history and contemporary pop culture. Readers will find a wide array of subject choices from fascinating crime figures like Al Capone to inspiring pioneers like

Margaret Mead, from the greatest minds of our time like Stephen Hawking to the most amazing success stories of our day like J. K. Rowling.

While the emphasis is on fact, not glorification, the books are meant to be fun to read. Each volume provides in-depth information about the subject's life from birth through childhood, the teen years, and adulthood.

A thorough account relates family background and education, traces personal and professional influences, and explores struggles, accomplishments, and contributions. A timeline highlights the most significant life events against a historical perspective. Bibliographies supplement the reference value of each volume.

PREFACE

As even the most casual reader will readily detect, this biography stands on the shoulders of the previous prodigious labor of two scholars in particular: Herbert Aptheker and David Levering Lewis.

I—and indeed all those who seek to understand W.E.B. Du Bois—am in their debt.

INTRODUCTION

W.E.B. Du Bois was stunned.

It was February 1951, and the diminutive—five feet six inches tall—and balding, caramel-colored intellectual, was well into his ninth decade when he was taken to criminal court, fingerprinted, made to empty his pockets, frisked for concealed weapons, and handcuffed.

This was a major setback for the man who had grown accustomed to being regaled because of his essential role in the founding of the NAACP (National Association for the Advancement of Colored People), his diligent labor as the "Father of Pan-Africanism," his doctorate from Harvard, his pioneering research on the unlamented African slave trade, his trailblazing book on Reconstruction or the post–American Civil War era, his thought-provoking novels, his globetrotting, and his race for the U.S. Senate from New York—a race he had lost ignominiously, just before his arrest.

But times had changed as Du Bois—who spoke in clipped, stentorian tones reflecting his upbringing in New England—would be the first to acknowledge. The Soviet Union, which had allied with the United States during the war against Hitler's Germany and Imperial Japan in the war that had concluded in 1945, was now widely viewed as—to use the epithet that came to be popularized later—the "Evil Empire," and Du Bois was now clamoring for friendship with Moscow, not least because of the prospect that nuclear war between his nation and this emerging antagonist could obliterate humanity. Indeed, the criminal charge—and prison term—he faced, that could effectively have killed this aging man, was that he had failed to register as an agent of an unnamed foreign power, which was presumed to the Soviet Union.

Five years after the nuclear destruction of Hiroshima and Nagasaki, Japan, Du Bois assumed the leadership of the Peace Information Center, an international nonprofit organization dedicated to banning nuclear weapons. Since the end of the Pacific War, tensions had risen between Moscow and Washington, both proud possessors of these weapons of mass destruction, and with the war that had erupted on the Korean peninsula in June 1950—where these two superpowers backed opposing sides—there was a real fear that a nuclear war could well ensue. So moved, Du Bois—who long had combined political and intellectual activism—took to the podium and the picket line as the leader of the Peace Information Center, as he expressed his alarm about this chilling turn of events.

This vanguard role was nothing new for William Edward Burghardt Du Bois. Born in Great Barrington, Massachusetts, on February 23, 1868, Du Bois grew up during the height of Reconstruction—the period that spelled hope for 4 million newly freed slaves of African descent. But this was to prove to be a false dawn as Du Bois—who ranks with Barack Obama, Martin Luther King, Jr., and Frederick Douglass as, perhaps, the most important African American of all time—was to spend his life in a nation that was scarred indelibly by racial segregation or Jim Crow legislation and policies. Yet, virtually at the moment he breathed his last breath—he died August 27, 1963, in self-imposed exile in Accra, Ghana—a new era was beginning, as the March on Washington, where Dr. King was to give his "I Have a Dream" speech, was initiating a new era.

In a perverse irony, Du Bois was unable to reap the harvest to which he had contributed so much, as he died before the passage in Washington of the Civil Rights Act of 1964 and the Voting Rights Act of 1965, both of which changed the face of the nation. During his storm-tossed life, Du Bois pursued virtually every avenue available to bring about the laws of freedom that did not materialize until he died. He embraced or flirted with a variety of ideologies, including racial integration, Black Nationalism, Pan-Africanism, and Marxism, while pursuing alternatively vigorous activism and rigorous scholarship. After graduating from Fisk University, he matriculated at the University of Berlin (his facility in German was more than adequate) and Harvard University, emerging as a leading scholar. He went on to pursue scholarship relentlessly at Wilberforce University and the University of Pennsylvania—it was there that he produced *The Philadelphia Negro: A Social Study*, one of the first exemplars of the emerging field of urban sociology.

But Du Bois came to see that it was insufficient to produce sterling scholarship when the people whose cause he served were writhing in agony as lynchings, debt slavery, massive unemployment, and coruscating racism were prevalent throughout the land of his birth. Thus, he turned to activism, first challenging Booker T. Washington, black America's preeminent leader, who had made his peace with Jim Crow and publicly disdained militant challenge to the status quo, counseling instead to focus on building commercial enterprises. From that challenge emerged the "Niagara Movement," then the NAACP itself in 1909, where Du Bois founded their popular journal, the *CRISIS*, which within a few years of its initial publication had garnered a hefty 33,000 subscribers. It was the NAACP that paved the way for desegregation, which was to accelerate after Dr. King's remarkable 1963 address.

Du Bois left the NAACP in 1934 in a dispute with its leadership—a dispute that was characterized as Du Bois pursuing a path of self-determination and black Nationalism viewed as inconsistent with the organization's professed belief in integration. This was at a time when black America had displayed keen interest in the plans and programs of the Jamaican émigré Marcus Garvey, whose "Back to Africa" cry and emphasis on self-determination had captured the imagination of millions both in the United States and the Pan-African world generally. That Du Bois would be accused of echoing Garvey was strangely ironic since they had clashed famously on ideological—and other—grounds. Yet, Du Bois had been a stalwart in the Pan-African movement, which posited the unity and commonalities of peoples of African descent both in Africa and its diaspora. It was not a great leap from Pan-Africanism to the ideological rift that developed between Du Bois and the NAACP in 1934.

Chastened, Du Bois returned to the academy—Atlanta University in his case—before returning to the NAACP in 1944, as a kind of "Minister of Foreign Affairs," where he was instrumental in shaping the post-war environment that led directly to decolonization in Africa and the establishment of an international human rights regime via the nascent United Nations (UN). It was from that perch that he filed a historically profound petition in 1946 at the UN that charged the United States with massive human rights violations against African Americans. Yet, as the United States moved from cooperation to conflict with Moscow, the cold war erupted and the leadership of the NAACP decided that having Du Bois on the payroll was inconsistent with their newly minted friendship with the political and economic leadership of the nation.

For it was during the cold war that Washington realized that it would be difficult at best to charge Moscow credibly with human rights violations, as long as a despicable and atrocious apartheid prevailed on these shores; as a result, Jim Crow had to go. But part of this bargain was that radicals and socialists in black America—like Du Bois—had to be marginalized.

Thus, after being forced out of the NAACP for the second time—this time in 1948—Du Bois decamped to the Council on African Affairs, where he heightened his friendship and camaraderie with others of similar ideological persuasion, such as, the famed actor, singer and activist, Paul Robeson. Leaders of the Council on African Affairs were among the first to raise the cry against apartheid in South Africa and campaign against colonialism in Africa as a whole.

Du Bois also campaigned for world peace—which is what led to his arrest in 1951—but as a result of a global effort, he was able to escape imprisonment. It was at that point that he had married his second wife—the writer and activist, Shirley Graham—who was almost 30 years younger than the now aging intellectual. A novelist, biographer, playwright, and activist, she was also a member of the Communist Party, and it was she who brought him closer to their ranks. In the struggle for socialism, he made a final attempt to bring justice and equality to African Americans. In 1961, just before moving permanently to Accra, Ghana, he joined the Communist Party; both acts, moving to Africa and joining the Communist Party, were viewed widely as a final repudiation of the land of his birth, though actually there was more involved. For what had attracted him to West Africa was an invitation by his former pupil Kwame Nkrumah, who led Ghana to independence in 1957, and this newly minted African state developed the ambitious goal of producing an *Encyclopedia Africana*—a gigantic series of volumes detailing the African experience from ancient to present times—and it was thought that Dr. Du Bois, though then in his early nineties, was just the man to insure that this important project would be completed. When he joined the Communist Party before choosing an African exile, he was also sending a message of rejection of the anticommunism that had led directly to war in Korea—and eventually Vietnam—and a sharp curtailment of civil liberties nationally with which he was intimately familiar.

But his dreams were not to be realized. Du Bois was to expire before the encyclopedia was completed. Yet, in returning to scholarship and returning to Africa, he had come full circle. Nevertheless, his Herculean legacy also includes an impressive record of activism, and a history of struggle on behalf of black America that continues to reverberate.

TIMELINE: EVENTS IN THE LIFE OF W.E.B. DU BOIS

1868 Born, Great Barrington, Massachusetts (February 23).

1888 Receives degree from Fisk University, Nashville, Tennessee.

1890 Receives degree from Harvard College.

1892 Begins graduate school, University of Berlin.

1895 Receives doctoral degree, Harvard University.

1896 Marries Nina Gomer.

1900 Participates in Pan-African Congress, London.

1903 Publishes *The Souls of Black Folk*, in which he challenges Booker T. Washington.

1909 Founds National Association for Advancement of Colored People (NAACP), and joins staff.

1934 Leaves NAACP in philosophical dispute and returns to teach at Atlanta University.

1944 Returns to NAACP as director of their efforts in the international arena.

1948 Fired from NAACP in political dispute.

1950 Runs for the United States Senate from New York State.

1951 Tried and acquitted for being agent of unnamed foreign power as result of peace activism. Marries Shirley Graham in wake of his wife's death.

1961 Joins the Communist Party-USA; moves permanently to Ghana, West Africa, in order to direct the *Encyclopedia Africana*.

1963 Dies in Ghana (August 27).

Chapter 1

BEGINNINGS

Nestled in the southwestern corner of Massachusetts in the Southern Berkshires and bordered by Connecticut to the south and New York to the west, Great Barrington—which historically has had a relatively small population of minorities—is not the kind of place where one would expect an African American leader to be born. But it was there that William Edward Burghardt (W.E.B.) Du Bois was born on a Sunday in 1868. His parents Alfred and Mary Du Bois had married just a year earlier in neighboring Housatonic. Du Bois later described the home into which he was born as "quaint, with clapboards running up and down, neatly trimmed," with a "rosy front yard" and "unbelievably delicious strawberries in the rear." It was, he said, a "rather nice little cottage" that was "furnished with some comfort."[1]

The anodyne nature of this village that was Great Barrington contrasted sharply with the places his ancestors had come from. Du Bois, like so many African Americans, has roots that extend deeply into the history of his homeland.

His mother, Mary Silvina, was born around 1831, and her son spoke of her in his customary rhapsodic words. She was "dark shining bronze," he said, with "smooth skin and lovely eyes; there was a tiny ripple in her black hair, and she had a heavy, kind face." He could have added that she had full lips and riveting eyes.[2] Little is known about her background—except that she was part of a local farming family. It was in approximately 1867 that she caught sight of Alfred Du Bois in Great Barrington. He was from a family of free Negroes, many of whom hailed from Poughkeepsie, New York, and were related to Dr. James Du Bois, an affluent doctor of French Huguenot origins.

Dr. James Du Bois did not join the revolt against British rule in North America, which led to the creation of the United States of America, and when London lost, he decamped to the Bahamas, then developed extensive interests in neighboring Haiti. (Ironically, many Huguenots, who mostly were Protestants, had fled France in the mid-17th century, not least due to ongoing conflict with the majority Catholic population; thus, many of them fled to South Africa where they comprised a significant percentage of the European minority that imposed apartheid on that land—the struggle against this miserable system was to become one of W.E.B. Du Bois's sacred causes.)

To this day Haiti occupies an exalted space in the imagination of black America. From 1791 to 1804 a bloody revolution rocked this Caribbean island nation that eventuated in that rarity of rarities—a successful slave revolt—leading to the creation of an independent republic. The Haitian Revolution had caused Paris to liquidate a good deal of its holdings in the Americas, leading to the Louisiana Purchase by the new government in Washington, D.C., and the territorial expansion of the United States. This revolution also concerned slaveholders in the United States, who worried that continued importation of enslaved Africans to the states would ultimately tip the numerical balance—à la Haiti—resulting in a replay of what had occurred there. It was in 1808 that decisive steps were taken to curb the slave trade to the United States.

Dr. James Du Bois returned to the United States a few years after the Haitian Revolution. One of his sons—Alexander—was on his way to becoming a shoemaker but changed course and, instead, became a small businessman in New Haven, Connecticut, the home of that citadel of higher education, Yale University. It was in the Nutmeg State that Alexander Du Bois married Sarah Marsh Lewis, a union that produced a number of children—including W.E.B. Du Bois's father,

Alfred Du Bois, who was born in Haiti; W.E.B. Du Bois's father's birth-place provided Du Bois a direct connection to the taproot of Pan-Africanism. Alfred Du Bois resided for a while in Haiti but, like so many others—before and since—he eventually migrated to the United States, where by 1860 he was pursuing various occupations—waiter, barber, cook—in New York. He eventually made his way to Massachusetts, where he met, wooed, and married Mary Silvina.

But their union did not last and not unlike Barack Obama, Du Bois grew up mostly without the influence of his father. Unsurprisingly, he became uncommonly close to his mother, a relationship that became ever closer when she endured medical setbacks, including a paralytic stroke that disabled the left side of her body that made her very dependent upon him. Forcing him to grow up quickly, this situation compelled W.E.B. Du Bois at an early age to become a caretaker and take a job after school. Simultaneously, Mary Silvina—abandoned by Alfred Du Bois—invested a great deal of emotion and effort in their offspring. She imparted a number of moral lessons to the young Du Bois that he absorbed fitfully, including the perils of imbibing alcoholic beverages (an indulgence that he did not pursue until he was a student in Berlin), smoking (also a habit he subsequently adopted), and the like.

So armed, Du Bois—one of the only African Americans in his public school—excelled. Not only did he please his mother with his studiousness, but he also created a way to escape from Great Barrington and build a better life for his family. Yet, the road out of Massachusetts was not obstacle-free. As an adult he was to recall graphically and dramatically a searing incident that occurred when he was a mere 12 years old. He and his classmates had decided to purchase cards and exchange them, but, as he recalled it with a lingering melancholy, "one girl, a tall newcomer, refused my card—refused it peremptorily with a glance. Then it dawned upon me with a certain suddenness that I was different from the others; or like, mayhap, in heart and life, and longing, but shut out from their world by a vast well."[3]

As he later recalled it, this event was a turning point for him, as it convinced him of the salience of race and racism: the study of race and the fight against racism was to come to dominate the rest of his life. Young and fatherless, black in a world of whites, Du Bois stumbled from time to time, once barely escaping forced detention after pilfering a neighbor's grapes.

Like the young Malcolm Little—who was to become Malcolm X—the authorities had concluded that Du Bois (who was to become a leading intellectual) would be better served if he were to learn a trade, a noble pursuit no doubt but one which would have deprived the planet of a fearsomely articulated intelligence. It was his high school principal, Frank Hosmer, who rode to his rescue, convincing the judge that a stiff reprimand would be sufficient.

Luckily, Du Bois was able to escape the snares that had entangled—and would continue to entangle—so many African American youth: he was lucky—but unfortunately, many of his compatriots were not. For it was at this juncture that the promise of Reconstruction was being drenched in a tidal wave of blood, as African Americans were being forcibly deprived of basic citizenship rights, disallowed from voting, and subjected to vile Jim Crow in schools, employment, and public accommodations. Lynchings were becoming ever more common as the victorious North had tired of conflict with the white South, which sought with vigor and enthusiasm to consign African Americans to the bottom of society.

Given a second chance in his young life, Du Bois did not disappoint. He accepted the challenge that had been laid down originally by his mother, then reinforced by Frank Hosmer. He buckled down and focused intently on his studies. His first published work appeared in the *New York Globe* in 1883, when he was 15 years of age. *The Globe* was a weekly newspaper, targeting African American readers, and was edited by Timothy Thomas Fortune (1856–1927), one of the leading intellectuals of his era. For the following two years, Du Bois published 27 different articles in this journal that was to become one of the more influential in black America, establishing himself early on as a force to contend with. Most of the pieces, in retrospect, seem rather mundane, often reflecting the quotidian comings and goings of the small town that was Great Barrington. Occasionally, however, Du Bois's words veered beyond the drearily ordinary. In the September 8, 1883, edition he informed his readers about his summer trip when he visited New Bedford, Albany, Providence, and other cities. He was "pleased to see the industry and wealth of many of our race" though he was "struck" by the "absence of literary societies, none of which did I see in any of the cities. It seems to me as if this of all things ought not to be neglected."[4]

Even as a teenager, Du Bois was straining to raise the intellectual level of African Americans, viewing this as a precondition for progress. Du Bois's predilections were also evident when the intrepidly youthful reporter covered a debate concerning whether Native Americans should be admitted as a students to the recently opened Hampton Institute—which had educated his soon-to-be rival, Booker T. Washington. The affirmative prevailed, he reported. He went on to contribute 300 closely argued words urging "colored men of the town" to "prepare themselves" for the coming local and state elections, since within the town, the "colored people . . . hold the balance of power . . . if they will only act in concert they may become a power not to be despised." This speech showcases his early interest in political mobilization as a tool of liberation, an interest that was to dominate his subsequent years.[5] Thus, he was pleased to report on the prospect of the "holding of a county convention of the colored Republicans," the political party of the departed Abraham Lincoln, which was simultaneously the vehicle of those few African Americans who were allowed to cast ballots: Frederick Douglass, a precursor of Du Bois as a political and intellectual force, declared that the Republican Party "[is] the ship, all else is the sea."[6]

Similarly striking about Du Bois's early dispatches is the critical role played by an institution that even then had become a leading institution in black America—the church. The African Methodist Episcopal Zion Church was a constant reference point for the young Du Bois. He was the recording secretary for their Sewing Society, comprised mainly of women, perhaps an expression of what was to blossom in the youthful Du Bois as a unique kind of feminism.[7]

Nevertheless, more revealing of the man he was to become was the trip he had discussed in one of his initial articles. In the summer of this pivotal year of 1883 he journeyed to the home of his grandfather, Alexander Du Bois, a man with whom he had the scantest of acquaintance. His grandfather was residing at that point in New Bedford, Massachusetts, a port town that had been an early residence of Frederick Douglass after he had escaped from slavery in Maryland and an abolitionist headquarters that featured a thriving community of Cape Verdeans and others from the Lusophone world. For Du Bois, who would eventually become a globetrotter of some renown, routinely dashing off to Europe, Asia, and Africa, this was the first extended journey of his young life. Along the way he was to absorb experiences that were to shape his adolescent consciousness. For example, in Narragansett Bay he was moved by a manifestation of what had become a challenger to the July 4 holiday in black America, August 1, the day when the emancipation of the enslaved in the British Empire was celebrated.[8]

Yet as stirring as this episode was and as indelibly as it marked him, it is evident that most important to his emerging career as a writer and activist was the time spent communing with his grandfather. Du Bois's grandfather, like Du Bois himself, was not tall but his bearing and carriage emitted an impression of great stature. Given the penury that characterized most African Americans of that era—including the life of Du Bois in Great Barrington—Alexander Du Bois was affluent relative to the times and the community from which he had sprung. His home contained a library and fine wines. As Du Bois stared in awe, Alexander Du Bois entertained New Bedford's finest: "They sat down and talked seriously," he reported later; "finally my grandfather arose, filled the wine glasses and raised his glass and touched the glass of his friend, murmuring a toast. I had never before seen such a ceremony," he said with wonder. "I had read about it in books, but in Great Barrington both white and black avoided ceremony. To them it smacked of pretense." Du Bois wrote of that time: "[I] sensed in my grandfather's parlor what manners meant and how people of breeding behaved and were able to express what we in Great Barrington were loath to give act to, or unable. I never forgot that toast."[9]

Alexander Du Bois was to pass away in 1887 but the scene in his home was to stay with his grandson for the rest of his life. His grandfather had become in a sense the model on which he was to construct himself: "Always he held his head high, took no insults, made few friends. He was not a 'Negro'; he was a man!"[10] Du Bois's tendency toward rhapsodizing about his grandfather was perhaps intensified by the emotional scars left by his father's absence.

Returning to Great Barrington energized, Du Bois expanded his literary efforts, becoming a correspondent for the *Springfield Republican*, a powerful and influential conduit for his ideas. Though a tender 16 years of age, he had become a paragon of seriousness, a model student, a budding intellectual. Graduating from high school in June 1884, the highly regarded Du Bois—who had studied Latin and Greek—provided stimulating remarks at the ceremony that hailed the abolitionist, Wendell Phillips. Already Du Bois was pointing himself in a direction that would lead to following in the enormous footprints of abolitionism.

But where was he to continue his studies? In the neighborhood was prestigious Williams College and in the vicinity was Harvard, considered widely to be the epitome of higher education in the United States. What was not in doubt was that his studies would not cease with high school, proceeding to university was not negotiable. Yet this was easier said than done for one as impecunious as Du Bois. Then there was the weighty matter of his disabled mother to consider—what would happen to her if he departed? Then with an abrupt sadness akin to a deus ex machina in a tragically well made play, Mary Silvina died of an apoplectic stroke in March 1885. Then divine providence intervened in the form of Frank Hosmer. He organized an informal committee of local bigwigs, the great and the good of Great Barrington, who pledged to underwrite Du Bois's education at Fisk University. That this school for Negroes in Nashville, Tennessee, was founded by the Congregational church was not coincidental, since it was precisely this denomination in Great Barrington that had contributed the bulk of the funds for his matriculation at Fisk. With the path of his next four years of life set, Du Bois proceeded to a land that only recently had been a battlefield in a gory war that had liberated the enslaved.

* * *

Often overshadowed by its larger and more affluent neighbor—Vanderbilt University—Fisk University in Nashville, Tennessee, had been initiated in 1866 by the American Missionary Association: like its peer as a historically black institution of higher education—Howard University—it too was named after an officer in the Union or U.S. army, in this case one who had commanded Negro troops during the Civil War. Early on it had garnered a global reputation because of the Jubilee Singers, who toured the planet on behalf of the university, raising funds and bringing attention to the institution Du Bois entered as a student in 1885.

1885 was a propitious time in America. The promise of Reconstruction had been drenched in tragedy, as federal troops were withdrawn

from the South because of enormous pressure from the defeated—
though still potent—Confederates who had sought to secede from the
United States and form a separate nation based on enslavement of Africans. Native Americans were being subjected to similar pressure and,
steadily, were being ousted from territory they once had controlled.
Labor unions, which had seemed to be on the march, were being driven
into penury. Given such an unforgiving social environment, it was not
surprising that as Du Bois was beginning his studies, ever insistent voices
were speaking out ever more dramatically against the idea of higher
education for Negroes; proponents of white-only education argued
that educating Negroes was pointless because Negroes were—supposedly—destined to be "hewers of wood" and "drawers of water."

Undeterred, Du Bois began his studies in September of the fateful
year of 1885, entering as a sophomore at the tender age of 17 since his
secondary school education in Great Barrington was viewed as providing him with a decided boost compared to his classmates, who mostly
hailed from the poorest precincts of the South. Quickly acclimating
himself to the peculiar folkways of Nashville, which included a kind of
racist segregation that was not as prevalent in Massachusetts, Du Bois
established residence at a dormitory named—ironically—after David
Livingstone, who had established a reputation as a shameless adven-
turer in Africa. Du Bois's adaptation may have been more arduous than
that of his classmates, who hailed from the comparatively tiny black
middle class—morticians, shopkeepers, physicians—and Southern
towns like Memphis, Little Rock, Atlanta, and Chattanooga; on the
other hand, Du Bois was much more accustomed to dealing with the
white community, who were well represented on the faculty at Fisk.
Hence, it was Du Bois who commented on the irony of a U.S. flag
bedecking the central building on campus, observing acidly, "may the
nation whose colors we fly protect the rights of those we educate!"[11]
This was not simply unnecessary sarcasm. Lynching was not unknown
in Nashville, and some students felt the need to arm themselves when
they sauntered to town. Though the U.S. Constitution was amended
to guarantee formerly enslaved Africans the right to vote and equal
protection under the law, these high-minded provisos were observed
more frequently in the breach. The end of Reconstruction and the
withdrawal of troops from the South indicated that the white elite of

the North and South, recently at each other's respective throats, had reconciled—at the expense of the Negro.

An excellent student, Du Bois rose rapidly in prominence on campus. It was not long before he was editor-in-chief of the university's newspaper, where he was not shy in sharing his often controversial opinions with readers. For example, he demanded that students raise funds for a gymnasium. By arguing for the university to be funded by African Americans themselves, he figuratively thumbed his nose at the Northern philanthropists who subsidized Fisk. Aware of the unique contribution of the Jubilee Singers, Du Bois repeatedly trumpeted the virtues of music developed by African Americans, notably the spirituals that he characterized as "the strangest, sweetest" in the world. He wanted the "Negro race . . . to build up an American school of music which shall rival the grandest schools of the past."[12] He was keen to note that "our race, but a quarter of a century removed from slavery, can master the greatest musical compositions."[13]

These words of Du Bois all were uttered in the student newspaper, and it was there that Du Bois burnished his growing reputation as an intellectual and thinker. It was in these pages that he expressed admiration for the black historian George Washington Williams and the activist cum journalist, Timothy Thomas Fortune—both of whom came to be role models for him in these ostensibly disparate spheres of history and journalism. Du Bois excelled in both spheres and graduated in June 1888. When he had spoken at his high school graduation he had hailed abolitionist Wendell Phillips, but in Nashville he chose to speak instead of the Iron Chancellor, Germany's Bismarck, who was in the process of forging his nation into a powerful force that was to shake the foundations of the world. Incidentally, this topic also served as a harbinger of where Du Bois would travel in order to enhance his intellectual armor in pursuit of his own effort to forge a powerful black America.

By the fall of 1888 he entered Harvard College in Cambridge, Massachusetts—where many in his hometown had wanted him to study in the first place—as a junior. He received his bachelor's degree in June 1890 and went on—with fellowships—to graduate study. In history his professors were Edward Channing and Albert Bushnell Hart, luminaries in the field; with the encouragement of the latter, in particular, he delivered a paper at the December 1891 meeting of the American

Historical Association that focused on the African slave trade. This paper anticipated the theme of his dissertation, which was to be published five years later.

That Du Bois would choose to make this particular topic his priority can be understood in the context of what was occurring as he was obtaining his advanced degrees. It was in 1884—just before he entered Fisk—that the leading European powers had met in Berlin to carve up Africa like a Thanksgiving turkey, dividing among themselves spheres of influence and colonization. That is how Germany wound up controlling the nation that was to become Namibia—larger than Texas and California combined in territory. This marked a new stage in the evolution of colonialism in Africa—a process that had been accelerated by the African slave trade. In 1886, as Du Bois was settling into Fisk, class warfare erupted in the form of fierce railroad strikes that rocked Missouri, Arkansas, and Kansas. The Knights of Labor were rising, and in June 1886, anarchists were accused of tossing a bomb that killed seven Chicago police officers in an incident known as Haymarket. As Du Bois was leaving Harvard, the legislature in Mississippi drafted a new constitution that effectively eliminated African Americans from the voting rolls: a two-dollar poll tax, a literacy test, disqualification from voting for petty crimes, and the ability to recite from memory and interpret arcane provisions of the state's constitution were among the measures adopted. Simultaneously, carnage exploded at the steel plant in Homestead, Pennsylvania, as a fierce strike erupted. This was occurring as a populist movement of discontented farmers and workers was surging—then ran aground not least because of an inability to overcome racism within the ranks.

Looked at in this telescoped fashion, Du Bois's return to his home state appears to be a smooth transition from the Deep South—but such was not the case. Massachusetts itself was no paradise for the Negro—it only seemed that way in comparison to Tennessee. Thus, one white Southerner objected to sitting next to Du Bois in a classroom at Harvard, and those who were Jewish and Catholics faced pervasive discrimination, which suggests a full-spectrum bigotry that is shocking by today's standards. Thus, he was rejected by the glee club and, generally, found it difficult to avoid the snobbery that permeated the core of Harvard: being black and not wealthy besides, Du Bois was bound to encounter rebuffs of all sorts. Such barriers shed light on the subsequent perception of

Du Bois's supposed aloofness. The fact was that it had been burned into his consciousness early on that there were those who sought to shun him because of the color of his skin: being conscious of the prejudices against him helped to generate within him a certain reticence and shyness. Yet, despite such indignities, Du Bois would not be swayed from his goal of educating himself while obtaining the credentials that would give him credibility in his crusades on behalf of African Americans.

He was one of a mere handful of African American students at Harvard, typical of the colleges and universities that abounded in the self-proclaimed "Athens" of the United States (Boston's self-important nickname), Harvard (unlike Fisk) was not founded expressly for African American students, and was not particularly friendly to them. Du Bois had managed to wangle a fellowship to continue his education and, perhaps, already feeling the burden of preparation to rescue his compatriots from lynching, racism, and exploitation, he displayed a discipline rare for one of his age. He rose at 7:15 A.M. for breakfast and 45 minutes later was hard at work poring over various texts and writing. Lunch arrived at 12:30 P.M., then there was more work from 1–4 P.M., then a trip to the gymnasium for an hour after that. By 5 P.M., he would relax, then take dinner from 5:30–7 P.M., where he would find time to read newspapers. Then it was more study—or taking in lectures or social visits—until 10:30 P.M., then to bed. Such rigor allowed him to reap dividends when he received his report card, where he excelled, graduating cum laude on June 25, 1890. As at high school and Fisk, he was chosen to give a commencement address, and suggestive of his intellectual evolution, he chose to speak of Jefferson Davis, the leader of the now defeated Confederate States of America, which had plunged the nation into Civil War in order to preserve slavery.[14] Moving from Wendell Phillips to Otto von Bismarck to Jefferson Davis, revealed where Du Bois was going—both intellectually and politically. For initially it was abolitionism that grabbed his imagination, then he looked abroad and was captivated by the consolidation of a modern German state, then he came back to the South to take a jaundiced look at the man who had become the symbol of fighting to the death to preserve slavery.

Consequently, though he studied subjects as diverse as geology, chemistry, political economy, and philosophy, he laid a firm foundation for his future campaigns by devoting substantial attention to the prickly topic of how peoples of African descent arrived in this hemisphere in the first place. With this topic in mind he chose to pursue an advanced degree at Harvard.

Du Bois had other reasons to remain in Cambridge. Beginning at Fisk, he had gained a reputation as a man who was not unattractive to the opposite sex. His appeal did not alter substantially at Harvard and given that he was a handsome bachelor obviously on the way to fame—if not fortune—it was inevitable that he would become an object of someone's affection. One young woman with whom he became involved was Maud Cuney of Galveston, Texas, daughter of Norris Wright Cuney, one of the most powerful African American politicians in the nation. Tall, lovely, and vivacious, she studied the piano at the New England Conservatory of Music. Assisting him in his courtship was the inheritance he had received from his grandfather, Alexander Du Bois, who had obviously been impressed when the teenage Du Bois had come to visit him. A moustache was sprouting on Du Bois's face, soon to be supplemented by a pointed beard. Typically well dressed and modest of mien, he cut a dashing figure on the streets of Cambridge and Boston. It was during this time that he made his way to Amherst, not far distant from Great Barrington, where his acute vision settled on the loveliness of the young ladies there, among which—he was to note—was "Fannie Bailey, hailing from Cambridge," who "was a symphony in purple."[15]

Yet, he was not sufficiently distracted to ignore his studies. Thus it was that he found himself in December 1891 in Washington, D.C., for the annual meeting of the American Historical Association, the capstone of the profession. His remarks on the African Slave Trade neatly summarized his—then—far-reaching conclusions: "If slave labor, was an economic god," said Du Bois, "then the slave trade was its strong right arm; and with Southern planters recognizing this and Northern capital unfettered by conscience it was almost like legislating against economic laws to attempt to abolish the slave trade by statutes."[16] It was such a display of scholarship that led Harvard to award Du Bois a Masters of Arts degree in June 1892.

By 1892, although slavery had officially ended, many African Americans were trapped in a form of debt slavery on plantations in the Deep South. Du Bois was in a unique category of African Americans who had been able to pursue higher education; however, he was not content with this formidable accomplishment. Du Bois applied for and received a fellowship from the Slater Fund, which made possible two years of graduate study—mostly in history and economics—at the University of Berlin. This opportunity was bittersweet since he would have to not only leave Maud Cuney behind but also leave all that was familiar for the uncharted territory of Germany.

Du Bois was also uncharted territory for Germany. The "Iron Chancellor's" effort to consolidate his nation and place it in a position to be a challenger to Britain and France for domination of the wealthiest continent had attracted Du Bois's attention early on. He informed his classmates at Fisk that the rise of Germany held acute lessons relevant to "the rise of the Negro people."[17] Unfortunately, what seemed to inflame the ire of Berlin was the fact that the territory controlled by Paris and London in Africa was much more extensive than that of Germany, a reality that the seizure of Namibia had not assuaged. Hence, in strolling the broad boulevards of Berlin, Du Bois could easily have been mistaken as a prize from Germany's newly minted African empire rather than the diligent student that he actually was. Fortunately funded by philanthropists (among which was Rutherford B. Hayes, who as U.S. President had effectively terminated Reconstruction a few years earlier), Du Bois was able to embark upon what was to amount to both an adventure and an education. For the Slater Fund awarded him a fellowship that made possible two years of graduate study—mostly in history and economics—at the University of Berlin. Indicative of the fact that he saw this accomplishment as not his alone but one that was designed to benefit a beset black America, he encouraged his classmates from Fisk to follow in his footsteps.[18]

In July 1892 the youthful Du Bois boarded a ship headed for Rotterdam, then Dusseldorf—the first German city in which he set foot. The Iron Chancellor had grand plans for this bustling and crowded metropolis, which even then was renowned for its Ruhr-fueled industry. One advantage that Du Bois held over the typical U.S. visitor was his flawless mastery of the German language (his dedication to learning German shows the extent of his fascination with Germany itself and the lessons black America could glean from its rise).

In the fall of 1892 Du Bois ambled into a classroom at the University of Berlin, founded in 1809. Despite its relative youth—dwarfed in this regard by Oxford, Harvard, and Charles University in Prague—the University of Berlin had attracted eminent faculty, including the philosopher Georg Hegel (whose ideas deeply influenced Du Bois), the historian Leopold von Ranke (whose attempt to promote a scientific view of history also influenced Du Bois), and the sociologist Max Weber (who Du Bois was to challenge eventually for his title as the most influential scholar in sociology).

Convinced that he was well on his way to attaining the credentials and knowledge that would allow him to help lift his people—only recently removed from enslavement—to ever greater heights, Du Bois buckled down to the rigors of graduate study in Berlin. Renting a room from a local family, Du Bois retained the rigorous discipline that had served him so well at Harvard. Despite his fluency in German, the youthful Du Bois, who maintained a lifelong sensitivity to slights—racist and otherwise—could often be spotted sitting alone or walking alone. In February 1893 on his 25th birthday he was—as was typical—alone and reflecting on the next period in his life with the vision and utter seriousness that was to become his hallmark. He pledged that he would not only attain great heights personally but, more important, this would be of profound moment for black America. "These are my plans," he cried, "to make a name in [social] science, to make a name in literature and thus to raise my race." It would be an error to mistake as megalomania Du Bois's equating his own rise with that of a much beleaguered black America. For a people who had been deprived systematically of education—at one point it had been a crime to allow a slave to learn to read and write—desperately needed intellectual candlepower, and, sadly, there were very few in Du Bois's position to obtain higher education: and he knew this fact all too well.[19]

So inspired, Du Bois felt it his duty to apply himself with iron regularity to his education; he became a devotee of a German culture he had come to appreciate, as embodied by the works of particularly writers such as Goethe and Heine; he imbibed a form of German Romanticism that was to be espied—by some analysts—in his coming fascination with Pan Africanism.

As the academic year was coming to a close in the late spring of 1893, Du Bois found it necessary to traverse the continent—or as much as his limited funds would allow. In visiting Switzerland, Hungary, and Austria, he had the opportunity to obtain a panoramic view of the persecution of various minorities, particularly those who were Jewish. Learning more how discrimination affected the lives of Jews in Europe helped him to contextualize what was befalling black America, and helped him recognize that the plight of his people was not wholly peculiar but shared commonalities with that of others. He also found time to visit Venice, and in Italy got as far south as Naples and, thus, was able to witness the kind of regional discrimination that had led to the acerbic aphorism that "Africa starts south of Rome." Throughout Europe, Du Bois often was mistaken for a "Gypsy" or Roma or a Jew; his experiences gave him a unique vantage point from which to comprehend Europe.

Perhaps inspired by his European peregrinations and struck by the abject poverty of those in rural areas of Europe—and the obvious parallels with black America—Du Bois launched a major study that was translated as "The Large and Small-scale System of Agriculture in the Southern United States, 1840–1890," shards of which were to inform a good deal of his subsequent research back in the United States. He also found time to study statistics—in some ways, the heart of social science—and the Protestant Reformation, an apt topic of study in the land of Martin Luther.

In the midst of travels and study, Du Bois would have been purblind if he had ignored what amounted to the strongest socialist movement then extant. Karl Marx himself had studied at the University of Berlin, and, like Du Bois, had been inspired to deepen both his activism and his research by what he had seen in Germany. Du Bois began attending socialist meetings in his neighborhood, and took notice of their spectacular electoral rise and the wafer-thin distinctions that separated one faction in this fractious movement from another.

Perhaps those who funded his education had gotten wind of this radical turn for the Slater Fund arrived at the decision to terminate financial support. This meant that he failed to win a University of Berlin doctorate. And so, after spending two action-packed and stimulating years in Berlin, Du Bois reluctantly retreated to Harvard, his second choice, to obtain his doctorate.

NOTES

1. W.E.B. Du Bois, *Dusk of Dawn: An Essay Toward an Autobiography of a Race Concept*, New York: Oxford University Press, 2007, 91; W.E.B. Du Bois, *The Autobiography of W.E.B. Du Bois: A Colloquy on Viewing my Life from the Last Decade of its First Century*, New York: Oxford University Press, 2007, 61; W.E.B. Du Bois, *Darkwater: Voices from Within the Veil*, New York: Oxford University Press, 2007, 5.

2. Du Bois, *Autobiography*, 62, 64.

3. W.E.B. Du Bois, *The Souls of Black Folk*, New York: Oxford University Press, 2007, 2.

4. *New York Globe*, September 8, 1883.

5. *New York Globe*, September 29, 1883.

6. *New York Globe*, October 20, 1883.

7. *New York Globe*, December 29, 1883.

8. *Providence Journal*, August 2, 1883.

9. Du Bois, *Autobiography*, 98.

10. Du Bois, *Autobiography*, 71.

11. *Fisk Herald*, November 1887.

12. *Fisk Herald*, November 1887.

13. *Fisk Herald*, April 1888.

14. David Levering Lewis, *W.E.B. Du Bois: Biography of a Race*, New York: Henry Holt, 1993.

15. *Boston Courant*, July 9, 1892.

16. W.E.B. Du Bois, "The Enforcement of the Slave Trade Laws," *Annual Report of the American Historical Association for the Year 1891*, Washington, D.C.: Senate Misc. Doc. 173, 52nd Congress, 1st Sess., 1892, 163–174.

17. *Fisk Herald*, September 1893.

18. *Fisk Herald*, November 1892.

19. Lewis, *W.E.B. Du Bois: Biography of a Race*, 47.

Chapter 2

DR. DU BOIS

After two years in Europe, Du Bois returned to the United States by boat, across the choppy waters of the North Atlantic. The plight of African Americans that had existed when he had left for Europe had yet to terminate: African Americans continued to endure lynching and disfranchisement as the promise of Reconstruction continued to be suffocated and strangled. The now 26-year-old scholar traveled in steerage, along with prospective European migrants who upon arrival in New York would immediately be deemed of a higher status than Du Bois, whose roots in the United States ran deep. Yet despite this obvious handicap, it was not long before he possessed one advantage that few have shared before or since: although he had failed to obtain a doctorate from the University of Berlin, he was able to "settle" for the same degree from Harvard, a credential that also placed him in the educational stratosphere of the entire nation.

He also was ready to enter more directly into the fray and seek to stem the tide that was capsizing his people. He applied to teach at several colleges designated for African Americans. After the Civil War, a number of these institutions had arisen—including his own Fisk—as the United States endured an apartheid-like educational system that even a prospective Harvard doctorate had difficulty penetrating. The first acceptance came from Wilberforce University in Ohio, appropriately named after the famed British abolitionist who had done so much to ban slavery. By late 1894 Du Bois was ensconced in the faculty there; he taught Greek, Latin, English, German, and history—a crushing load of courses that hardly left time for the research and writing he craved.

On the outskirts of Dayton, this area had thrust itself into the consciousness of African Americans as the home of Paul Laurence Dunbar, who by the time of Du Bois's arrival was in the process of establishing himself as a skilled and talented poet of no small notoriety. Wilberforce was also quite close to nearby Yellow Springs, the home of Antioch College, which was to become a lodestar for student activism in years to come. But in 1894 Du Bois had good reason to feel that he had descended from the lofty altitude signaled by Cambridge and Berlin to the depths of academia, as Wilberforce's sparse and spare facilities—particularly in what was of crucial importance to the scholar: the library—hardly met the standard to which he had grown accustomed. From the concrete canyons of major metropolises, Du Bois now found himself in the midst of cornfields as far as the eye could see. Having cultivated a finely manicured beard (which was to complement his increasingly balding pate)—and often sporting a deftly carved cane and elegant gloves, Du Bois was instantly identifiable on a campus replete with students often a generation removed from enslavement.

His dapper appearance could not mask his seemingly inexhaustible ability to work, leading some to believe that he must have survived without sleep. For within months of his arrival, Du Bois had finished his masterful Harvard dissertation, "The Suppression of the African Slave Trade to the United States of America, 1638–1870," a landmark in the field of history. It was in June 1895 that his Harvard professors placed their imprimatur on this exemplar of historical excavation, conferring upon him the title for which he was to be known for the rest of his life—Dr. Du Bois.

His Harvard instructors maneuvered to insure that his scholarship was published—a rarity for doctoral dissertations, which are routinely consigned to obscurity on dusty library shelves. Instead, the significance and profundity of Du Bois's work was ratified when it appeared in book form as the first monograph in the famed series known as Harvard Historical Studies.

More than a century after it was first pored over by eager readers— and unlike many of its late 19th-century peers—Du Bois's book continues to withstand the test of time. Constructed from primary documents (parliamentary and colonial records, federal and state legislation, census figures, court cases, journalistic accounts), "The Suppression of the African Slave Trade to the United States of America, 1638–1870" was a reflection of the gathering consensus that had taken hold at Berlin, Johns Hopkins, Harvard, and like-minded institutions that history should be built, to the extent possible, from such eyewitness accounts. Given such firsthand verification, it was hard to dispute Du Bois's conclusion that indicted the United States—its nationals and authorities— for its promiscuous participation in the African Slave Trade, even after it was thought to have been banned in 1808. This odious commerce, Du Bois had concluded, received a de facto sanction from Washington, not least because of the weighty influence of slaveholders in government; moreover, the immense market for enslaved Africans that then existed in Cuba and Brazil was much too profitable for U.S. slave dealers to ignore. This conclusion—bold for the times—has been verified by today's scholarship, though this work was grounded in assertions made by Du Bois decades earlier.[1]

Du Bois's masterpiece served as a precursor for the work of the Trinidadian scholar, C.L.R. James, in that Du Bois's work connects the epochal Haitian Revolution to France's hurried sale of the Louisiana Territory to the United States.[2] Du Bois also knew that it was the turmoil in Haiti that convinced slave traders in the United States that the better part of wisdom would be to avoid importing more enslaved Africans—thus risking the dire prospect of "Africanization" or creating a racial ratio disadvantageous to the enslavers. Du Bois also recognized the significance of slavery for the U.S. economy, then on a glide path to becoming the planet's weightiest; this observation anticipates the implication of the scholarship of yet another Trinidadian scholar, Eric Williams.[3]

Decades later, Du Bois was to subject his first book to withering—and, perhaps, unfair—criticism, lamenting his inattention to Marx (economics) and Freud (psychology) in explicating the horrors of enslavement.[4]

Nevertheless, the fact that this book continues to be consulted and quoted suggests its ongoing relevancy.

Even as Du Bois was putting the finishing touches on this manuscript, the very modern idea that now governs academia—"publish or perish"—was not altogether absent from his world. He had good reason to believe that if he was able to garner attention as a published scholar, his chance of being rescued from the relative backwater of Wilberforce would be greatly improved.

But Du Bois did not envision for himself a life solely as a scholar cloistered in the ivory tower and, consequently, early on, found time to comment on pressing matters of public import: the death of human rights leader Frederick Douglass was just such an event. Born enslaved in Maryland, Douglass was able to escape bondage for a new life in Massachusetts and New York, where he penned works about his life so riveting that they continue to be read; he then became the leading antislavery campaigner of his era, which brought him on more than one occasion to tumultuous and rapturous crowds in Europe. On February 20, 1895, Douglass died—strikingly—just as his putative successor, Du Bois, was establishing himself as the leading tribune of black America. A memorial service for Douglass was held at Wilberforce on March 9, and Du Bois, the youngest faculty member, addressed those assembled. In praising Douglass for his steadfastness and vision, accidentally and serendipitously—or not—he sketched the role he was to play in the coming century.[5]

Though only 27 years of age and weighted down with a burdensome teaching load, Du Bois was still able to draw attention to himself—as he did with well-received remarks about Douglass—and attract the attention of others who were renowned, such as the elderly and graying 76-year-old Alexander Crummell, who had come to Wilberforce in the spring of 1895 to address students and faculty. An Episcopal cleric, a heralded intellectual, a man who had toiled in Liberia (the West African state settled by "free" Negroes from the United States), and a contemporary of such eminences as Martin Delany, Edward Wilmot Blyden, and Henry Highland Garnet, Crummell also foreshadowed a brand of Pan-Africanism that Du Bois was later to embody. In Du Bois's canonical text, *The Souls of Black Folk*, Du Bois rhapsodizes about this fortuitous encounter and intimates how it shaped his own accelerating consciousness. "Tall, frail and black he stood," said Du Bois, "with simple dignity and an unmistakable air of good breeding." Theretofore, Du Bois's life had been shaped by his high school principal in Great Barrington and his professors at Harvard and Berlin but now he had the rare opportunity to meet face-to-face a man who too was African American, who too had devoted his life to "racial uplift." As much as his grandfather, from that point forward, Du Bois chose to walk in the large footprints of Alexander Crummell.[6]

Douglass's death and Crummell's arrival on campus were twin shocks to the young Du Bois, reminding him at once that time was short and the need for successors to giants who were passing away or in their dotage was great. While Du Bois was bogged down in a blizzard of classes, others were stepping forward to fill the vacuum left by the passing of Douglass. At the Cotton States International Exposition on September 18, 1895, Booker T. Washington—who was to become Du Bois's antipodal foil for years to come—shook the South and the nation. A founder of Tuskegee, which continues to be a beacon of higher education in Alabama, Washington in his "Atlanta Compromise" offered to accept the Jim Crow regime, which mandated racist segregation and severe restrictions on the right to vote, in return for the white South accepting minor steps forward in black progress in the realms of business and agriculture. "Cast down your buckets where you are," Washington advised, "by making friends in every manly way of the people of all races by whom we are surrounded." In exchange, said Washington, Euro-Americans must cast down their buckets "among those people who have, without strikes and labor wars, tilled your fields, cleared your forests, [built] your railroads and cities." At a time when obstreperous trade unions and angry farmers were stirring the streams of discontent, powerful elites were bound to lend an ear to the comforting idea that African Americans would not contribute to this overall disarray. Washington was not a spellbinding orator, unlike Douglass, for example, but his words were no less riveting to those who were listening. "In all things that are purely social we can be as separate as the fingers," he said with a display of his digits, "yet one as the hand in all things essential to mutual progress."[7]

In coming years, Du Bois was to confront Washington, though initially he seemed as taken by the words of the Wizard of Tuskegee as any.

"Let me heartily congratulate you upon your phenomenal success at Atlanta—it was a word fitly spoken," Du Bois enthused. "Here might be the basis of a real settlement between whites and blacks in the South, if the South opened to the Negroes, the doors of economic opportunity and the Negroes cooperated with the white South in political sympathy."[8]

Perhaps Du Bois was snowed under by classes and lectures, perhaps he did not pay careful attention to the demobilizing import of the Wizard's words, perhaps he was shading toward opportunism—whatever the case, he did not emerge initially with full-throated opposition to Washington. Meanwhile, Wilberforce had its diversions, including the friendships of Paul Laurence Dunbar and the military man Charles Young—both emblems of the "Talented Tenth" of Negroes, that Du Bois was to hail subsequently. There was another friendship that the attractive young bachelor also developed during that time. Often besieged by dinner invitations and social engagements by those who viewed him as a handsome betrothal catch, Du Bois ultimately retreated from this snare when he met Nina Gomer. She was his student. Her family resided distant from his, in Cedar Rapids, Iowa. Wilberforce was not their only commonality. Like Du Bois, she too was an African American who had roots in the Francophone world, Alsace in her case. They were married on May 12, 1896, in her hometown. Though they remained married for decades, their relationship was star-crossed and it is fair to say that he did not find true marital bliss until his second marriage—when he was an octogenarian—to the writer and activist, Shirley Graham.

With a Harvard doctorate in hand by 1895 and a marriage a scant year later, Du Bois had attained two notable landmarks. Yet he was still trapped at Wilberforce, teaching a crushing load of classes and finding it difficult to escape the swamp of petty politics that too often was the norm in college life and was exacerbated by the debilitating Jim Crow that inherently generated frustrations and anger with hardly an outlet.

But rescue from this dilemma came in the form of a letter from the University of Pennsylvania in Philadelphia, an Ivy League institution of some repute, that offered him a position—not as a professor (Jim Crow veritably forbade this) but as an investigator, who would conduct a study of African Americans in this major metropolis. Philadelphia in 1896 had the largest African American population in the nation and, perhaps, the most influential. Philadelphia had spawned one of the

more significant religious denominations among African Americans—
the African Methodist Episcopal faith. Philadelphia was also home to
the Society of Friends—or the Quakers—who had helped to generate
one of the strongest abolitionist movements in the nation during the
antebellum era and later produced Bayard Rustin, a chief theoretician
of the civil rights movement and top aide to Dr. Martin Luther King, Jr.

But, like other U.S. cities, Philadelphia had been unable to escape
the pestilence of racism, as bloodily racist attacks on African Americans
had become as much a part of the city's landscape as the sprawling oasis
of greenery that was Fairmount Park. Part of the problem in the City
of Brotherly Love—as was the case nationally—was that those African Americans who could vote were aligned with the party of business
elites, the Republican Party, while the white working class was aligned
traditionally with the Democratic Party. Since African Americans were
also overwhelmingly working class, this meant that the working class
was torn asunder on a political axis, which generated enormous tension
and frequent firefights between black and white workers.

This was the fractious climate into which Du Bois and his newly be-
trothed was thrust. The nation was not doing much better than Philadelphia itself, as the challenge of the Populist movement, generated by
farmers outraged by falling crop prices and unions motivated by falling wages, was continuing to shake the stability of the nation. Then
there was the rising influence of the Progressive movement of whom it
was said they would steal the clothes—and programs—of the Populists, whenever the latter went swimming; the tension across America
was creating a momentum for change akin to a gigantic snowball hur-
tling down a steep mountain. As political conflict escalated, there were
those who were interested in accumulating more information about
black Philadelphia, whose votes could tip the balance in close elections,
hence the invitation to Du Bois to organize a study of this sector.

There were about 40,000 African Americans living in Philadelphia
and its crowded, densely populated neighborhoods that served as a virtual incubator for all manner of maladies. They were overwhelmingly
poverty stricken and life—in the phrase of Thomas Hobbes referring to
his native England—was "nasty, brutish and short."

Thus it was that the dapper Dr. Du Bois, attired quite fashionably
as was his wont, found himself canvassing black Philadelphia for data
to use in his pioneering sociological study, *The Philadelphia Negro*.

Du Bois's friend, the historian Herbert Aptheker, calculated that Dr. Du Bois expended 835 hours in interviews involving 2,500 households during a 90-day period of intensive research commencing in August 1896: this research involved talking with approximately 10,000 men, women, and children all told.[9] Piling fact upon fact and statistic upon statistic, Du Bois mounted a devastating indictment of the calloused condition black Philadelphia was accorded, that was all the more devastating because of its scientific veneer. This book, along with his first book on the African slave trade, not only established him as the premier scholar in black America but also served as bookends of an era, documenting rigorously the perilous journey African Americans had made from slavery to freedom.

His epochal study of Philadelphia in some ways mimicked a similar study conducted decades earlier by Frederick Engels that examined the working class in Manchester. Unlike Engels, who as an affluent businessman and close comrade of Karl Marx was only moonlighting as a social critic), Du Bois actually lived among those who were the target of his research. Thus situated, Du Bois was able to produce an exhaustive examination of every aspect of black life: history, demography, family, migrations, education, occupations, health, organized life (especially in the churches), prisons, pauperism, alcoholism, housing, amusements, class differentiations, contact across the color line, voting, and political activity. Du Bois's study even goes as far as including a word to concerned whites about their responsibility for the dire situation he describes so meticulously.

It was becoming increasingly difficult to ignore the intellectual firepower that Du Bois was unleashing in defense of black America. Meanwhile, back in Philadelphia, Du Bois, who had reached his 29th birthday in 1897, also experienced the joy of the birth of his firstborn, a son, Burghardt, born on October 2. This added responsibility did not lessen his anxiety at the thought that his temporary academic appointment at the University of Pennsylvania was expiring within a few months of this exhilarating birth. Though he was producing scholarship of an extraordinary character at a relatively young age, Du Bois was confronted with the distinct possibility of unemployment, adding a peculiar poignancy to his explications in *The Philadelphia Negro* concerning the toxicity of joblessness. Seeking to preempt this unsavory possibility,

Du Bois thrust himself further into the national spotlight by publishing in the celebrated *Atlantic Monthly,* which had a justifiable reputation as a beacon of intellectualism. It was here that he introduced his now famous line, "the Negro is a sort of seventh son, born with a veil, and gifted with second-sight," and began to develop the idea of "double-consciousness" that he subsequently expanded upon in his soon-to-be-published classic, *The Souls of Black Folk*: Du Bois grappled with the inexorable anxiety that flowed from the enslavement and abuse of those then known as U.S. Negroes coupled with the reality that there appeared to be no possibility of returning to the African homeland. It was here too that Du Bois flung caution to the winds and raised searching and disturbing questions about black America's primary gatekeeper—Booker T. Washington—who then had the power to advance (or retard) the career of a scholar then contemplating the possibility of unemployment. Yes, Du Bois said, the industrial training then sanctified at Tuskegee was not unwelcome but, he continued, in an implicit rebuke of Washington's "Atlanta Compromise," "the power of the ballot was [needed] in sheer self-defense." Taking a more comprehensive view of the Negro's plight than that suggested by Washington, Du Bois added portentously, "work, culture, liberty—all these we need, not singly but together, gained through the unifying idea of Race."[10]

Du Bois's words were an early signal that the delicately cast compromise brokered by the Wizard of Tuskegee would not be greeted with unanimous glee. Also percolating in Du Bois's ever active consciousness was another notion that would soon emerge and roil the waters of black America. For it was in *The Philadelphia Negro* that Du Bois adumbrated the idea of the "Talented Tenth," the purported "best" among African Americans—those like Du Bois himself—who would lead the masses to the Promised Land. This thesis—as much as anything else that he wrote or did—contributed to the ultimately misleading idea that Du Bois was an "elitist," somehow disconnected from those for whom he purported to speak. Later, of course, Du Bois was to revise this controversial notion to the point that the "Talented Tenth" came to resemble a self-sacrificing political vanguard. In any case, Du Bois added ballast to this conception by pleading for a scientific study of the realities of the "Negro Problem." Though Du Bois's call to study the "Negro Problem" has been much reviled and discussed, scholarly neglect of African

Americans often meant that those who were thought to speak on their behalf often were flying blind, wholly unaware of the nuances and crevices of Negro life that would make for reasonable policy prescriptions on their behalf.[11]

Thus, even his jab at the "Atlanta Compromise," with all the danger for his career that it suggested, could not obscure Du Bois's increasing prominence. Ironically, it was Atlanta University itself—a historically black school in the Wilberforce tradition, albeit with a higher profile in basic research—that offered him a post that he quickly accepted, moving to the "City Too Busy to Hate" by 1897. Hard by the serpentine Chattahoochee River, Atlanta housed a sprawling complex of Negro colleges, including the schools that came to be known as Morehouse and Spelman. A bulwark of the erstwhile Confederate States of America, Georgia had been devastated during the Civil War, emerging afterward with bruised feelings—notably among the Euro-American elite—toward the United States, feelings that were inevitably visited upon a long-suffering African American population. Atlanta was a citadel of Jim Crow, the ramified system of racist segregation that defined the Deep South, and was a frequent site of lynchings—and worse.

It was not the kind of place—it was thought—that Du Bois would find congenial but at this juncture he did not have many options, despite his sterling doctorate from Harvard. Quickly Du Bois plunged into a maelstrom of beaver-like busyness that included teaching, speaking engagements, polishing manuscripts, writings for popular publications—and more. It was here that Du Bois was to spend 12 long and transformative years of triumph and travail that were so engaging that it was to this city that Du Bois later returned for another decade of residence, beginning in 1934.

Atlanta University, being situated in a major metropolis, had more allure and charm than that possessed by Wilberforce. Du Bois taught courses in economics, history, and sociology, among others—while also finding time to play competitive tennis. The sight of Du Bois rushing to whack a small ball across a wide net humanized him in the eyes of his students, many of whom were intimidated by his classroom presence, which was deeply influenced by the martinets who had instructed him in Berlin.

Du Bois felt, however, that his lasting contribution would be in the realm of research, and in 1897 he initiated a renowned series of studies on such disparate matters involving African Americans as poverty rates, wages, churches, business enterprise, and the like. These studies involved the dispensing of numerous questionnaires to collect data necessary to illuminate the plight of African Americans; Du Bois was a pioneer in collecting and scrutinizing mounds of data, from which he was able to draw conclusions and construct the narratives of his studies.

By dint of tireless labor and a steady stream of publications, even before a new century dawned and an old one concluded, Du Bois was becoming better known widely as a model of scholarly rectitude—and, possibly, an antipode and alternative to the model provided by Washington. For example, in March 1899 Du Bois delivered a series of lectures at Hampton Institute in Virginia, Washington's alma mater. "It is doubtful," said one well-informed commentator, "if any visiting lecturer has ever more successfully won the admiration and swayed the thoughts of the students here."[12]

At roughly that same moment—that is, by 1898—the United States had embarked on a new departure, waging war against the tottering Spanish Empire and emerging triumphant with domination over Cuba, Puerto Rico, and the Philippines. During this same era, the United States had collaborated in dislodging indigenous rule in Hawaii, and, in the process, had become a budding imperialist power—though still far distant from the leader in this realm: Britain. Bringing under the U.S. flag many more millions of "non-Europeans" created strains within the United States itself that Du Bois was among the first to notice. On the one hand, many white Southern politicos resented the notion that their beloved nation was being "overrun" by these "non-Europeans." On the other hand, there were those—particularly among the Northern elite—who were happy to see their nation accumulate more markets for export goods and more cheap labor to be exploited.

All the while, Du Bois continued to labor tirelessly. By 1898 the Bureau of Labor Statistics of the U.S. government had begun publishing some of Du Bois's special studies that focused on African Americans, particularly in the South. Yet amidst the blizzard of memoranda and conference papers, lectures and pamphlets, books, and detailed letters,

Du Bois endured a staggering blow that was to pierce his psyche. It was in April 1899 that the ghoulish lynching of Sam Hose—an African American farmer from the area surrounding Atlanta—occurred. Hose got into a bruising fracas with a white counterpart—that led to the latter being shot and killed. In retaliation, a white lynch mob brutally tortured, immolated, and killed Hose. As was often the case with these ritual executions, the mob of thousands of Euro-Americans who had witnessed this outrage and/or killed him distributed Hose's various body parts as souvenirs. Du Bois was depressed and stunned by this macabre exercise, and promptly marched to the office of the editor of the local paper, Joel Chandler Harris—soon to garner fame as a popular writer notorious for vicious stereotypes of African Americans—to deliver a protest for publication. As he walked in distress to his appointed designation, Du Bois little knew that like ham hocks in the window of a butcher shop, Hose's mangled knuckles were on display in a store window—when he espied this ghastly sight, Du Bois could hardly contain himself and wept uncontrollably.

It was beginning to dawn on him that scholarly productivity—no matter how enlightening or rational or exquisite—was simply not enough to confront the mammoth magnitude of prejudice and hate that African Americans had to confront. Hose's lynching occurred as another monumental event occurred—the brutal coup that dislodged African American officeholders in Wilmington, North Carolina, which also led to those that voted for them fleeing far and wide. As if that were not enough, it was during this same period of angst and pain that his son passed away. He had come down with diphtheria, a common illness of an unhealthy era, and died on May 24, 1899. As his son was wailing in agony, Du Bois frantically had sought to reach one of the few African American physicians in segregated Atlanta who would be willing to treat his rapidly diminishing loved one. Of course, white doctors would not deign to attend to an infant not of their racial group. Infant mortality among African Americans was endemic during this era, which Du Bois well knew, but—unsurprisingly—the shock of this tragedy being visited upon his own family was almost too much to bear. In his much honored book, *The Souls of Black Folk,* he reserves pride of place for reflections on this catastrophic heartbreak. "A perfect life was his," he moaned, "all joy and love, with tears to make it brighter—

sweet as a summer's day beside the Housatonic. The world loved him; the women kissed his curls, the men looked gravely into his wonderful eyes, and the children hovered and fluttered about him."[13] Burying one's child is thought to be a tragic calamity that indelibly marks the parent: certainly this was true in Du Bois's case. More than this, this misfortune also left a deep imprint on his marriage, and though he and Nina Gomer remained married for decades, there was a certain distance between them after their son's death—a distance that was often punctuated by frequent periods of separation between them.

Du Bois had witnessed Jim Crow up close as a teenager in Nashville and now its poison had permeated the fabric of his being with the horrific Hose lynching and the death of his first born. Such experience was moving him perceptibly from the tranquil groves of the academy to the rough-and-tumble world of activism. This transition would inexorably involve a bruising confrontation with the strategy and tactics of Booker T. Washington, yet, ironically, his stellar academic credentials led to Tuskegee offering him a post for the 1900–1901 academic year. That is how he found himself in February 1900 at Washington's campus—at the Wizard's invitation—in what amounted to a job interview. Amidst the buildings mostly constructed by the labor of students and bearing the names of the titans of Northern capital—Phelps, Huntington, Parker—was a larger community where Jim Crow reigned.

Simultaneously, Du Bois was being considered for a high-level post as an administrator of the public schools of Washington, D.C., the capital city of the rising power that was the United States. Although Washington, D.C., was racially segregated, it was not segregated to the extent of Atlanta or Tuskegee, and thus held some attraction for both Du Bois and his spouse. Moreover, though it had yet to assume the title it garnered in the 1960s—"Chocolate City"—Washington, D.C., contained a sizeable African American population (a real attraction for a social scientist of Du Bois's bent) and numerous amply stocked libraries and archives, notably the library at Howard University (the self-proclaimed "capstone" of Negro education) and the Library of Congress, not to mention what was to become the U.S. National Archives.

As it turned out, offers were tendered neither from Tuskegee nor Washington, D.C., and the disappointed Du Bois had good reason to believe that Booker T. Washington was behind it all. A simmering conflict between these two men was now metastasizing into a boiling and rancorous dispute, the ramifications of which were to shape black America for decades to come.

Licking his wounds, Du Bois returned to what had become his second home, Western Europe. It was a propitious moment to do so. In 1896 Ethiopia resisted Italy's attempts at colonization, and, therefore, became a beacon of hope and pride for black America. A few years later war erupted in South Africa between the British Empire and the "Boers," or the descendants of the mostly Dutch migrants who had begun migrating to the Cape of Good Hope in the mid-17th century; if nothing else, Africans had reason to think that white racial solidarity might be fraying. Then in 1905 Japan defeated Russia in a war that seemed to suggest that the rapaciousness of white supremacy had hit a formidable stumbling block. In the middle of this vortex of change, Du Bois crossed the Atlantic once more, this time to England and France.

In July of this fateful year, 1900, he attended the first Pan-African Congress in London as secretary of the congress, and later that summer he decamped to France, where he served as an organizer of the American Negro Exhibit, which was part of the United States building at the World's Fair in Paris. Both stops were important but, as it turned out, it was London that echoed through the ages for it was here where the radical idea was formalized that peoples of African descent should unite based on their commonality of concern, that is, opposition to labor exploitation and support for decolonization. This idea was led by those of the diaspora, such as Du Bois and the Trinidadian barrister Henry Sylvester Williams, but was intended for peoples of African descent wherever they might be.

Hence, from July 23 to 25, 1900, at Westminster Town Hall in southwest London and on leafy Chancery Lane, Du Bois presented profound words that continue to resonate to this very day. In the opening paragraph of this manifesto addressed "To the Nations of the World," appear the tossed-down gauntlet, "the problem of the twentieth century is the problem of the colour line, the question as to how far differences of race, which show themselves chiefly in the colour of the skin and the texture of the hair, are going to be made, hereafter, the basis of denying to over half the world the right of sharing to their utmost ability the opportunities and privileges of modern civilization." Du Bois urged that peoples of African descent "take courage, strive ceaselessly, and fight bravely, [so that] they may prove to the world their incontestable right to be counted among the great brotherhood of mankind."[14]

This crucial gathering did not emerge from out-of-the-blue, for African American interest in Africa had not flagged over the centuries. This was reflected in the names of religious denominations (e.g. the African Methodist Episcopal faith or the Abyssinian Baptist Church in Harlem) or the continued interest in Ethiopia or the efforts by African American missionaries in Africa. Thus, it was not terribly surprising when this July 1900 meeting proved to be such a rousing success. Among the participants were Benito Sylvain of Haiti, who exuded this reinvigorated Pan-Africanism, as he had served as a top aide to Ethiopia's emperor.

The ambitions of this trailblazing meeting were rather modest: there was no full-throated demand of immediate independence of the African and West Indian colonies, for example. Yet it was undeniable that this London confab was a shot over the bow at the colonizers, and that a turning point had been reached that signaled the imminent demise of colonialism, which had denuded Africa in particular of wealth, just as the slave trade had been responsible for uprooting millions of Africans and depositing them in the Americas as slave laborers.

Thus, what came to be known as the First Pan-African Congress was an auspicious opening of what was to become a critically important century. That Dr. Du Bois was present at the creation of this new departure was an indication that this man who had emblazoned his name in the annals of academia was now entertaining broader goals. That these ambitions would bring him into conflict with Booker T. Washington was easily foreseeable.

NOTES

1. For example, Gerald Horne, *The Deepest South: The United States, Brazil and the African Slave Trade*, New York: New York University Press, 2007, passim.

2. C.L.R. James, *The Black Jacobins: Toussaint L'Ouverture and the San Domingo Revolution*, New York: Vintage Books, 1989.

3. Eric Williams, *Capitalism and Slavery*, Chapel Hill: University of North Carolina Press, 1994.

4. W.E.B. Du Bois, *The Suppression of the African Slave Trade to the United States of America, 1638–1870*, [Harvard Historical Series Number 1], New York: Longmans, Green, 1896.

5. W.E.B. Du Bois, "Douglass as a Statesman," *Journal of Negro History*, 49 (October 1964): 264–268.

6. Du Bois, *The Souls of Black Folk*, 103–109.

7. Louis R. Harlan, *Booker T. Washington: The Making of a Black Leader, 1856–1901*, New York: Oxford University Press, 1972, 218.

8. W.E.B. Du Bois to Booker T. Washington, September 24, 1895, in Herbert Aptheker, *The Correspondence of W.E.B. Du Bois, Volume I*, Amherst: University of Massachusetts Press, 1973, 39; Lewis, *W.E.B. Du Bois: Biography of a Race*, 175.

9. W.E.B. Du Bois, *The Philadelphia Negro*, Millwood, NY: Kraus-Thomson, 1973, 16.

10. W.E.B. Du Bois, "Strivings of the Negro People," *Atlantic Monthly*, 80 (August 1897): 194–198, 195.

11. W.E.B. Du Bois, "The Study of the Negro Problem," *Annals of the American Academy of Political and Social Science*, 11 (January 1898): 1–23.

12. *Southern Workman*, 28 (April 1899): 149–151.

13. Du Bois, *The Souls of Black Folk*, 99–102.

14. "To the Nations of the World" in *Report of the Pan-African Conference*, 23–25 July 1900, London, *W.E.B. Du Bois Papers, University of Massachusetts-Amherst*.

Chapter 3

WHEN TITANS COLLIDE

Du Bois's tenure at Atlanta University occurred as the nation in which he resided witnessed an ossifying of Jim Crow. It was in 1896 that the U.S. Supreme Court in the profoundly significant case, *Plessy v. Ferguson*, placed its imprimatur on the system of "separate but equal" (which amounted to separate and unequal); this racist system often descended to the level of absurdity, for example, "separate but equal" graveyards, "separate but equal" Bibles to swear witnesses in courtrooms, no intermarriage across the color line, or mandates that workers of various ancestries were forbidden to peer out of the same windows in factories. This totalizing—actually totalitarian—regime seemed so pervasive and formidable that inevitably a number of African Americans decided that the better part of wisdom was figuring out how to make one's peace with Jim Crow by rationalizing deprivation of the vote and lynching and all the rest. Foremost among these advocates was Booker T. Washington, who seemingly had taken the measure of Du Bois—who he probably envisioned correctly as a potentially dangerous rival—by inviting him for a job interview (or, more likely, an inspection) in February 1900.

While the nascent Progressives were not above pilfering the policy clothes of Populists, the latter were swimming toward the mainstream.

Washington similarly seemed to adopt as his own ideas and data generated by Du Bois. Thus, in 1901, Washington founded the National
Business League — an organization of actual and would-be entrepreneurs — which became the apex of the Tuskegee notion that building
enterprises and generating prosperity was the surest way to confront Jim
Crow. Yet in assessing the promise and prospects of this still negligible
class of businessmen, Washington had to rely upon studies conducted
by Du Bois.

Still, despite this reliance, Washington—and many of the white businessmen of the North upon whom he relied—was deeply suspicious of
African American intellectuals like Du Bois, fearful of their critique of
accommodation to Jim Crow and how a rejection of the separate but
equal doctrines could influence Negroes at large. Washington's bene-
factors in the North were fearful of Du Bois's ideas about unions and his
developing socialist ideology, which—they thought—could portend
expropriation of their wealth and enterprises. On the other hand, there
were some among Washington's coterie who decided that co-opting
Du Bois might be the wiser course. Thus, in 1902, Du Bois received an
invitation to leave Atlanta for Tuskegee with a promise of a substantial
increase in salary. Among those counseling that he do so were the finan-
cier Jacob Schiff; the president of the Long Island Railroad, William
Baldwin, Jr.; and other captains of industry such as Robert C. Ogden,
J. G. Phelps Stokes, and George Foster Peabody, all of New York.

Understandably, Du Bois proceeded cautiously in mounting full-
fledged opposition to the powerful Washington. After all, Du Bois was
a young man with a family, and, given his trenchantly articulated viewpoints, uncertain job prospects. He had reason to think that the Tuskegee
Wizard had not only blocked a possible job in Washington, D.C., but
also "facilitated" his failed visit to Alabama in February 1900. Washington was not a man to trifle with, in other words.

This much Du Bois knew. Thus, a scant year after his earlier journey
to rejection in Tuskegee, February 1901 found Du Bois again in Alabama,
this time for a conference in which Washington's cautious ideas served
as the centerpiece. An impressed Du Bois took to the pages of the widely
circulated *Harper's Weekly* to sing the praises of this gathering, brushing
aside misgivings.[1] Du Bois even expressed interest in spending personal
and intimate time with Washington, though apparently this wish was

not fulfilled. For his part, in his lavishly praised autobiography, Washington recalled fondly the time before Du Bois's later visit to Alabama: "there came to me what I might describe as almost the greatest surprise of my life," he said brightly. "Some good ladies in Boston arranged a public meeting in the interests of Tuskegee," which "was attended by large numbers of the best people of Boston, of both races. This meeting," said Washington with his usual class-tinged brio, "was attended by large numbers of the best people of Boston, of both races." Washington addressed the assembled, along with Paul Laurence Dunbar, and, the Wizard added pointedly, "Dr. W.E.B. Du Bois read an original sketch."[2]

Washington, born a slave in 1856 on a Virginia farm, was a mere 12 years older than Du Bois—but his experiences in bondage and growing up in the harshness of the South, gave him a perspective that differed substantially from that of his academically trained counterpart. By dint of tireless labor and shrewdness, Washington had built an empire headquartered at Tuskegee but he also had a far-reaching influence on the Baptist church—the parishioners of this largest of the black denominations extended throughout black America. His allies were potentates of the leading black fraternal orders. He controlled the editorial policies of nearly all of the black weekly newspapers through subsidies and, in a few cases, through outright ownership. Through his close ties to the presidencies of Theodore Roosevelt and William Howard Taft he controlled lucrative patronage posts, a power that was wielded deftly to reward his backers—and punish those not so blessed. Crossing Washington was a must to avoid.

Moreover, Du Bois presumably did not know—but well could have suspected—that the crafty Washington was, typically, a double-dealer. That is, though piously disclaiming any interest in voting rights for African Americans, he covertly worked behind the scenes to fund lawyers to challenge suffrage restrictions in Alabama and Louisiana. He battled racist discrimination that stained railway cars in Tennessee and elsewhere.[3] If Du Bois suspected this kind of progressive activity, there would be little reason for him to challenge this deviousness—not to mention that confronting Washington seemed to be a sure route to ostracism, isolation, and, possibly, financial disaster. Thus, Du Bois was upset with Washington's *public* posture, which seemed to portend a great leap backwards for black America.

Besides his prodigious labor and the desire to avoid running afoul of the influential Washington, there were other reasons for Du Bois to avoid ensnaring tensions. For a few years after the death of his son, he and his wife were blessed to give birth to a daughter, Nina Yolande. Moreover, Du Bois was developing friendships—with the Atlanta educator John Hope in the first place—that tended to occupy more of his time. Yet, as things turned out, his talks with the insightful Hope served as a sounding board for his increasingly distressed opinions of Washington's initiatives. Thus, it would be an error to assume that Du Bois's diplomatic effort to avoid alienating the powerful Washington was akin to a surrender to Tuskegee's agenda. Du Bois continued to call for more analytical studies of black America, on the premise that knowledge was a useful precondition for alleviation of pain; by publishing a detailed study of one typical Georgia county that contained more than a modicum of African Americans, Du Bois was engaged in a kind of proto-political warfare.[4] Besides, even Washington—a man to be feared—could hardly object to gathering data.

In line with his effort to convey basic data to the nation, Du Bois penned a comprehensive examination of the economic realities of the dual education system in the former slave South, which doomed African American youth to inferior education and reduced life's opportunities. Du Bois painstakingly showed the awful inadequacies of a separate-but-equal education; he also demonstrated that much of the money to support this obscenity came directly from African Americans themselves, and thus, in his view, financial support from the United States government for education was necessary. Simultaneously he produced two nearly book length studies on the inferior housing Negroes had to endure.[5] Immersing himself in the grim realities of black America, Du Bois produced an analysis on the impact of the economic downturn that gripped the nation at the turn of the century and how the downturn had devastated African American lives.[6]

Du Bois was a pioneer in exposing the grimy underbelly of the convict lease system, which led to mass arrests of African American men in particular, then turning them over to plantations and other employers for brutal labor. In a prescient comment, Du Bois concluded that by referring to "that sort of social protest and revolt which we call crime," we elide the wider point that "we must look for remedy in the same reform of these wrong social conditions, and not in intimidation, savagery, or the legalized slavery of men."[7]

As a relentless social science investigator, Du Bois was privy to information about the condition of African Americans that indisposed him to accept Washington's roseate acceptance of Jim Crow. Thus, it was easy to see why Du Bois may have concluded that Washington was too clever by a half—and had to be confronted; Washington's public opposition to the antiracist struggle, irrespective of his progressive subterfuges on behalf of positive causes, were too demobilizing and damaging, particularly in the midst of the unfortunately predictable waves of lynchings. Thus, in mid-1901, Du Bois wrote a review of Washington's highly praised autobiography in a widely circulated journal. It was a "partial history of the steps which made him a group leader," Du Bois sniffed, that exposed "but glimpses of the real struggle which he has had for leadership." Yes, conceded Du Bois, it was true that Washington had not invented that which had brought him fame (and scorn from a growing number of African American activists), in other words, industrial education or training blacks for proletarian posts (bricklaying, carpentry, mechanics, etc.), which often were disappearing because of automation or fiercely racist competition: this training at Tuskegee was accompanied by a disdain for the liberal arts, the study of foreign languages, and that which had propelled Du Bois. Du Bois also argued that the autobiography glossed over how much Washington compromised his ideals in order to secure the support of white elites. What Washington did, charged Du Bois, was to "put life, unlimited energy and perfect faith into this programme" and thereby converted the program into virtual dogma. Washington had triumphed, Du Bois said accusingly, because he had accepted Jim Crow in the South and "by singular insight he intuitively grasped the spirit of the age that was dominating the North," in other words, the "spirit of commercialism." In contemplating the Wizard's philosophy, Du Bois was aghast: "it is as though Nature must needs make men a little narrow to give them force." Du Bois went further, saying, "[Washington] pictures as the height of absurdity a black boy studying a French grammar in the midst of weeds and dirt. One wonders how Socrates or St. Francis of Assisi would receive this!"[8]

After crossing the Rubicon and confronting Washington publicly, Du Bois kept up a steady drumfire of opposition against the Wizard. While

the fabled Tuskegee Machine was counseling—at least publicly—meek
acceptance of the vulgarity of racist segregation, Du Bois led a delegation of African Americans to protest the notion that the public library
in Atlanta should be confined to whites only.[9] While Washington was
telling African Americans to keep their heads down and labor tirelessly
and silently, Du Bois with rising temper averred that his people "never
will abate one jot or title from his determination to attain in this land
perfect equality before the law with his fellow citizens."[10]

Meanwhile, as Du Bois was raising an ever-insistent voice against
accommodation to Jim Crow, Washington disagreed—at least publicly.
John Hope, the antilynching crusader Ida B. Wells-Barnett, Du Bois,
and a growing coterie who came to be known as the Talented Tenth
were appalled by Washington's attitude, and, more and more, they were
not afraid to say so. Among this increasingly disgruntled group was the
famed attorney and novelist, Charles Waddell Chesnutt. "I take a firm
stand for manhood suffrage, and the enforcement of the constitutional
amendments. I stake no stock whatever," he groused to Du Bois, "in these
disenfranchisement constitutions."[11] These intellectuals perceived accurately that Washington had another agenda, which was to demonize
his opponents with slighting words, which was not only anti-intellectual
(and quite dangerous for the besieged community of African Americans
who needed thoughtful strategies to escape from their plight) but was
also dangerous in the obtaining climate of the violent and powerful Ku
Klux Klan and other proponents of Jim Crow. In the argot of the era,
Du Bois and his comrades were deemed to be "uppity"—and such an
explosive charge in the then prevailing climate could lead directly to
fatalities, as the history of lynching amply demonstrated.

Yet Du Bois and his allies would not retreat. Soon, their dispute was
to be characterized as a death-match between the Tuskegee Machine
and the Talented Tenth. This was true—but it was more than this. For
from the bad old days of slavery to the exhilaration of its abolition—
and beyond—there had been a fundamental ideological split among
African Americans that inflamed the Du Bois–Washington confrontation. During slavery, there were those like Frederick Douglass who counseled confrontation with the slave system, and Martin Delaney, another
justly celebrated abolitionist, who looked abroad for aid to and solidarity with the enslaved. Then there were others who felt that bondage

was eternal and it was futile to oppose it. Today, there are those like Justice Clarence Thomas of the U.S. Supreme Court who disparage confrontation and others such as the Reverend Jesse Jackson who take a diametrically opposite tack.

It was during the uncertain post-Reconstruction years that Du Bois published his classic and perhaps best-known book, *The Souls of Black Folk*, a series of essays that included a devastating critique of one Booker T. Washington. A mere 265 pages, this book—one of the classics in the English language—emerged from its Chicago publisher in 1903, and catapulted Du Bois to center stage in black America. Over the decades it has sold hundreds of thousands of copies. Several of its chapters had been published earlier—in somewhat altered form—in magazines: however, the essay on Booker T. Washington, which was considered adventurous and bold at the time, was largely new, and it was momentous in that it publicized the fundamental differences that separated the two men. These differences led to the development of the Niagara Movement in 1905 and then, in 1909, its successor, the National Association for the Advancement of Colored People (NAACP). The influence of *The Souls of Black Folk* ricocheted not only throughout black America but also the Pan-African world. Casely Hayford, a west-African lawyer and author, who was then making his mark in the nation that was to be called Ghana, told Du Bois of the "pleasure" he had derived from his book.[12]

As is apparent in the book, Du Bois has obvious affection for his people. He clearly believes that they had a special and ennobling mission to perform for humankind, as their oppressed condition was encased in their great and dramatic artistry. The book radiates with what could easily be characterized as a Black Nationalist consciousness, which prefigures this trend's efflorescence in the movement of the Jamaica-born Marcus Garvey (who, ironically, famously crossed swords with Du Bois shortly after Washington's death in 1915). The book also reflects a keen awareness of Du Bois's realization that African Americans were tied inexorably to darker peoples worldwide—which too was a response to his nation's most recent imperialist turn, as evidenced by the seizure of Hawaii and the ouster of Spain from Puerto Rico, Cuba, and the Philippines.

Each essay is a sparkling jewel. One essay gives a touching assessment of Alexander Crummel, a man who had served as a role model for him.

Another provides a painfully explicit treatment of the death of his first-born son, Burghardt. At a time when those of African origin allegedly lacked humanity, the very title of this remarkable book forcefully rejected such a notion. This distillation of the humanity that characterized African Americans—a radical thought for the time—continues to give the book vitality, even as the idea of their inhumanity has dissipated. Du Bois accomplishes this exacting task by citing Negro spirituals—of the kind that the Fisk Jubilee Singers had made famous—throughout. Du Bois's unique ability to evoke the awful present while peering over the horizon to detect the shape of the future, is no better glimpsed than in the signature line of the volume: "the problem of the Twentieth Century," he intoned portentously at the dawn of this new century, "is the problem of the color line," a weighty point that he had enunciated previously. It was Du Bois who remarked that "the relation of the darker to the lighter races of men in Asia and Africa, in America and the islands of the sea" was the crux of decades to unfold.[13] Yet in framing this question, Du Bois presupposed that it was a problem that was hardly insoluble (if it were, it would hardly be worth a remark), and thus, he anticipated the anticolonial wave that was to envelope the planet by the time of his death.

That is not all. Again, Du Bois posed a question in this worthy volume that continues to resonate: "How does it feel to be a problem?" With these few words, he captured the vexing dilemma of African Americans who could not be seen in their humanity or even as distinct individuals but, instead, as little more than exemplars of a "problem people." He did not stop there. It was in this book that Du Bois articulated yet another theme that was to illuminate the black condition while igniting a debate that rages to this day. For it was here that Du Bois remarked that the African American "ever feels his two-ness," that is, being "an American, a Negro; two souls, two thoughts, two unreconciled strivings." In other words, the African American has "two warring ideals in one dark body, whose dogged strength alone keeps it from being torn asunder." Heretofore, dissenting and radical African American thinkers had—like Martin Delany or Henry Highland Garnet—counseled expatriation or separation as the preferred road for the Negro. Those like Douglass had advised that complete assimilation was the way out of the awfulness of racism. Du Bois sliced the Gordian knot—or perhaps, more precisely, untied it—by acknowledging that there was a recurring tension between the two viewpoints that was unavoidable. *The Souls of Black Folk* is a book, in short, for the ages

Despite the wealth of ideas in the book, what riveted the attention of many readers of that time was Du Bois's frank airing of his differences with Booker T. Washington, a man whose power of retaliation was both fearsome and predictable. Du Bois's challenge was not only articulated on his own behalf but he also purported to speak for the Talented Tenth, who railed against the Tuskegee Wizard's disparagement of intellectual accomplishment and political engagement. Du Bois's book caused a debate to erupt in black America that was to result in a more formal and organizational challenge to Tuskegee's hegemony. Du Bois had been a man of words and study but with the publication of this book, he was to be propelled more overtly into the arena of activism, and soon his name was to equal that of Booker T. Washington in fame and high regard.

Buoyed by this newfound recognition, which included more requests for public speaking and literary contributions, which in turn brought larger and larger audiences (often predominantly of Euro-Americans, interestingly enough), he chose not to dilute his message to make it go down easier; instead, he sharpened his sword, affirming that racism in the United States was a form—albeit an especially virulent form—of elitism and class oppression. This too was a breakthrough of sorts, marking a great leap forward from the thinking of Douglass and, certainly, Washington. This bombshell was delivered in Manhattan at the Twentieth Century Club, many of whose members were both outraged and frightened by the explosion of labor militancy, anarchism, and socialism that Du Bois's words about class seemed to portend. In recent years, Populists had rocked the countryside while labor militants in the Knights of Labor had been busily organizing factories and anarchists were enmeshed in the "propaganda of the deed," which did not exclude targeted assassinations of the rich and the powerful. Socialists were on the march on both sides of the Atlantic, and the Industrial Workers of the World (whose greatest strength was in the mines and timberlands of the far West and the vessels that delivered both exports and imports) had had a spurt of growth as well. Du Bois, who had witnessed many of these trends while in Europe, seemed to be suggesting that the plight of African Americans was not far distant from the situation faced by those targeted by the radical left and that an alliance of more than convenience was in order.

His perception was fueled by the associations he had developed, among which was his tie to S. M. Sexton of the United Mine Workers (UMW). It was early in 1903 that Sexton informed Du Bois that his union had "always welcomed the Negro" into its ranks. "Many Negroes hold responsible offices both in local and state organizations" of the UMW, he said.[14] Of course, it was in the very nature of their labor that miners—enmeshed in what may have been the most hazardous occupation of all—exuded solidarity; in the bleakness and darkness underground with sooty faces all around, obliterating distinctiveness, and a necessity to rely upon one's fellow worker in order to leave the mine alive, miners had come to exemplify a class solidarity across racial lines that contrasted sharply with the policy of other unions. Nevertheless, the members of the Twentieth Century Club had to realize that failing to ease the burden pressing down on the Negro was likely to bring such an alliance closer to fruition.[15] Du Bois did not reassure these elites when he announced shortly thereafter, "I have many socialistic beliefs," not to mention "sympathy with the movement" itself.[16]

Of course, the high and mighty could attempt to ignore Du Bois and give even more support to the Tuskegee Machine. Thus, Du Bois sought to block this passageway by escalating his assault on Booker T. Washington, informing a reporter from the journalistic empire of William Randolph Hearst that "we refuse to kiss the hands that smite us"—unlike the Alabamian. He went on to say that "the way for black [people] today to make these rights the heritage of their children is to struggle for them unceasingly, and [if] they fail, die trying."[17] But Du Bois chose to assail not just the puppet but also the puppeteer. For he pursued the then audacious maneuver of denouncing the Jim Crow titans of the U.S. Senate, including "Pitchfork" Ben Tillman of South Carolina and James Vardaman of Mississippi, the two leading voices of not only Negro disenfranchisement but overall defenestration.[18] Today, it is difficult to imagine how courageous it was to criticize these men who were not above launching lynch mobs.

It was Du Bois's example that no doubt caused others to enter the fray. Foremost among these was William Monroe Trotter, a fellow Harvard man who continued to reside in Boston, where he toiled as a gutsy

and plucky writer whose frequent flaying of the Tuskegee Machine ri-
valed those of Du Bois. At a now renowned event in Boston, Trotter received word that Washington was coming to town to address members
of his National Negro Business League who were gathering at the African Methodist Episcopal Zion church on Columbus Avenue. It was a
hot summer day in 1903—July 30 to be exact—when Trotter and his
hearty band erupted, and seemingly rushed the podium to confront
Washington physically. Pandemonium reigned, along with shouting
and cries of anguish. Punches were thrown. Apparently a police officer
who had rushed to the scene was stabbed. Washington could only gape
in amazement as some of Trotter's comrades bellowed in his direction,
"We don't like you," a sentiment that they then were acting out in dramatic fashion.[19]

The Trotter-led demarche was symptomatic of a growing militancy
in black America, a refusal to accept supinely the veil of oppression. The
convulsion in Boston was a rejection of Washington—his surreptitious
activism aside—and his call to building enterprises, a directive that made
no sense considering that Negro entrepreneurs were a prime target of
lynch mobs, as their very existence violated the basic precepts of white
supremacy. As difficult as the struggle might have been, there was no escape from the battle for basic rights, particularly voting rights.

Yet just as Du Bois had sought to reconcile the contrasting philo-
sophies of Douglass and Delany by writing eloquently about "double-
consciousness"—the ability to think of oneself as both "American" and
"African"—Du Bois continued to think (at least for a while) that he
could bridge the choppy waters that separated Trotter from Washington. Thus, he continued to seek an entente between the two, including
planning for a confab to that end to be held in Manhattan at Carnegie
Hall in early 1904. It was an opportunity for a "heart to heart talk with
Mr. Washington," Du Bois said hopefully, though he must have known
that the Wizard would not have found the agenda appealing since Number One on this list was "full political rights on the same term as other
Americans"—though it was followed by a concession to the Tuskegee
Machine: a call for "industrial education for the masses." Yet Du Bois
made it clear that the Atlanta Compromise was not the guiding light
he had in mind for this gathering: he concluded, "the general watch
word must be, not to put further dependence on the help of the whites

but to organize for self help, encouraging 'manliness without defiance, conciliation without servility.'"[20]

Still, in addressing the influential donor, George Peabody, Du Bois sought to bridge the gulf that was separating Trotter and Washington; he criticized Trotter's "lack of judgment," and noted that he possessed "less and less faith in Mr. Washington," who was "leading the way backward."[21]

Agreeing that "we ought to have as far as possible, all shades of opinion represented," Washington seemed to meet Du Bois half way; however, he also said that "our people are in the South [and] we should be very sure that there is a large element in the conference who actually know Southern conditions by experience," and "to [not] depend too much on mere theory and untried schemes of Northern colored people"—a direct jab at Du Bois's Talented Tenth.[22]

Ritualistic bowing to the necessity of Negro unity in a hostile environment ultimately could not bridge the increasingly wide chasm that separated Trotter from Washington, and the Carnegie Hall gathering predictably failed to lead to an entente between the warring factions.

This was so in no small part because, perhaps, even more than Trotter, it was Du Bois who was growing more distant from Washington. While Du Bois was sympathetic to unions, Washington thought they were little more than folly. Washington was disdainful toward women's suffrage—Du Bois decidedly was not. While Du Bois spent most of his life in cosmopolitan sites such as Philadelphia, Atlanta, and New York, Washington resided in rural Alabama. There was a fundamental difference in these men's respective ideologies that simply making nice with each other could not overcome. It was inevitable that their paths would diverge. Yet more than the individual differences that separated these two men, their respective paths represented alternative modes of handling Jim Crow—resistance versus accommodation. This difference took organizational form when Du Bois helped to initiate the Niagara Movement, then the NAACP.

Meanwhile, the opposition that had congealed to block the ascendancy of Washington's ideology had broadened into a full-scale challenge that would transform black America and the nation as a whole. On January 13, 1905, a meeting was held at the office of William Trotter in Boston. The capital of the Bay State was an appropriate venue for this important confab for although Boston was a citadel of abolitionism, it was not above enforcing Jim Crow measures. Hence, at this meeting a decision was made to seek a meeting with President Theodore Roosevelt with the aim of compelling him to command his attorney general to uphold the 15th Amendment (mandating the right to vote for the formerly enslaved) in cases that reached the U.S. Supreme Court. Second, this group demanded that the White House enforce the Interstate Commerce Clause of the Constitution with regard to curbing Jim Crow on trains in particular. Finally, these comrades of Du Bois wanted the Roosevelt regime to encourage national aid to education in the most needy states.

These three demands—the right to vote, curbing Jim Crow, and education—were not only to become the hallmark of the Niagara Movement that Du Bois was to spearhead that same year, 1905, but was to be the epicenter of the civil rights earthquake that erupted in the 1950s. Still, Roosevelt chose not to meet with Du Bois and his crew, not least because he was decidedly favorable to the Tuskegee Machine.[23]

Yet in some ways, the opposition from the White House was not the most impregnable roadblock encountered by Du Bois and his fellow dissidents. The fact was that the Tuskegee Machine had a virtual stranglehold on the many newspapers that catered to African Americans, and ever since the first of this genre—*Freedom's Journal*—had come into existence in 1827, these organs had been essential in shaping consciousness and attitudes among this often besieged community. Thus, Du Bois complained bitterly, "in order to forestall criticism of certain persons [Washington's] money has been freely furnished [to] a set of Negro newspapers in the principal cities," and the continuously lengthening list of black newspapers included the prime organs in New York City, Chicago, Boston, Washington, and Indianapolis, among other metropolises. And this filthy lucre came directly from Tuskegee. These funds, carped Du Bois, had come in part as a "direct bonus, part in advertising & all of it has been given on condition that these papers print certain matters & refrain from other matters. This movement has been going on now for 3 or 4 years." Du Bois groused in March 1905, "until [this situation is now] notorious among well-informed Negroes & a subject of frequent comment."[24]

This was no minor matter since Washington's veritable control of the newspapers (the major means of communication in an era before radio and mass profusion of telephones) gave him almost untold influence, which made it exceedingly difficult for anyone, including Du Bois, to carve out an alternative agenda to Washington's. Thus, by confronting Tuskegee, Du Bois had placed himself in a vulnerable and sensitive position. Washington had a record of crushing opponents with little hint of mercy. Moreover, Washington had powerful winds at his back, something that Du Bois well knew. As Du Bois put it, "he has the support of the nation, he has the political patronage of the [Roosevelt] administration, he has apparently unlimited cash, he has the ear of the white press."[25]

As was his wont, Du Bois not only chose to challenge Washington's undue influence on the press but, in addition, chose to construct an alternative. As a college student he had served as the editor of the *Fisk Herald*, and had long expressed an interest in building his own journal to intervene forcefully in the battle of ideas. This opportunity arose in the midst of his jousting with Washington when he accepted the opportunity to serve as editor of a journal—*Moon: Illustrated Weekly*—which was published on Saturdays at a printing shop on Memphis's famed Beale Street. He was still teaching at Atlanta University, still conducting groundbreaking research, still challenging Washington, and yet, he found the time to take on another pressing responsibility. *Moon* had the distinction of being the first illustrated weekly in black America and attracted a slew of advertisers, including real estate companies, dentists, insurance companies, and the like. But then as now, launching a new publication was more than a notion and this journal that began with such promise in 1905—was defunct within a year. Undaunted, Du Bois quickly proceeded to launch a brand new publication, *The Horizon: A Journal of the Color Line*, which he owned and edited, though it was printed in Washington, D.C.

Both of these publications prefigured his trailblazing editorship of the *Crisis*, which lasted for more than two decades, beginning in 1910. All of these journals displayed his lifelong concerns: a dedicated interest in Africa and a concerted sympathy for the poor and working class. Crossing swords with the Tuskegee Machine had led Du Bois to the realization that scholarship was simply not enough to undermine the towering edifice that was Jim Crow, which is why during the summer of 1905, Du Bois and his comrades found themselves in Canada, where they forged an agenda that meant nothing less than a major course correction for black America.

NOTES

1. W.E.B. Du Bois, "Results of the Ten Tuskegee Conferences," *Harper's Weekly*, 45 (June 22, 1901): 641.

2. Booker T. Washington, *Up from Slavery*, New York: Penguin, 1986, 270.

3. David Levering Lewis, 258–259.

4. W.E.B. Du Bois, "The Negro as He Really Is," *World's Work*, 2 (June 1901): 848–866.

5. W.E.B\. Du Bois, "The Home of the Country Freedmen," *Southern Workman*, 30 (October 1901): 535–542. (other phases of this study appear in the same journal in the June, September, November, December, and February 1902 editions).

6. W.E.B. Du Bois, "The Savings of Black Georgia," *Outlook*, 69 (September 14, 1901): 128–130.

7. W.E.B. Du Bois, "The Spawn of Slavery, the Convict Lease System in the South," *Missionary Review of the World*, 14 (October 1901): 737–745.

8. W.E.B. Du Bois, "The Evolution of Negro Leadership," *Dial*, 31 (July 1, 1901): 53–55.

9. W.E.B. Du Bois, "The Opening of the Library," *Independent*, 54 (April 3, 1902): 809–810.

10. W.E.B. Du Bois, "Hopeful Signs for the Negro," *Advance*, 54 (October 2, 1902): 327–328.

11. Charles Waddell Chesnutt to W.E.B. Du Bois, June 27, 1903, in Herbert Aptheker, ed., *The Correspondence of W.E.B. Du Bois: Volume I, Selections, 1877–1934*, Amherst: University of Massachusetts Press, 1973.

12. Casely Hayford to W.E.B. Du Bois, June 8, 1904, in Herbert Aptheker, ed., *The Correspondence of W.E.B. Du Bois: Volume I, Selections, 1877–1934*, Amherst: University of Massachusetts Press, 1973, 76.

13. W.E.B. Du Bois, *The Souls of Black Folk: Essays and Sketches*, Chicago: McClurg, 1903, 35, 49, 59.

14. S. M. Sexton to W.E.B. Du Bois, February 22, 1903, in Herbert Aptheker, ed., *The Correspondence of W.E.B. Du Bois: Volume I, Selections, 1877–1934*, Amherst: University of Massachusetts Press, 1973, 50.

15. Du Bois's weighty words were reported widely, indicative of their explosive importance; see *Boston Transcript*, February 21, 1904; *San Antonio Gazette*, April 17, 1904; *Des Moines Register Leader*, October 19, 1904; *Savannah News*, October 19, 1904; *Denver News*, October 19, 1904; *Chicago Tribune*, December 16, 1904.

16. W.E.B. Du Bois to I. M. Rubinow, November 17, 1904, in Aptheker, *Correspondence, Volume I*, 82.

17. *World Today* (Chicago), 6 (April 1904): 521–523.

18. W.E.B. Du Bois, "The Problem of Tillman, Vardaman," et al., *Central Christian Advocate*, 49 (October 18, 1905): 1324–1325.

19. *Boston Globe*, July 31, 1903. See also Ruth Ann Stewart, *The Life of Portia Washington Pittman, The Daughter of Booker T. Washington*, Garden City, NY: Doubleday, 1977, 50–51.

20. W.E.B. Du Bois to Kelly Miller, February 25, 1903, in Aptheker, *Correspondence, Volume I*, 53. See also Herbert Aptheker, "The Washington-Du Bois Conference of 1904," *Science and Society*, 13 (1949): 345–351.

21. W.E.B. Du Bois to George Peabody, December 28, 1903, in Aptheker, *Correspondence, Volume I*, 67–68.

22. Booker T. Washington to W.E.B. Du Bois, November 8, 1903, in Aptheker, *Correspondence, Volume I*, 53–54.

23. Alexander Walters to W.E.B. Du Bois, January 13, 1905, in Aptheker, ed., *Correspondence, Volume I*, 92–93.

24. W.E.B. Du Bois to William Hayes Ward, March 10, 1905, in Aptheker, *Correspondence, Volume I*, 96. See also August Meier, "Booker T. Washington and the Negro Press," *Journal of Negro History*, 38 (January 1953): 67–90.

25. W.E.B. Du Bois to Oswald Garrison Villard, March 24, 1905, in Aptheker, *Correspondence, Volume I*, 98–102.

Chapter 4

PRESENT AT THE CREATION

Why would African Americans who were interested in blazing a new trail for black America in the early years of the 20th century choose to meet in Canada?

The northern neighbor of the United States long had been a sanctuary for African Americans escaping enslavement; the British Empire, of which Canada had been a prime part, had abolished human bondage well before the United States, and even before that hallowed time, this huge colony had evinced a decided sympathy for abolitionism. More than half a century before Du Bois's arrival in Ontario, Frederick Douglass had arrived in Seneca Falls, New York—about a hundred miles away on Lake Ontario—to demand equality for women. As Douglass and his compatriots arrived in upstate New York, enslaved Africans in the United States by the thousands were escaping bondage by following the "North Star" to freedom in Canada. When John Brown made his powerful antislavery raid in 1859 at Harpers Ferry, Virginia, the basic planning for this epochal event had taken place in Canada. Certainly, those who were worried about the reach of the Tuskegee Machine's snooping would feel more comfortable meeting in a jurisdiction where the government was not thought to be an ally of Booker T. Washington. Indeed, during the War of 1812, Canadians—contrary to the way this war was perceived south of the border—harbored the disturbing impression that the United States wanted to seize their homeland. Over the years Canadians had developed a healthy skepticism of the beneficence of the United States, an ethos shared by many African Americans; thus, this huge and sprawling nation was a logical choice for a meeting of black America's leading dissidents. Ironically, these dissidents had wanted to meet in Buffalo, New York, but—predictably—a surge of Jim Crow had compelled them to seek refuge across the border.

Thus it was that 29 men and one teenage boy arrived on July 10, 1905, at the charming and venerable Erie Beach Hotel in Ontario, Canada's richest and most populous province. Their clarion cry had been endorsed by 59 men—subsequently, the dearth of women in what came to be called the Niagara Movement would become a source of contention—from 16 states and the District of Columbia. The mission they chose to accept was no less than the bold reinvention of the politics of black America. To that end they devised a structure that included a Press and Public Opinion Committee with the preeminent among them, Du Bois and Trotter in the leadership, suggestive of the desire to confront the overwhelming control exerted over newspapers by the Tuskegee Machine. Du Bois was also elected as the chief administrative officer of this group and was also selected to draft the primary document that emerged from their urgent huddling.

Their now celebrated "Declaration of Principles" bore the indelible imprint of Du Bois's thinking with its anguished lamentation of what had befallen African Americans, its bitter denunciation of Jim Crow, and its interest in class-based organizations such as trade unions, which although hopeful, was still clear-eyed about the reluctance among many union leaders to embrace the darkest among us.

As things turned out, the founding of the Niagara Movement occurred at a fortuitous moment. While acknowledging that "the color line belts the world," Du Bois remarked that Japan's defeat of Czarist Russia in a bloody war in 1905 signified the beginning of the end of "white supremacy."[1] This was a startling assertion in light of contemporaneous developments in Du Bois's own backyard. For as Du Bois was drafting his prescient words about white supremacy, one of the worst pogroms against African Americans that had occurred up to that point broke out in Atlanta in September 1906.

By the 1880s, Atlanta had become the hub of an ever-growing economy, with its population soaring from 89,000 in 1890 to 150,000 in 1910. Rapid change and growth are often unsettling; competition for employment frequently is heightened in such a circumstance, and reactions against alleged "foreign" elements fuels xenophobia and fear. It was in this context that Tom Watson—who had been catapulted into prominence as a Populist, fighting the malefactors of great wealth—devolved into a race-baiting reactionary, eager to castigate African Americans. When in 1906 local newspapers reported inflammatorily that white women had been assaulted by black men, a racist and murderous riot took place. Thousands of whites fell upon and viciously beat every African American they could lay hands on. Blacks were ejected from trolley cars and chased, and the sidewalks soon were bathed in blood. Strikingly, a number of African Americans had armed themselves and were able to beat back the howling mobs—but others were not so lucky, falling victim to bloodlust. Among the former, however, was Du Bois, who at a moment of tension, grabbed a shotgun in order to protect his family. Nonetheless, at most two whites died as a result of this riotous episode, whereas an estimated 40 Negroes were killed.[2]

The riot was a sobering reminder of what Du Bois and the Niagara Movement were up against. As if that were not enough, in that same year—1906—in Brownsville, Texas, a gun battle involving Negro soldiers occurred. This was on the border with Mexico, as tensions with this southern neighbor were waxing, as a revolution was brewing that would transform this nation and the borderlands generally. In response to this outbreak of violence, all the Negro men of these segregated units were ordered discharged—dishonorably—by President Roosevelt. Ultimately, this harsh decision was reversed, but there is little doubt that this incident soured Du Bois further on Roosevelt and his party, the Republicans, for which those few Negroes who could vote had cast their ballots.[3]

These events helped fuel an escalation of Du Bois's ongoing radicalization. In his own journal, *Horizon*, he declared himself a "Socialist-of-the-Path," that is, he endorsed government ownership of railroads, coal mines, and certain factories. As he saw it then, in the "socialistic

trend . . . lies the one great hope of the Negro American." He was not
in accord with the Socialists on all matters; yet, he added tellingly, "in
trend and ideal they are the salt of this present earth."[4] Shortly thereafter, Du Bois joined the Socialist Party itself, and though his party
affiliations varied thereafter, such viewpoints remained with him to
his death.[5]

On the other hand, Du Bois's disaffection with the hegemonic GOP
was reflected in a series of what he termed "heart-to-heart talks with
the Negro American voter." The first offering in this series noted tartly
that "aside from special consideration of race, the policy of the Democratic party is the best policy for this nation." He chose to elide this party's horrible racism, which included an ongoing alliance in the Deep
South with the terrorists known as the Ku Klux Klan, because the Democratic party was more favorable to the cause of organized labor (and
organized labor's cause "is the cause of black laborers") and because the
party was seen as more hostile to both monopolies and imperialism,
as manifested most dramatically in Cuba and the Philippines.[6] Thus,
Du Bois announced boldly in 1908, the "Democratic Party deserves a
trial at the hands of the Negro," and that "the best thing that can happen in the next election will be a big black [William Jennings] Bryan
vote." Bryan was a silver-tongued Nebraskan whose stem-winding
perorations long had captured the imagination of the nation.[7] When
Bryan was defeated at the hands of the Republican, William Howard
Taft, Du Bois noted acidly that "we did not happen to have the power
in the last election of deciding who should be President but we will
have the power in certain future elections."[8] Du Bois's newfound affection for the Democrats—which was to blossom decisively with the
rise of Theodore Roosevelt's kin, Franklin—can be interpreted as a
rejection of the GOP, which, he thought, had "forfeited its claim to the
Negro vote."[9]

This was a growing sentiment among African Americans, propelled
in large part by Roosevelt's ejection of Negro soldiers from service after
the Brownsville episode and his blatant kowtowing to racist sentiment
in order to reassure the doubting that he was not as close to the Negro
people as his relationship with Booker T. Washington may have indicated.[10]

It was in such an unforgiving atmosphere that the Niagara Movement chose to meet again, this time on August 15, 1906, at a site pregnant with meaning—Harper's Ferry. It was here in 1859 that the heroic John Brown had sought to spark a massive slave uprising and, instead, helped to foment a Civil War that had the same effect: abolition. Du Bois did not disappoint, as the Blue Ridge mountains that had resonated with cries of emancipation decades earlier now rang with his call for enforcement of the U.S. Constitution, specifically the 14th Amendment proviso for reduction in the congressional representation of states where African Americans were deprived of the vote. Yet Du Bois did not simply stop there. He went on to make demands that have yet to lose relevance: "We claim for ourselves," he said, "every single right that belongs to a freeborn American political, civil and social; and until we get these rights we will never cease to protest and to assail the ears of America. The battle we wage is not for ourselves alone but for all true Americans. It is a fight for ideals, lest this, our common fatherland, false to its founding, become in truth the land of the thief and the home of the Slave—a byword and a hissing among the nations for its sounding pretensions and pitiful accomplishments."[11]

Though claiming equality today seems to be the most commonplace of common sense, in 1906 this was far from the case. Negroes could be lynched—brutally murdered—by simply hinting that they were equal: this was the quotidian application of the doctrine of white supremacy. Consider, for example, that as Du Bois was heroically raising his voice in opposition to Jim Crow, the Reverend T. Nelson Baker—who was also African American—was chiding Negro youth for refusing to adhere to segregated arrangements in Nashville, a town that Du Bois knew all too well. Baker suggested that Jim Crow resulted not from the diktat of white supremacy but, instead, from the supposed "defects" of African Americans themselves. He berated what he saw as the "chronic state of whining and pouting" among these youth, and argued that the "degradation of Negro women"—they were routinely subjected to sexual harassment by white men—was driven by the women's supposed "perverted aesthetical taste" for these men.[12]

The Reverend Baker was only expressing what was then the prevailing nonsense about the presumed "bestiality" of the Negro, and, therefore, Du Bois's rising in opposition to his diatribe should be seen as courageous as it was at that juncture. It was "sad," said Du Bois, that the Reverend Baker would speak so disparagingly of his own people; this "vicious and wanton attack which you have made on educated Negro womanhood—the nasty slur on the chastity of that class of Negro women to which my wife belongs and the young women whom I teach every day [belong]—is the most cowardly and shameless thing I have recently read." Du Bois did not flinch in stoutly "expressing to [Baker] my indignation and my righteous contempt for a man who thus publicly maligns that very class of women to which his own wife and mother belong."[13]

It was not only the Reverend Baker who was compelled to endure Du Bois's testy rebukes. Joining him in being castigated was the noted Boston attorney, Samuel May, Jr., son of the staunch abolitionist, the Reverend Samuel J. May. After May, Jr., expressed support for Jim Crow, Du Bois reprimanded him. He argued that "segregation of any set of human beings, be they black, white or of any color or race is a bad thing, since human contact is the thing that makes for civilization and human contact is a thing for which all of us are striving today."[14]

Baker and May should not necessarily be viewed as outliers; in many ways, they represented the mainstream of what passed for "respectable" opinion. It was Du Bois and the Niagara Movement that seemed to be beyond the pale. Thus, David Wallace, a civil rights activist, who was about to move from the relatively mild racial climate of Chicago to the decidedly more chilly atmosphere in Chattanooga, Tennessee, reminded Du Bois that "there are many who dare not, for good reasons, speak or contribute openly who ought to know of that method of rendering substantial aid to a cause which, I am sure, lies close to [many] Negroes' and many white men's hearts." Thus, reluctantly, Wallace concluded that though he might "later find it possible to be associated with you openly but for the present my resignation is final." Though he added, "you shall have a secret comrade in me."[15]

With all due respect to Wallace, what the Niagara Movement needed were men—and women—bold enough to stand openly by Du Bois's side. Nevertheless, the anger and fury in Du Bois's words, in his retort to Baker and, above all, in his declaration on behalf of the Niagara Movement marked a watershed in the evolution of the politics of black America. It marked the beginning of the end of the accommodation to Jim Crow represented by the Tuskegee Machine and the rise of a fierce militancy that eventuated in the founding of the NAACP in 1909.

Now with organizational heft behind him in the form of Niagara, Du Bois attacked the Tuskegee Wizard. Taking to the pages of the *Moon*, which he had helped to initiate, he excoriated the regression Negroes had been forced to take under Washington's less than inspiring leadership. Disenfranchisement had spread like mushrooms after a brisk spring rain, as had separate—and inferior for blacks—train cars.[16]

This was the grim reality that greeted the beleaguered members of the Niagara Movement as they gathered in Oberlin, Ohio, in August 1908. The GOP was rapidly deserting the Negro, while the Democrats—albeit having more union support—were not above dalliances with the Ku Klux Klan. The leafy and bucolic Midwestern college town of Oberlin was known for its antiracism, having admitted Negro students even before the Civil War erupted, and it continued to boast of its abolitionist credentials. Yet Oberlin in its uniqueness stood starkly as something of an admonition to the nation as a whole where such progressive sentiments were hardly evident. The meeting in Oberlin had been preceded by the Niagara Movement's meeting in Boston, Trotter's hometown and site of his disruption of Booker T. Washington's conference, which had catapulted these dissidents into organizing an alternative movement.[17]

Du Bois was general secretary of this organization, which carried the hopes of so many under such adverse conditions. Traveling southward Du Bois spoke before an energized crowd of 500 cheering Negroes at the Shiloh Baptist Church in Washington, D.C., whose pastor, the Reverend J. M. Waldron, was a fellow member of the Niagara Movement. "It is high time to take steps to show our power," Du Bois bellowed, but the hopefulness of Oberlin and Boston could not obscure the grim realities that obtained.[18]

In short, despite the yeoman efforts of Du Bois and his fellow strugglers, the path to freedom led steeply uphill. Increasingly, the mainstream press was pitting Du Bois against Washington—to the detriment of the former. One journal claimed that it was Du Bois who was "ashamed" of being a Negro since he demanded a swift end to racist discrimination (presumably, the unashamed welcomed racism). A restrained Du Bois could only respond that he found it "very extraordinary that you should regard the man who stands up for his rights as being ashamed of himself."[19] His life in Atlanta easily confirmed this reality, if there was any doubt. Jim Crow reigned supreme, which meant that the city's commodious library was barred to him. The mass transit system had severe Jim Crow restrictions, which he and his spouse, Nina, would not deign to patronize. They too were excluded from the better retail stores, which did not leave either in an ideal mood. Then there were the general indignities to which they were subjected, such as, having to be careful about which water fountain from which to take a cold drink on a hot day or what park bench upon which to rest after a taxing stroll.

Subjected to such casual cruelties, Du Bois, a proud man, was understandably resentful, and, like many Negroes, was quick to discern slights from whites who seemed oblivious to the blows to which he was subjected on a routine basis. Thus, he developed a reputation for possessing a cold reserve that, fundamentally—to the extent it existed—was a reflection of the circumstance in which he found himself as a black man who had to be quite careful in expressing himself or displaying any visible emotion, lest it engender an extremely adverse reaction.

Of course, there were compensations. One was the easy relationship he developed with Mary White Ovington, a reformer and socialist. Born three years before Du Bois, as the Civil War lurched to a close, she became a social worker of note with sterling expertise. Strikingly beautiful with blonde hair and penetratingly blue eyes, he came to rely upon her because of her deep understanding of urban poverty—based upon experience in both New York City and London—and her even deeper recognition of the necessity for far-reaching change in the United States and the world. Ultimately, she was to become essential in helping Du Bois to launch the NAACP. Yet Jim Crow cast a shadow over this friendship too, for he was unable to set foot in the lobbies of the hotels in which she resided when she visited Atlanta; such restrictions placed an undue strain upon their relationship.

But the strain was insufficient to bar her participation in a momentous gathering, for it was on May 31, 1909, that Du Bois hosted in New York City the modestly titled "National Negro Conference" (sometimes referred to as the "National Committee on the Negro"), which marked the founding of the much awaited NAACP. In addition to Du Bois, also present at the creation of this momentous organization were Ovington, Oswald Garrison Villard (a lineal descendant of the famed abolitionist, William Lloyd Garrison), and William English Walling (like many of the participants, a man of socialist beliefs). It was Walling's chilling and expansive account of the anti-Negro riots that rocked Springfield, Illinois—the city that propelled Abraham Lincoln—that was the proximate cause of this august meeting.

It seemed that the terribly tumultuous events that some had thought were only indigenous to the Deep South (e.g., Du Bois's own Atlanta) were spreading northward at a dangerous pace, removing any idea that there might be a sanctuary or haven for an increasingly besieged population. For it was in this otherwise drab and unprepossessing Midwestern town that white mobs rampaged through the streets for weeks, setting fire to black businesses, beating up blacks whenever they found them, and demanding that two black inmates—both accused of crimes against whites—be handed over to them by the county sheriff. It took 5,000 federal troops to restore calm and order. It was all a familiar story. Again, the press was complicit for it was on August 14, 1908, that the *Illinois State Register* reported in hysterical terms the alleged rape of a white woman by a black man; it was "one of the greatest outrages that ever happened in Springfield," it was reported with fury barely abated. It was a "premeditated assault," and "no effort should be spared to find the black viper." Weeks later, the woman in question, Mabel Hallam, would confess to having fabricated the entire story.

As this catastrophe was unfolding, also concluding was the first genocide of the new century, as Imperial Germany intentionally devastated the Herero and Nama peoples of the nation that is now Namibia—in southwest Africa—in a brutal battle over land and resources, in a prophetic but little-noticed rehearsal of what was to befall Europe a few decades later. As this awful genocide was ending, on the other side of the world in Australia, Jack Johnson, an African American boxer stirred fury when he decisively defeated—and pummeled—a white opponent. Johnson's victory was a setback not accepted supinely in the United States and elsewhere. The upset spurred a search for a "White Hope" who could beat Jackson and put him in his place. In such a fetid and fervent atmosphere, Du Bois—and those who joined him in New York City in 1909—knew that they had to build an organization to confront the bestiality that seemed to be encircling the globe. They had arrived at this realization not least because as Du Bois declared remarkably, "Negro slavery exists on a large scale in the United States today."[20] He was referring to the pervasive debt peonage that had entrapped too many Negroes in a system whereby they grew crops for a landlord but somehow never escaped debt and a convict-lease system based upon casual mass arrests of Negro men particularly, who were then hired out to employers with none too tender mercies.

Thus, the need was crying and urgent when Du Bois arrived in New York City for this important meeting. He was pleased with his handi-work. The "net result" of this epochal gathering, he announced, was "the vision of future cooperation, not simply as in the past, between giver and beggar—the older ideal of charity—but a new alliance be-tween experienced social workers and reformers in touch on the one hand with scientific philanthropy and on the other with the great strug-gling mass of laborers of all kinds, whose condition and needs know no color line."[21] As Du Bois then saw it, African Americans were "girding themselves to fight in the van of progress," not only for themselves but also for "the emancipation of women, universal peace, democratic gov-ernment, the socialization of wealth and human brotherhood."[22] This democratically capacious and profoundly altruistic vision of the strug-gle of African Americans, which was established and first articulated by Du Bois, was to be the keynote of their human rights crusade for the rest of the century. Thus, Du Bois also was well aware that racism was a crosscut saw that did not slice in only one direction and that the battle for equality on behalf of African Americans was not for them-selves alone. In a short reflection, purposefully entitled, "The Souls of White Folk," he recorded that because of racism these "souls" were "daily shriveling and dying [in] the fierce flame of the new fanaticism." He went on to ask, "Whither has gone America's proud moral leader-ship of the world?"[23]

Not least because of the depth and pervasiveness of this kind of white racial chauvinism that then existed, which Du Bois knew so well, perhaps it should come as no great surprise that there was initial con-troversy as to whether Du Bois himself should play a leading role in the nascent NAACP, even though he was its guiding spirit and best-known Negro in the organization of this important body. Part of this was reflected in Du Bois's star-crossed relationship with Oswald Garrison Villard. Born four years after Du Bois, this grandson of William Lloyd Garrison, the renowned abolitionist, and son of Henry Villard, a railroad magnate, founding president of the behemoth General Electric and owner of the influential *New York Post*, the younger Villard was not a man to be trifled with—an idea he, above all, took quite seriously. It was fortunate that he took a clear interest in the plight of the Negro, for in 1897 he took control of the *Post* whose influence stretched beyond the already powerful sway of Manhattan. He also owned the weighty journal of ideas, *The Nation*, and his philanthropies had included generous donations to Booker T. Washington—a source of some friction with Du Bois, even before their contretemps over the direction of the NAACP.

The proximate cause of their latest controversy was the unusual fact that both had been working on biographies of the heroic John Brown, the white man who gave his life in 1859 in a failed attempt to foment an insurrection among the enslaved. Unfortunately—for Villard—he was beat to the chase by Du Bois, whose justly praised volume was published in 1909, a year before that of his competitor. Du Bois considered this book one of his favorites, and it did not help things when Villard—in a move of questionable ethical dimensions—chose to review his colleague's biography in a sharply ungenerous and ungracious manner. Villard adamantly denied that the review in question was "written with the intent of giving an unfair drubbing to a supposedly rival book of mine," as he proceeded to turn the tables and charge Du Bois with perpetuating an "injustice" with his allegation. "I do not think there can be too many books about the John Brown period," said Villard with perspicacity though his statement evaded the point about the dubious nature of his own review of Du Bois's work.[24]

For Du Bois had poured heart and soul into his rehabilitation of Brown, a man then widely viewed as a calloused madman, a wild-eyed zealot, and a bloodthirsty fiend. By Du Bois's own admission, this biography of vindication was more of an interpretation than an attempt to dredge up new revelations via immersion in primary sources. Yet, more than a justification of Brown's militant abolitionism, this book also marked an evolution for Du Bois in the way it commingled scholarship with advocacy. In this, it differed from his earlier work, particularly his first book on the African Slave Trade.

The conflict between Villard and Du Bois settled down to the extent that it was possible, as Du Bois chose to leave Atlanta University and join the staff of the newly born NAACP as its leading African American operative: with that, the ongoing challenge to the Tuskegee Machine that had been percolating for years reached a decisive and transformative stage.

"Of course," said Walling to Du Bois in mid-June 1910, "we shall be able to pay you what is right and proper during the first year—$2,500, plus your expenses—and shall fully hope to employ you in after years, perhaps even at an increasing salary"; the Socialist leader conceded that the "main sacrifice will be yours, in leaving a position which you have filled with such credit, and probably with such satisfaction to yourself, for so many years."[25]

This was true. This was an immense sacrifice for Du Bois for he would leave not only his family behind in Atlanta to migrate to a bustling and crowded Manhattan but also his scholarship—his other love—in order to plunge headfirst on behalf of a despised minority into the rough-and-tumble politics of a hostile atmosphere.

What was to follow proved to be of monumental significance for both Du Bois and black America. For it was not preordained that this fledgling grouping would take flight—not to mention becoming a battering ram against Jim Crow in a process that lasted decades. As for Du Bois, the longest sustained piece of work by him was his editorship of the Crisis, organ of the NAACP; this magazine appeared each month under his editorship from its first number, dated November 1910, through June 1934, when he and the organization he had helped to found, came to a parting of the ways. In the earlier volumes very nearly the entire journal was written by him; later, departments of the magazine appeared by him—signed and unsigned—as did particular essays often signed by him. This journal had a dramatically profound impact on black America, solidifying militant opposition to the accommodation of Tuskegee and blazing an alternative path. Yet its impact soared far beyond the realm of politics. In the first issue, November 1910—years before the "Harlem Renaissance" was proclaimed as a turning point in the arts—attention was called to the fact that "New York is becoming an art center for colored people," with such performers as Bert Williams, Cole and Johnson (comprised of Bob Cole, J. Rosamond Johnson, and James Weldon Johnson), and Will Marion Cook and the Clef Club Orchestra of 130 musicians under James Reese Europe. The first issue of the journal ended with the listing of 11 relevant books: 1 on Cuba, 8 on Africa. and 2 biographies, of John Brown (by Villard) and of his lineal ancestor, William Lloyd Garrison (by Lindsay Swift), indicative of Du Bois's political acuity in stroking carefully a man with whom he had only recently been in conflict.

Just as the success of the NAACP was not a certainty, the triumph of the *Crisis* was not predetermined either. This Du Bois knew more than most, given his experiences with the *Moon* and the *Horizon*. Even before Du Bois's deflating experiences with journalism, there had been the rise—and fall—of *Freedom's Journal*, beginning in 1827, and the varied experiences of Frederick Douglass in this field, none of which survive (unlike the *Crisis*). Suggestive of the extraordinary nature of this journal is that even today it would not be easy nor simple to launch a magazine of ideas with a progressive and antiracist message. That in the foreboding and forbidding days of 1910 a journal could be launched with 5,000 initial subscribers at the rate of $1 per year—or 10 cents a copy for a 16-page edition—remains a wonder.

Officially, Du Bois was director of publicity and research at the infant organization, lodged at 20 Vesey Street in the crowded confines of lower Manhattan. Unofficially, there was a considerable amount of wrangling in the upper reaches of the group not only about Du Bois's role but what the organization would become. Contrary to what the NAACP is today, at the beginning there was substantial backing for the idea that it should be primarily a white group dedicated to black uplift, and this viewpoint contrasted with what was emerging as the consensus view: an interracial group dedicated to a protracted struggle for equality. Undoubtedly, Walling, a millionaire, and Ovington, a social worker, were the progenitors of the NAACP—yet, it is also true that Du Bois quickly became the public face of the group and his labor, as much as anything else, helped to guarantee its extraordinary longevity. Yet also present at the creation of what became the NAACP was an all-star team of African Americans, including Ida B. Wells-Barnett, the justly celebrated antilynching crusader; Mary Church Terrell, the multilingual descendant of one of black America's most affluent families; and a sprinkling of suffragettes, including Fanny Garrison Villard, Inez Milholland Boissevain, and Isabel Eaton. Their collective triumph in defeating the vision that called for a less ambitious, less racially diverse grouping, was signaled in its very name: in highlighting the advancement of "Colored People"—as opposed to the Negro or the Afro-American— the point was adumbrated that the agenda would be expansive, encompassing the darkest among us, wherever they might be. This expansive vision was also reflected in the group's organ, which was formally entitled *The Crisis: A Record of the Darker Races*.

Indicative of the ambitiousness of what the NAACP intended was the selection of their first president. Born in 1845, Moorfield Storey had served as secretary to the legendary abolitionist Senator Charles Sumner and was thereafter one of the leading attorneys in the nation and had been a president of the American Bar Association. More telling about his political tendencies was his service as president of the Anti-Imperialist League. He brought his anti-imperialist beliefs to the NAACP, until his untimely death in 1929. The relationship between the courtly Storey and the hardworking Du Bois was to be of exceedingly important significance for black America during the tenure of their relationship, which lasted from 1910 to 1929.

For it was during that important period that the NAACP journal edited by Du Bois took the nation by storm. Black businesses flocked to take out advertisements, providing another revenue stream beyond the subsidy from the group's board of directors. Businesses who bought advertising were followed rapidly by a good deal of the nation's major historically black colleges and universities, including Fisk, Howard, Shaw, Virginia Union, and Wilberforce (conspicuously, Tuskegee and Washington's alma mater, Hampton, were not among these distinguished advertisers). By bringing these eminences on board, Du Bois had succeeded in co-opting them, giving them a stake in the journal's—and the organization's—success. By April 1912, circulation skyrocketed to 22,500. By way of comparison, Jesse Max Barber, founder and editor of the *Voice of the Negro*, established in 1904 in Atlanta—before being forced to evacuate to Chicago because of the pogrom there—told

Du Bois directly that the largest number of copies ever printed by his publication was 17,000 in that same year, 1912.[26]

In 1912 both the nation as a whole and black America as a part of this whole were reaching a momentous fork in the road; it was a timely moment for hungry eyes to be poring over the luster of Du Bois's prose. For by the time of this bump in circulation, a revolution had erupted on the nation's southern border, as Mexico was undergoing the first radical transformation of the century. This radicalism infected numerous Mexican Americans and then spilled over to those African Americans with whom they shared numerous neighborhoods along the 2,000-mile border stretching from Texas to San Diego that separated the United States from its neighbor. Moreover, black America remained upset by what had befallen Negro soldiers in Brownsville, and now young men from some of those same regiments were now duty-bound to patrol a border where revolutionary violence had become endemic. In addition, other nations had begun to fish in these troubled waters, as Japan and Germany began to cultivate allies in the borderlands, thereby further jeopardizing U.S. national security.

As things evolved, it was becoming ever clearer that Jim Crow—which could cause Mexican Americans and African Americans to lend a willing ear to real and imagined foes of the United States—was jeopardizing U.S. national security. It was Du Bois's genius that he was the first Negro leader not only to acknowledge this sensitive conjuncture but, more than that, to take advantage of it to the detriment of Jim Crow and the benefit of black America.

NOTES

1. W.E.B. Du Bois, "The Color Line Belts the World," *Collier's*, 28 (October 20, 1906): 20.

2. Mark Bauerlein, *Negrophobia: A Race Riot in Atlanta, 1906*, San Francisco: Encounter Books, 2001; Gregory Mixon, *The Atlanta Riot: Race, Class and Violence in a New South City*, Gainesville: University Press of Florida, 2005.

3. W.E.B. Du Bois, "The President and the Soldiers," *Voice of the Negro*, 3 (December 1906): 552–553.

4. *Horizon*, February 1907.

5. W.E.B. Du Bois, "The Economic Aspects of Race Prejudice," *Editorial Review* (New York), 2 (May 1910): 488–493.

6. *Horizon*, July 1908.

7. *Horizon*, September 1908.

8. *Horizon*, November-December 1908.

9. *Horizon*, August 1908.

10. *Horizon*, November-December 1908.

11. W.E.B. Du Bois, "The Address to the Country," 1906, *W.E.B. Du Bois Papers-University of Massachusetts-Amherst*.

12. *Congregationalist and Christian World*, 91 (April 7, 1906): 508.

13. W.E.B. Du Bois to Reverend T. Nelson Baker, April 14, 1906, in Aptheker, ed., *Correspondence, Volume I*, 117.

14. W.E.B. Du Bois to Samuel May, Jr., December 10, 1907, in Aptheker, ed., *Correspondence, Volume I*, 138.

15. David R. Wallace to W.E.B. Du Bois, October 16, 1908, in Aptheker, ed., *Correspondence, Volume I*, 142.

16. *Moon: Illustrated Weekly*, March 2, 1906.

17. *Daily Republican*, (Springfield, Massachusetts), August 29, 1907.

18. *Washington Post*, October 1, 1907.

19. *Kansas City Star*, February 7, 1908.

20. *Cincinnati Times-Star*, December 5, 1910.

21. W.E.B. Du Bois, "The National Committee on the Negro," *Survey* (New York), 22 (June 12, 1909): 407–409.

22. *New York Times*, December 12, 1909.

23. W.E.B. Du Bois, "The Souls of White Folk," *Independent*, 69 (August 18, 1910): 339–342.

24. Oswald Garrison Villard to W.E.B. Du Bois, November 26, 1909, in Aptheker, ed., *Correspondence, Volume I*, 158–159.

25. William Walling to W.E.B. Du Bois, June 8, 1910, in Aptheker, ed., *Correspondence, Volume I*, 169–170.

26. J. Max Barber to W.E.B. Du Bois, March 2, 1912 in Aptheker, ed., *Correspondence, Volume I*, 176–177.

Chapter 5

A NEW PATH

Du Bois's leadership of the NAACP indicated that black America was embarking on a new path. Booker T. Washington had not disappeared but he did not have behind him a membership organization comprised of the Negro masses, and though he had bribed and browbeaten a good deal of the Negro press, he also did not have under his administration an organ of opinion that was growing by leaps and bounds.

Yet, by 1912, the left-handed, balding, and diminutive Du Bois might have acknowledged more directly why the Tuskegee Machine might have chosen to accommodate the powerful for it was evident then that this small planet was entering a time of bloodlust and violence that was of particular consequence for black America, which tended to get pneumonia when the nation as a whole was enduring a head cold. For it was not just the Mexican Revolution that had exploded—the Great War that was about to burst forth in Europe in 1914 would require a meaningful complement of Negro soldiers, who were to suffer mightily before this conflict ended.

All was not gloom and doom, however, for moving from the comparative parochialism of Georgia to the relatively cosmopolitan New York was liberating for Du Bois. Jim Crow was less intense in Manhattan than

Atlanta, and, besides, coincidentally, Du Bois was part of a great migration from South to North that was to transform the nation. For it was
at this precise moment that Harlem (the multiblock neighborhood of
northern Manhattan that encompassed a great university [Columbia]
and a very good college [City College of New York], was speckled with
tenement buildings, and underpinned by a rumbling subway system) began to receive thousands of migrants of African descent from the former
slave South and the Caribbean basin. The island of Manhattan is only
12 miles long, and Harlem is a relatively small part of that but its size
was (and still is) belied by the magnitude of this neighborhood's contribution to the politics and culture of the nation. But what was occurring
in Manhattan was occurring simultaneously in Chicago (as Negroes departed Mississippi), Philadelphia, and Boston (as Negroes departed the
Carolinas). The migrations to these cities were occurring for similar
reasons: racist terror was pushing Negroes northward; the boll weevil
devastated agricultural crops, and northern factories began to ramp up
production in anticipation of supplying a European market that was gear-
ing for war, which necessitated more workers that could not be supplied
altogether by immigration, given that there were fewer immigrants due
to the same impending conflict.

     As Negroes escaped the Deep South, they obtained the right to vote
and participate more freely in organizations like Du Bois's NAACP.
This provided jet propulsion to his efforts and shook up politics nationally. Du Bois also took advantage of his migration northward by plung-
ing more directly into the operations of the Socialist Party (SP), whose
ranks he had joined earlier. Yet Du Bois remained flummoxed by the
party's unwillingness—or inability—to tackle racism forthrightly. He
took his concern directly to an audience of 1,000 Socialists—almost all
white—on January 20, 1912.[1] The SP was of the opinion that the Socialist Utopia would resolve the prickly matter of racism, that it was
inextricably tied to the innards of capitalism, and, thus, this august organization tended to disdain the difficult day-to-day battles against intrac-
table problems like lynching. This was all well and good in theory, but
it was a hard proposition to sell to African Americans seeking to avoid
gory and ferocious lynch mobs: rather than wait for utopia, they might
decide to heed the siren songs emanating from Tokyo and Berlin to the
effect that this nation's rulers were simply too beastly for redemption.

Du Bois insisted that disenfranchisement of African Americans was not simply a matter for them alone—whose resolution had to await the establishment of socialism—but that this deprivation vitiated democracy as a whole. The disenfranchisement of African Americans virtually guaranteed the rule of Dixiecrats and demagogues, and made next to impossible the rise of any to their left, socialists least of all.[2] "There is a group of ten million persons in the United States toward whom Socialists would better turn serious attention," he reminded his fellow party members, referring to his fellow Negroes.[3] He was pleased to observe in the *Crisis* in December 1911 that the SP was "the only party which openly recognizes Negro manhood"; thus, he opined, "is it not time for black voters [to] carefully consider the claims of this party?" Likewise, he continued, one of five workers in the nation were African American, and, he added prophetically, "the Negro Problem then is the great test of the American Socialist," a test that this party failed generally.[4] On the other hand, all of Du Bois's engagements with the socialists were not as problematic for he shared membership in the organization with both Walling and Ovington, and their shared ideology improved their own collective functioning within the NAACP.

Despite the SP's manifest weaknesses, Du Bois clung to the socialists like a life raft in a storm-tossed sea for the alternatives were so unpromising, a bitter reality that was manifest in the pivotal election year of 1912. For as revolution brewed in Mexico and loomed in Europe, presidential candidates at home included the elephantine incumbent, William Howard Taft of the GOP, whose party had for years now seemed embarrassed and discomfited by the support of Negroes; Theodore Roosevelt, running on a third party ticket, who, despite his bluster against entrenched monopolies, exposed disdain for the Negro when he cruelly mistreated the soldiers of Brownsville; and finally, the Democrat, Woodrow Wilson, a native of Virginia (though he had been yanked into prominence as President of his alma mater, Princeton University, which became a launching pad for his election as Governor of New Jersey), who did nothing to dislodge Old Nassau's distaste for admitting Negro students and seemed to be more a man of the Old South than of the more enlightened precincts of central Jersey.[5] In August 1912, Du Bois informed readers of the *Crisis* that if he could assure the presidency to the socialist Eugene Victor Debs, he would do so, for of all the candidates "he alone, by word and deed, stands squarely on a platform of human rights regardless of race or class."[6]

Wilson emerged triumphant—the first southerner since Zachary Taylor and the first Democrat since Grover Cleveland to enter the White House—which only meant that Du Bois and the NAACP had to work that much harder to destroy Jim Crow. Though a member of the Socialist Party, Du Bois knew that given the construction of the Electoral College and the winner-take-all nature of U.S. elections, his choice could not prevail. Thus, he advised a vote for Wilson, hoping, praying that the working-class base of his Democratic Party would somehow come to its senses and pursue a path of concord with a mostly working-class African American community. Not for the first or last time, this fervent wish proved unavailing. Yet so strongly did Du Bois hold to this belief at this time, that he chose this precise moment to resign from the Socialist Party. This resignation did not spell the end of his attempt to entice these radicals to pay much more attention to those most likely to respond to their entreaties. "There is a group of ten million persons in the United States toward whom Socialists would better turn serious attention," he said referring to African Americans in what was becoming a mantra.[7] "The Negro Problem then," he maintained, he repeated as if it were a magic incantation, "is the great test of the American Socialist."[8] Of course, Du Bois's political dalliances with the left were not limited to himself alone. In one of the first editions of the *Crisis* he edited, it was reported that in Guthrie, Oklahoma, representatives of various Negro organizations denounced the GOP leadership and urged the "Negroes of the state to support the entire Socialist ticket" and called for the enfranchisement of women.[9]

Thus, the "Negro Problem" was also a "great test" for Du Bois himself that he rarely failed to pass. This was reflected in his first novel, *The Quest of the Silver Fleece*,[10] which was published in the immediate aftermath of the founding of the NAACP. It was an attempt to provide a realistic portrayal of the impact of cotton, racism, and peonage in the nation in the early 20th century, as Upton Sinclair and Frank Norris had done about the same time with meat and wheat. The Negro characters—particularly the women—are strong, and the whites are drawn in varying form, that is, the hesitant liberal, the evil Bourbon, the courageous and dedicated white opponent of racism (also a woman and perhaps inspired by Mary White Ovington, the NAACP founder). The lasting significance of this work is that it portends the arrival of the Harlem Renaissance, a remarkable flowering of literature and the arts among African Americans that was to erupt more than a decade later.

Nevertheless, Du Bois had come to recognize that placing all his eggs in the basket of the United States itself, when it came to the destruction of Jim Crow, may not have been a fool's errand—but it was not far from it. Having spent considerable time in Europe and being aware of the direct challenge provided by Japan in particular—whose defeat of Russia in 1905 he had hailed as a signpost in the global struggle against white supremacy, Jim Crow's close cousin—he knew that extending his political tentacles abroad was eminently desirable. Making this goal even more appealing was the fact that the Tuskegee Machine had an international component of its own. In 1910 Washington himself was in London, where he opined that the plight of the Negro was well on its way to being resolved. John Milholland, a NAACP founder, happened to be in London at that time and immediately informed Du Bois that this wild distortion of the Wizard had to be refuted—which Du Bois promptly did.

Meanwhile, Du Bois became aware of an important gathering that was to occur in London in July 1911. Du Bois coordinated the U.S. delegation of this First Universal Race Congress and took the opportunity to interact with the novelist and futurist H. G. Wells; a crusader against colonialism in the Congo, Sir Roger Casement; and a leading politician, J. Ramsay MacDonald. Though this London confab presented a rare opportunity to advance the global struggle against Jim Crow, Du Bois was reluctant to abandon his battle station in Manhattan. "We are just getting into working shape the NAACP," he said. "It has been far more successful than we dreamed but not successful enough to stand at the moment my prolonged absence."[11]

Nevertheless, one constant in Du Bois's seemingly contradictory political career was his engagement with the international community. He knew that the plagues and vicissitudes visited upon African Americans—white supremacy, massacres, and the like—were not unique to North America, and, thus, bonding and building alliances with others abroad similarly situated was crucial. Moreover, he also knew that the balance of forces globally (Was white supremacy on the upswing or a downslide? Was the United States growing or diminishing in influence?) was an ultimately critical factor in determining the destiny of African

Americans and this could best be gauged beyond these shores. Thus, Du Bois crossed the choppy waters of the Atlantic once more to commune with a thousand delegates, representing what was loosely termed "fifty races," who had gathered in the Fishmongers' Hall. "When fifty races look each other in the eye, face to face," he enthused, "there arises a new conception of humanity and its problems."[12]

This gathering in London ratified Du Bois's faith in global alliances, which he was to pursue to his dying days. Yet this far-sighted viewpoint was not shared universally within the leading circles of the NAACP, the organization for which he toiled. More to the point, Oswald Garrison Villard, a leading member of the organization's board and a man with whom he had crossed swords previously, continued to dog his every move, seemingly uncomfortable with the idea that Du Bois—as an African American—would be seen as preeminent in an organization dedicated to Negro advance. Du Bois was not comforted by the well-known reality that Villard's wife, whose roots in the Deep South ran deep, contradicted her spouse's abolitionist heritage by refusing to have Negro—or Jewish—guests at their home. Villard himself tended toward imperiousness, and the ever sensitive Du Bois, keenly attuned to the poisonous nature of Jim Crow, found it easy to interpret this attitude quite negatively.

As so often happens, Du Bois's absence from the office due to his lengthy sojourn in London allowed these tensions to fester and boil over. Referring bluntly to the "passage of words between us in the board meeting," Du Bois acknowledged Villard's assertion that "you do not think further co-operation between us in the work of the association is possible." Du Bois begged to differ but made it clear in words that contradicted the essence of Jim Crow that "I count myself not as your subordinate but as a fellow officer," adding pointedly, "I decline to receive orders from anyone but the board."[13]

Villard did not cease in his attempt to rein in Du Bois, clip his wings, and place him under tighter control. "Mr. Villard has been frank from the beginning," Du Bois contended. "He opposed my coming to the position in the first place and has systematically opposed every step I have taken since. He has told me plainly," he cried, "that he should not rest until I and the 'Crisis' were 'absolutely' under his control or entirely outside the organization." As Du Bois saw things in words that echo through the ages, "Mr. Villard is not democratic. He is used to advising colored men and giving them orders and he simply cannot bring himself to work with one as an equal." For Du Bois, the NAACP had reached a critical juncture for "in most organizations of this kind the problem has frankly been given up as insoluble and usually an entire force of one race or another is hired. It has been my dream to make this organization an exception," he insisted, "and I have tried desperately and have failed." This was premature pessimism but more timely was his assertion that "if in this Association white and black folk cannot work together as equals; if this Association is unable to treat its black officials with the same lease of power as white, can we fight a successful battle against race prejudice in the world?"[14]

Joel Spingarn, a Jewish American, replaced Villard as chairman of the NAACP board in January 1914 (though he remained a member of the board), and Du Bois's relationship with this literary scholar and his brother, a noted attorney, was much closer than that with Villard. Yet he too reproached Du Bois for what he perceived as his less than comradely attitude to cooperation with others on the board; but the editor of the *Crisis* said without hesitation, "[yes,] my temperament is a difficult one to endure. In my peculiar education and experiences it would be miraculous if I came through normal and unwarped."[15] Du Bois may have been overly self-effacing here. It was true that he already had developed a reputation for being standoffish, though this was more a product of shyness and a reticence born in being an African American who often found himself amongst Euro-Americans who were less than diplomatic. For example, Villard thought the journal Du Bois edited should have spent more time highlighting the crimes of Negroes, as opposed to documenting the massive crimes targeting Negroes.

The heart of the dispute, in sum, was the *Crisis* and its unvarnished reporting of lynchings, colonialism, and the ugliness of white supremacy; this warts-and-all portrait was made all the more problematic—in the eyes of some—by it being engineered by an African American. Du Bois had threatened to resign, which would have been disastrous for a fledgling organization struggling to establish its credibility in the face of the stiff challenge provided by the Tuskegee Machine. The reality was that the nation as a whole—and not even the NAACP Board, who were deemed to be among the angels—were ill-prepared for the scalding and scolding magazine that Du Bois had produced. It appeared each month under his editorship from its first number, dated November 1910, all the way through July 1934, when he departed the organization as a direct result of tensions that his conflicts with Villard had foreshadowed. In its early stages very nearly the entire magazine was written by him; subsequently, departments appeared by him—signed and unsigned—as did particular essays often signed by him.

Looking back at this still stimulating journal, one is still struck by the militancy of it, particularly when contrasted with its peers—before and since. The very first issue—in November 1910—sets the tone with graphic reports on black men who in self-defense killed their bosses and were now facing death. In December 1910, he reports on physical resistance by Negroes in Oklahoma to efforts to disenfranchise them. In November 1911, he—once more—notes that in recent weeks there were reports of 14 Negro men being killed in the South, but that 10 white men were killed by Negroes in the South during this same time frame. This idea of militant self-defense was a repetitive one and was unsettling to the fiercest advocates of Jim Crow. This prescient approach of Du Bois—which prefigured the ideas of Malcolm X and the Black Panther Party, which were thought to be unique when they emerged decades later—reached a crescendo in the May 1913 when he penned a startling editorial, "The Vigilance Committee: A Call to Arms," in which he observed casually though explicitly that "there is scarcely a community in the United States where a group of colored people live that has not its vigilance committee." In an italicized paragraph Du Bois unequivocally states that "*the object of the National Association for the Advancement of Colored People is to offer a central headquarters and a collective force to ensure the greater effectiveness and permanence of such committees.*" Few things could be more unnerving to the perpetrators of racist violence than the idea that intended victims would fight back ferociously.

In May 1911, he declaimed at length on the paradox that racism often took the form of special attack against African Americans precisely because they had attained some element of economic independence, the condition that they had been told would eliminate racism! This was the cruel dilemma that the Tuskegee Machine, which was premised on the notion of economic independence for Negroes, could not or would not confront.[16]

Du Bois was not simply a cloistered member of the literati, churning out intriguing articles and reviews. He had become a chief organizer of the NAACP, often touring the nation speaking before appreciative audiences bedazzled by his erudition. Thus, it was in July 1913 that he completed a lengthy lecture tour, covering 7,000 miles and bringing him before audiences aggregating 18,000 people. Those he addressed were overwhelmingly African American, and he "thanked God" that he had "the privilege of working for them."[17]

Thus it was with fits and starts that the NAACP gradually took off to assume its still preeminent position in black America. At the wheel was Du Bois as this historic process was launched. Yet, seemingly, this mighty task was insufficient to assuage Du Bois's apparently insatiable appetite for labor. For in between editing what had become a leading journal and speaking before adoring audiences, Du Bois also found time to pursue a punishing schedule of writing, publishing his still enlightening book *The Negro*. This book is a pioneering effort at depicting within one volume the entire scope of Africa's past (a Herculean task surely), but Du Bois does not stop there. He goes on to contextualize the position of African-derived peoples in the United States, Latin America, and the West Indies, as he demonstrates the relationship between the exploitation of Africa and the rise of capitalism and imperialism in Europe and the United States. Rather modestly, Du Bois pointed to limitations of his previous research, his own linguistic limitations, especially in terms of African languages (a number of which have descended into desuetude since *The Negro* first emerged in 1915) and the brevity of the effort, as precluding the possibility of his being a definitive treatment of the capacious topic. Still, he hoped that his effort would "enable the general reader to know as men a sixth or more of the human race."[18]

Increasingly, Du Bois was coming to see that the beleaguered plight of Africans and African Americans alike was not merely a matter that afflicted them alone. Instead, as World War I erupted in 1914, he had arrived at the weighty conclusion that Europeans' and Euro-Americans' (particularly) squabbles over the spoils and carcass of a weakened Africa was a major source of war (with Africans having been snatched from their homelands and dragged to North America being early evidence of this extremely stressed situation). Weeks after the guns had

sounded in Sarajevo, Du Bois appeared before an attentive audience of
900 in New Hampshire. The weather was cold and inclement but Du
Bois's penetrating words burned hot. He insisted that "the present [war]
is caused by the jealousy among leading European nations over colonial
aggrandizement." Compared to France and Great Britain, who had garnered the lion's share of colonies, most notably in Africa, Germany had
arrived tardily at the colonial feasting table, and the onset of war was,
among other things, an attempt to rearrange the status quo. Yet amidst
the often deafening roar of the present, Du Bois had the perspicacity to
peer over the horizon and around the corner to espy China's awakening, which had been signaled by the overthrow of royalty there a few
years earlier: China's rise will be "irresistible," he prophesied.[19]

Subsequently, Du Bois expanded upon his controversial thesis in one
of his more influential writings, "The African Roots of War," published
May 1915. "In a very real sense," wrote Du Bois, Africa was the prime
cause of the war. The battering of this continent was highly profitable—to some. The title of this article says it all and also points to
decolonization and the uplift of Africa as a route to erode the linea-
ments of war. There too he spoke hopefully of the "awakening leaders"
of China, India, and Egypt. He suggested too that African Americans
had a pivotal role to play in this profound historical process.[20] In Du
Bois's estimation, descendants of enslaved Africans in the Caribbean also
had an essential task to perform. For in the midst of preparing for publication his influential article on the roots of war, he seized the opportunity to visit Jamaica for the first time, where he bumped into a young
man whose name came to be linked with his controversially—Marcus
Mosiah Garvey—who was tarrying in his native Jamaica before migrating to the United States. At a dinner in honor of Du Bois, the Mayor
of Kingston, and the U.S. Consul, Du Bois again spoke of the intercon-
nections of the struggles of colored peoples of the world and the central
role of Africans in the Western Hemisphere in the movement that had
come to be known as Pan-Africanism.[21]

Du Bois's journey to the Caribbean seemed to reawaken his awareness of the importance of this region, which included his own familial
beginnings. For from 1905 to 1941, the United States maintained a cus-
toms receivership over Haiti, followed by the direct intervention by the
U.S. military. It was in July 1915, shortly after his return from Haiti's

neighbor Jamaica that U.S. Marines stood by as the congress in Port-au-Prince approved a Washington-selected president for this beset nation. Figuratively—if not literally—at gunpoint, this man, appointed by President Wilson, signed a treaty under which U.S. citizens appointed by Washington controlled the nation's finances, police, public works, and the like. After the dissolving of the Haitian Congress by the U.S. military, a new constitution allowing foreign landownership was "approved." (Interestingly, this constitution was drafted by Wilson's assistant secretary of the navy, Franklin Delano Roosevelt.)

Thus, shortly after returning from Jamaica, Du Bois took his objections to Washington's Caribbean policy directly to President Wilson: "The United States has throughout the world a reputation for studied unfairness toward black folk," he charged. "The political party whose nominee you are is historically the party of Negro slavery." Changing course on Haiti, Du Bois suggested, would go a long way toward assuaging the widespread concern in the Pan-African world about U.S. policy.[22] The President chose not to respond.

Though he was to be accused of inconsistency and ideological reversals, Du Bois was interested in global issues throughout his long life, and he continued throughout his lengthy career to connect global concerns with the concerns of his homeland. He was among the first to acknowledge early on that as long as Africans abroad were being pulverized, African Americans too could hardly escape battering. There was a global correlation of forces that virtually dictated that, for example, a nonviolent civil rights protest could erupt after World War II, whereas it might have been drenched in a tidal wave of blood and gore after World War I. So, despite President Wilson turning a blind eye and a deaf ear to his insistent pleas, Du Bois did not flinch from pressing his global concerns on the White House, even as the scene at home showed little signs of improving. For as Du Bois was raising his eloquent voice against U.S. intervention in Haiti, he was also objecting strenuously to the simultaneous intervention in neighboring Mexico, as it was enmeshed in the first great revolution of the 20th century, an intervention made even more problematic by the dispatching south of the border of Negro troops in search of Pancho Villa, the celebrated revolutionary.[23]

Perhaps Woodrow Wilson—an unreconstructed segregationist—decided to ignore Du Bois's entreaties due to the NAACP's constant prodding of Wilson on so many different fronts. Not least due to the ministrations of NAACP lawyers, the U.S. Supreme Court ruled unconstitutional Oklahoma's preferential registration of white voters—the first opinion to nullify a state law under the 15th Amendment. Then the NAACP prevailed in a case from Louisville, which—at least on paper—guaranteed the right to buy decent housing. With Du Bois, an intellectual turned propagandist at the helm of a monthly magazine that was growing by leaps and bounds, the NAACP seemed to be reaching a new stage in its lengthy battle with the Tuskegee Machine.

This perception took on a sad reality when late in 1915 Booker T. Washington passed away. He had taken ill in New York City and with his typical bullheadedness rebuffed the counsel of his physicians and took a train to Tuskegee. But his body was wracked by all manner of maladies, seemingly induced by an especially virulent sexually transmitted disease, and the train ride to Alabama turned out to be his final journey. At his final resting place in Alabama, there then arose an imposing statue of the Wizard of Tuskegee seemingly lifting a veil of ignorance from a bent Negro beneath him. Critics charged that Washington and the policies he fought for had actually placed a veil of ignorance over African Americans. Du Bois, who had been catapulted into the public arena not least due to his challenge to Washington, was balanced in his analysis of his frequent sparring partner. Yes, he was "the greatest Negro leader since Frederick Douglass and the most distinguished man, white or black" to come from the Deep South since the conclusion of the Civil War. And, yes, the educational institution he constructed at Tuskegee and his desire to build businesses were both admirable. Yet, Du Bois could not avoid the conclusion that Washington erred grievously in downplaying disenfranchisement and his public approach of acquiescing to the most egregious aspects of white supremacy. Du Bois could have added that Washington's program had little purchase for an African American community in the midst of a great migration from South to North that would transform this community for all time. More than this, Washington's program, such as it was, seemed to accept the status quo rather than challenge it.[24]

Washington's acceptance of the status quo had been adamantly rejected by Du Bois and the NAACP, and with Washington's passing, the opportunity was created for the rise of the "New Negro" and the

"Harlem Renaissance," both of which embodied a militancy that the Tuskegee Machine abjured. This confrontational style was exemplified when Du Bois and the NAACP decided to protest *The Birth of a Nation* (a production from the then-infant motion picture industry). Based upon a novel by Thomas Dixon and directed by Hollywood's first wunderkind, D. W. Griffith, this film was a caustic history lesson meant to glorify the "lost cause" of the Confederacy, which had plunged the nation into the Civil War, which led to over 600,000 deaths—equivalent to over 5 million on a per capita basis if calculated on today's population. The movie was intended to inflame with its scenes of a dainty white woman committing suicide rather than submit to the bestial passions of an African American man pursuing her (actually a white actor in blackface acted in this scene as the filmmakers chose not to hire Negro performers). Reconstruction following the Civil War, which Du Bois was to portray in one of his more celebrated works as an era of democratic promise, here was presented as an era of rampant corruption and venality.

The film raked in huge profits and was shown—and praised—in Wilson's White House. Sensing immediately the power of this new medium that was cinema, Du Bois leapt into action. On May 30, 1915, 2,000 protesters packed an energetic meeting held at Boston's Faneuil Hall that sharply criticized this cinematic assault. Du Bois gave the main address, in which he contrasted the film, its content, and its spirit with what actually occurred during Reconstruction.[25]

The Birth of a Nation emerged at a time when lynching was skyrocketing, residential segregation was ossifying, and Jim Crow showed no signs of dissipating. The results were predictable: it was not unusual for white patrons of this cinematic provocation to launch attacks upon Negroes upon departing movie houses. Simultaneously, civil libertarians fretted that protesters might violate the free speech rights of moviemakers if they could prevail upon the authorities to shut down this outrage. Not for the last time, civil libertarians and civil rights advocates disagreed: in his justly praised autobiography, *Dusk of Dawn*, Du Bois observed that coincidentally enough the "number of mob murders so increased that nearly one hundred Negroes were lynched during 1915 and a score of whites, a larger number than had occurred for more than a decade." It was "dangerous to limit expression," Du Bois opined. "Yet without some limitations civilization could not endure." It was a "miserable dilemma," he concluded—but one whose brunt he did not shirk.[26]

The upside of this controversy centered on a racist extravaganza that propelled more positive developments, for this film inspired the NAACP to become more involved in Hollywood, seeking to intercept noxious scripts, spur the hiring of Negro performers, and, ultimately, galvanize a new generation of Negro filmmakers.

For Du Bois, his festering irritation with Hollywood was merging with his growing disapproval of the current occupant of the White House. He was coming to regret his past support for Wilson but the U.S. political scene did not offer an array of pleasant alternatives. There was "little to choose," he lamented, between "these two great parties," referring to Wilson's Democrats and the Republicans.[27] Du Bois had long been a fierce advocate of women's suffrage, and it was at this juncture that the journal he edited, the Crisis, took a page from that movement's playbook by advocating a "Negro Party [along] the lines of the recently formed Woman's Party." Barring that, Du Bois felt that African Americans, like picky diners at a Chinese restaurant, should select discriminately from an array of possible options, including candidates from the two major parties, the Socialists and, possibly, their own political organ. As for the presidential candidates, Du Bois suggested that his constituency should vote for the Socialist—or stay home. These were unappetizing selections since the labor-backed Socialists were reluctant to confront racism directly, envisioning the proclamation of the socialist commonwealth as the only way out for the Negro—in the meantime, presumably suffering was the only available option—while the two major parties were either in league with the Ku Klux Klan (Democrats) or so wedded to Big Business (the GOP), they could hardly ally effectively with a mostly working-class Negro community.[28]

Still, Du Bois seemed most disappointed with the Socialists, who he seemed to think should be in the vanguard of the antiracist struggle; instead they seemed to be perpetually lagging in this all-important realm. Their passivity towards fighting racism, he thought, cast the gravest doubt upon their sincerity and vitiated the possibility of their ever mounting effective action.[29]

Given his staunch opposition to President Wilson, friends and enemies alike were stunned when Du Bois lent support to what was probably the most controversial decision of Wilson's presidency—the decision to enter World War I on April 2, 1917. Du Bois's decision to support Wilson was even more surprising given his intimate knowledge of Germany—particularly its language and culture—and the presumed immunity to the anti-Berlin hysteria that it provided, hysteria that was then coursing throughout the land. To be sure, Du Bois then thought that positive developments could emerge from this conflict, not least since the major powers—notably the United States, Britain, and France—were so heavily dependent on troops of African descent. It was in that spirit that he appeared on a platform with Lajpat L. Rai, the great anticolonial crusader from British India.[30] The two friends addressed a session on the plight of the colonized and the oppressed shortly after Wilson's fateful decision. Sponsored by the Intercollegiate Socialist Society and held in Bellport, Long Island, it was there that Du Bois announced portentously that the war then raging should be fought in the hope that a result might be the enhancement of the independence of colored peoples, including Indians, a result that would enhance the otherwise dreary lives of African Americans.[31]

He was to be proven wrong in the specific—for as Du Bois knew better than most, this was an unjust war, a war grounded in the division of colonial spoils, that could hardly eventuate in a just result. But he was correct in the general—African Americans in particular began to realize that a crucial factor in determining their fate was precisely what was occurring in the world at large.

NOTES

1. *Socialist Call*, January 21, 1912.

2. *New York Times*, November 3, 1912.

3. *New Review* (New York), 1 (January 11, 1913): 54–57.

4. *New Review*, 1 (February 1, 1913): 138–141.

5. See Kathleen Wolgemuth, "Wilson and Federal Segregation," *Journal of Negro History*, 44 (April 1959): 158–173.

6. *Crisis*, 4 (Number 4, August 1912): 170–171.

7. *New Review*, 1 (January 11, 1913): 54–57.

8. *New Review*, 1 (February 1, 1913): 138–141.

9. *Crisis*, 1 (Number 2, December 1910). See also Charles F. Kellogg, NAACP, Baltimore: Johns Hopkins University Press, 1967.

10. W.E.B. Du Bois, *The Quest of the Silver Fleece: A Novel*, Chicago: A. C. McClurg & Co., 1911.

11. W.E.B. Du Bois to "My Dear Madame," February 28, 1911, in Aptheker, *Correspondence, Volume I*, 173–175.

12. David Levering Lewis, *Biography of a Race*, 441.

13. W.E.B. Du Bois to Oswald Garrison Villard, March 18, 1913, in Aptheker, *Correspondence, Volume I*, 181.

14. W.E.B. Du Bois to Mary White Ovington, April 9, 1914, in Aptheker, *Correspondence, Volume I*, 188–191.

15. W.E.B. Du Bois to Joel Spingarn, October 28, 1914 in Aptheker, *Correspondence, Volume I*, 203–207.

16. W.E.B. Du Bois, "Violations of Property Rights," *Crisis*, 2 (Number 1, May 1911): 28–32, 32.

17. *Crisis*, 6 (Number 3, July 1913).

18. W.E.B. Du Bois, *The Negro*, New York: Henry Holt, 1915.

19. *Manchester Leader* [N.H.], November 16, 1914.

20. W.E.B. Du Bois, "The African Roots of War," *Atlantic Monthly*, 115 (May 1915): 707–714.

21. *Jamaica Times*, May 8, 1915.

22. W.E.B. Du Bois to President Woodrow Wilson, 3 August 1915, in Aptheker, *Correspondence, Volume I*, 211–213.

23. Gerald Horne, *Black and Brown: African-Americans and the Mexican Revolution, 1910–1920*, New York: New York University Press, 2005, passim.

24. *Crisis*, 11 (Number 2, December 1915). Du Bois's words on Washington were reproduced and circulated widely. See, for example, *Chicago Evening Post*, December 13, 1915; *Sioux City Journal* [Iowa], December 7, 1915.

25. *Boston Traveller and Evening Herald*, May 31, 1915.

26. W.E.B. Du Bois, *Dusk of Dawn: An Essay Toward an Autobiography of a Race Concept*, New Brunswick, New Jersey: Transaction Publishers, 1983, 240.

27. *Crisis*, 12 (October 1916).

28. *Crisis*, 12 (November 1916).

29. W.E.B. Du Bois, "The Problem of Problems," *Intercollegiate Socialist*, 6 (December 1917–January 1918): 5–9.

30. Gerald Horne, *The End of Empires: African-Americans and India*, Philadelphia: Temple University Press, 2008.

31. *New York Evening Post*, September 22, 1917.

Chapter 6

CONFLICTS

Rather quickly, Du Bois's support for U.S. entry into what was then called the Great War was proven to be misguided. This fundamental error, combined with his feud with Marcus Garvey, who had sought to seize the mantle of the now departed Booker T. Washington, cast a shadow over Du Bois's subsequent career—among the Black Left as a result of his misjudgment of the war and among Black Nationalists as a result of his confrontation with the roly-poly migrant from Jamaica.

On the other hand, those so bold as to oppose the war often found themselves harassed, under indictment, or, in the case of immigrants, deported. As an officer of the NAACP, already under siege, adopting positions beyond the mainstream on such a fundamental matter as war and peace was not easy. A strategic objective of the association and its erudite staffer was the inclusion of African Americans at all levels of U.S. society, including the military—but did this mean backing each and every goal of a military, which at point was brutally occupying Du Bois's ancestral homeland, Haiti?

This issue came to the fore in the case of Charles Young, one of a very few black graduates of West Point and a friend of Du Bois from the 1890s, when both were teaching at Wilberforce. During an often tense 28 years of active duty, Young had served the U.S. Army in the U.S. West, in Haiti, in Liberia, and during the revolutionary tumult in Mexico. Then, after much agitation by the NAACP and its allies, the War Department established in 1917 a center for the training of Negro officers in Des Moines. Young, by then a lieutenant colonel, was generally expected to be the officer in charge. But that spring, Young was subjected to a medical examination that uncovered high blood pressure in the 49-year-old officer. In the face of pressure from African Americans and persistent efforts by Young himself (he rode on horseback from Ohio to Washington, D.C., to demonstrate his physical stamina), the spotlight was shone brightly on his troubling case. This demonstration was to prove wanting, despite Du Bois's adamant intervention.[1]

But the larger question was this: was there an inherent tension, if not contradiction, in Du Bois's and the NAACP's stance of integration and the tasks performed by those doing the integrating? Could you demand inclusion of Negroes in the military without conceding that the military had a role to play that often was deleterious? Black Nationalists of Garvey's stripe began to resolve this tension by reconsidering the entire notion of Negro inclusion into what many saw as a bankrupt society; instead, Garvey and others called for repatriation to Africa or otherwise building a Negro Nation. Ultimately, Du Bois's tenure with the NAACP was to run aground because of a similar tension: how did one oppose racial segregation and push for inclusion through the vehicle of organizations that oft times were based on a tight Negro unity?

Thus, Du Bois and the NAACP were elated when in the midst of war preparation, 700 Negro men were commissioned as officers, while others were given high appointments in the Departments of War and Labor; the Red Cross followed suit by promising to employ Negro women as nurses (later, they reneged). Moreover, Du Bois was influenced by the pro-war attitude of his NAACP comrade, Joel Spingarn. It was in that context that Du Bois made a decision that was to bring him grief—at least from the Black Left and Black Nationalists—for years to come: in June 1917, Du Bois was asked to serve in a projected special bureau whose purpose was, supposedly, to "satisfy" the grievances of Negroes but was justifiably seen by his critics as little more than intelligence gathering for the U.S. authorities. This was the background for his notorious July 1918 *Crisis* editorial "Close Ranks," which contained the fateful sentence: "Let us, while this war lasts, forget our special griev-ances and close our ranks shoulder to shoulder with our own white fel-low citizens and the allied nations that are fighting for democracy." It would have been bad enough if he had stopped there but in a rhetorical flight, for which he was well-known, Du Bois—who more than most had reason to resist the anti-Berlin hysteria—asserted, "that which the German power represents today spells death to the aspirations of Ne-groes and all the darker races for equality, freedom and equality."

Although the offer of an intelligence post to Du Bois was withdrawn (just as the Red Cross' promise of hiring African American women had been), the controversy continued, for good reason.

How could it not? How could the Du Bois of the "African Roots of War," the Du Bois of stern denunciation of Jim Crow become the Du Bois of July 1918 who offered to make a "constructive attempt to guide Negro public opinion by removing pressing grievances of colored folk which hinder the prosecution of the war"?[2] Many black Americans had a hard time swallowing this approach. One comrade of William Monroe Trotter was "amazed beyond expression. I believe that we should do just the reverse of what you advise"; actually, said Byron Gunner, the war "was the most opportune time for us to push and keep our 'special griev-ances' to the fore."[3]

Decades later it remains difficult to comprehend altogether Du Bois's attempt to reverse field and contradict much of what he had espoused. On the other hand, James Weldon Johnson, who was the chief admin-istrator of the NAACP, had served in the U.S. diplomatic corps in Central America at a time of great turmoil, which suggested that a pre-cedent had been set for NAACP leaders toiling on behalf of Washing-ton and, more precisely, extending the battle for inclusion of Negroes to all levels—including the inner sanctums of power. Again, the larger question—which would erupt in the 1960s when "integration" became the watchword of the Black Freedom Movement—was, in the phrase of the brilliant writer, James Baldwin, should one choose to "integrate" a burning house?

In that vein, Du Bois continued his pro-war drumbeat. In August and September 1918, the Crisis implored, "This is Our Country. We have worked for it, we have suffered for it, we have fought for it; we have made its music, we have tinged its ideals, its poetry, its religion, its dreams."

What the *Crisis* did not ask was, how could an unjust war for redivision of colonial spoils benefit African Americans?

This issue may have occurred to Du Bois himself, for hard on the heels of his misbegotten effort to enlist in military intelligence, his beaver-like energy turned in the opposite direction: the fate of the colonized, particularly in Africa, as a result of the war, began to rivet his imagination. Even before this juncture, Du Bois had addressed the cosmopolitan readers of the *New York Post* warning them that the silence about Africa's future was ominous for those who wished a democratic outcome of the war.[4] Thus it was that early December 1918 found Du Bois headed eastward across the swirling waters of the Atlantic destined for Paris. He had been preceded by President Woodrow Wilson, who was headed to Versailles with the aim of forging a peace settlement for a conflict that had led to the deaths of 21 million civilians and combatants. Du Bois, on the other hand, was on a mission for the NAACP to serve as special representative with the portfolio of insuring that what occurred at Versailles was not disadvantageous to those of African descent. This would include convening yet another Pan-African Congress, though unlike the earlier one, it would be clear who was in charge: Du Bois. This congress would also include an investigation of the treatment of Negro soldiers—including 200,000 African Americans, as reports streamed in concerning the maltreatment of Negro soldiers during the just concluded conflict.

Upon arriving in France, the Du Bois who had contemplated working on behalf of U.S. military intelligence vanished to be supplanted by the Du Bois who had become the very apostle and tribune of Black Liberation. He informed NAACP members about his proposal for moving Africa away from European domination and towards control by Africans themselves, which would open the door to mass migration by African Americans to Africa, an idea that Garvey, ironically, came to embody. Du Bois, however, denied that this was a "'separatist' movement" since, he counseled, "the African movement means to us what the Zionist movement must mean to the Jews, the centralization of race effort and the recognition of a racial fount."[5]

As it turned out, only a handful of the 58 delegates from 16 nations, protectorates, and colonies that attended the Pan-African Congress had intimate day-to-day knowledge of Africa. Even Du Bois, the convener, had yet to visit the continent—and at this gathering he was not alone in this deficiency—though it was heartening that Haiti was well-represented, given its historic role as a Pan-African citadel. Still, the opening session was quite impressive with the delegates seated at long green tables attired in business suits and frock coats.[6]

Du Bois was buoyed by his presence in France, which soon was to become a site of exile for a generation of African American intellectuals and artists it embraced, including Josephine Baker, Richard Wright, and James Baldwin. "Vive La France!" chortled Du Bois as he hailed France's public celebration of the role of African soldiers most notably in preventing her defeat, after the French had almost wholly ingested propaganda about German superiority, a notion eroded in the battlefields of Marne and Verdun.[7] France's hospitability, however, did not necessarily extend to the Pan-African Congress, a congress that was thought to have anticolonial overtones, held on its soil. The "American Secret Service [was] at my heels," Du Bois complained later, though Europe, presumably, was beyond their remit. Yet the Pan-African Congress was held nonetheless, and "the world fight for black rights is on," he exclaimed. Rather ambitiously, he proclaimed, "we plan an international quarterly, 'Black Review,' to be issued in English, French and possibly in Spanish and Portuguese." Du Bois expressed hope about the formation of the League of Nations, sensing that if appeals to Washington went unheeded, the league might lend a willing ear. As for his other mission, Du Bois—who only recently had urged black Americans to "close ranks" in support of the war—now expressed shock at how Negro troops were being mistreated. Already it seemed that Du Bois was edging and inching away from his startling pro-war stance, observing, "under similar circumstances, we would fight again. But by the God of Heaven, we are cowards and jackasses if now that the war is over, we do not marshal every ounce of our brain and brawn to fight a sterner, longer, more unbending battle against the forces of hell in our own land."[8]

No doubt Du Bois was chastened by what he discovered concerning the brutishness directed toward Negro troops: even the most ingenuously trusting naïf would have had difficulty in supporting a war in which men were treated so horribly.[9] To his credit, Du Bois did not let his initial error infect his subsequent actions, for he collected documents about this scandal and dutifully published them for the benefit of a wider audience. Readers of the *Crisis* learned that Paris was informed that their citizenry's less than hostile attitude toward U.S. Negroes was a threat to Washington's security. Rather angrily, the U.S. authorities announced, "the French public has become accustomed to treating the Negro with familiarity and indulgence." The authorities argued that such solidarity had to end since it was an "affront" to U.S. "national policy" since Washington was "afraid that contact with the French will inspire in black Americans aspirations which to them [Euro-Americans] appear intolerable."[10]

Thus, if requesting African Americans to "close ranks" on behalf of this war was the most egregious and fundamentally flagrant error ever committed by Du Bois, it is striking that within months he sought to make amends, advising Negro soldiers who only recently had wielded weapons: "We Return. We Return from Fighting. We Return Fighting."[11]

Yes, they did—because they had to—for Negro troopers were at times murdered in their uniforms as the former slave South leapt to reassert its dominance over those who might have imbibed subversive ideas in the freer air of France and had the effrontery to act likewise. Dixie's worst nightmare took place in August 1917 when armed Negro troops in the Jim Crow bastion that was Houston, Texas, went on a rampage, attacking white police officers and others in retaliation for real and imagined provocations.

What ensued thereafter was the Red Summer of 1919, as pogroms were launched against black men and women in Chicago, East St. Louis, and elsewhere.

The great migration from the Deep South to these industrial sites was unfolding, driven by the war's need for labor to staff industrial plants and the difficulty faced by the traditional source—European migrants—in crossing the submarine-infested Atlantic. The war's end also meant there was no longer a need to maintain any kind of diplomacy toward the domestic foe—the Negro—and open season upon them quickly ensued, a direct rebuff to Du Bois's naïve notion that this conflict would bring benefits. Now breathing fire, Du Bois instructed his troops in the NAACP that "when the armed lynchers gather, we too must gather armed." His words rising in intensity, he exhorted, "we must defend ourselves." Strikingly, fueled with the radicalism that only a trip to Paris—and the witnessing of bloody pogroms—could bring, Du Bois went on to hail the "one new Idea of the World War—the idea which may well stand in future years as the one thing that made the slaughter worthwhile—is an Idea which we are like[ly] to fail to know because it is to-day hidden under the maledictions hurled at Bolshevism."[12]

Du Bois was reacting to the reality that in the midst of the war, communists had seized power in Russia and then pledged to assist Africa in fighting European colonialism. Though he may have had occasional conflicts with the domestic counterparts of the Bolsheviks in the U.S. Communist Party, Du Bois remained a partisan of what became the Union of Socialist Soviet Republics (USSR) from its inception. Du Bois's ties with the USSR were ultimately to lead to the real threat of imprisonment. But Du Bois at this moment could hardly know what fate awaited. In any case he was then overjoyed with the growth of *Crisis*, which had skyrocketed from sales of 9,000 in 1911 to 104,000 by mid-1919: he must have concluded that he was doing something right.[13]

Nevertheless, Du Bois's paeans of praise for Bolshevism cannot be understood outside of the context in which he was operating, that is, the gnawing perception that African Americans had few allies in North America and were fighting a desperate battle for survival, and, like the United States itself when faced with this daunting prospect in World War II, Du Bois saw no alternative to seeking an ally in Moscow. The events in Elaine, Arkansas, in which scores of African American sharecroppers were slaughtered and hundreds jailed after they protested against their cruel fate, provided further substantiation—if any were needed—about the desperate plight of those Du Bois was sworn to serve. With aching precision, Du Bois took to the pages of the mainstream press to plead on their behalf but at a certain point he had to wonder if justice could actually be found in a nation founded on the principle of enslavement of Africans.[14]

*   *   *

By 1918, Du Bois was 50 years old and, increasingly, viewed as the preeminent intellectual leader among African Americans. To be sure, he was spending ever increasing amounts of time away from his spouse and seemed to be married in name only—yet, his public persona seemed to be reaching for the stratosphere. Yes, there were bumps in the road, the failed attempt to join U.S. military intelligence being foremost among them: but, ironically, the perfervid essence of Jim Crow, which automatically cast African Americans unilaterally into the profoundest depths of Hades, made it difficult for the talented amongst them—for example, Du Bois—to be embraced, converting them whether they chose to or not into dissidents of various types.

Such brutal ironies inexorably drove an intellectual like Du Bois to his typewriter: 1920 witnessed the publication of his sixth book. The final draft of *Darkwater* was actually completed in 1918 on his 50th birthday and captured nicely the essence of its creator in that it was a curious mélange of autobiographical reflections, trenchant commentary, poetry, fictional musings, and the like. Yet among the odds and ends, standing out starkly in these pages was his pivotal essay, "The Damnation of Women," a heartfelt assault on the centuries-long brutalization of African American women in particular. This essay, emerging at a time when the right of women to vote was about to be ratified, was quite timely.

Yet it could not be denied that some among his constituency had lost confidence in Du Bois because of his dalliance with U.S. military intelligence, and such doubts created an opening not only for the rise of one Marcus Garvey but created fertile soil for a raging debate between the two—a debate that has survived the passing from the scene of both men. Garvey, a Jamaican, was deeply influenced by Du Bois's former sparring partner, Booker T. Washington, but it would be an error to see their conflict as simply a replay of what had occurred at the turn of the 20th century. To the contrary, Du Bois and Garvey had much in common, which may have made their contretemps all the more ferocious. Recognizing that the destiny of the diaspora was tied intimately to the fate of the continent, both men had a deep and abiding interest in Africa. They believed that African Americans would receive better treatment if Africa itself were to revive, and this meant that both men placed a premium on anticolonialism, which brought both into conflict with London, Paris, Brussels, and Lisbon.

Another commonality of the two men was their roots in the Caribbean basin. Garvey's rise was difficult to separate from the mass migration of those from the so-called British West Indies (Jamaica, Trinidad, Barbados, etc.) to New York City in particular, where they came to comprise a formidable component of the overall Negro population. Emerging from small islands where those of African origin were the overwhelming majority, they brought a determined militancy to the United States, as many were unaccustomed to taking a racial backseat.

Their relationship commenced innocently enough. Garvey, who was born in Jamaica in 1887 and died in 1940 in London, first visited the

United States in March 1916; a year earlier he had been in correspondence with Booker T. Washington, who urged him to come to the United States—ominously, by the time Garvey arrived, Washington was dead. Nonplussed, one of Garvey's first efforts in the United States was to hold a meeting with a lecture by himself and musical entertainment, at Saint Mark's Hall at West 138th Street in Harlem. The lecture concerned Jamaica, and the meeting's purpose was to help Garvey's nascent organization form industrial farms. Thus, on April 25, 1916, Garvey visited Du Bois's office but found him out of town so, quite graciously, he left a note asking if the famed intellectual would "be so good as to take the 'chair' at my first public lecture." Du Bois just as graciously declined.[15]

By mid-1920 Garvey's forces had grown exponentially, and he then paid Du Bois the ultimate compliment: "At the International Convention of Negroes to be held in New York during the month of August," he told his soon-to-be bitter rival, "the Negro people of America will elect a leader by the popular vote of the delegates from the forty-eight States of the Union. This leader, as expected, will be the accredited spokesman of the American Negro people. You are hereby asked," Du Bois was informed, "to be good enough to allow us to place your name in nomination for the post."[16] This was during an era of good feeling between the two, as Du Bois referred glowingly to Garvey as "an extraordinary leader of men," and one who had "with singular success capitalized and made vocal the great and long-suffering grievances and spirit of protest of the West Indian peasantry." At this juncture, Du Bois was evidently moved by the spectacle of Garvey's Universal Negro Improvement Association (UNIA), which had been organized a few years earlier with the goal of uplift of Africa and Africans. However, a premonition of the storm clouds that were to ensue were glimpsed in Du Bois's terse response to Garvey's offer, responding stiffly that "under no circumstances can I allow my name to be presented."[17]

But just as Du Bois stubbed his toe on the boulder that was military intelligence, Garvey too had his flaws, which caused the NAACP leader to pursue him with a determined ferocity. For although, like Du Bois, Garvey had spoken highly of the Bolsheviks and Irish anticolonialists, unlike Du Bois, the Jamaican had sought an alliance with the terrorist Ku Klux Klan on the premise, inter alia, that both would be satisfied if African Americans decamped en masse from North America.[18] Thus, despite their commonalities, Du Bois went to some length to distinguish himself from the Jamaican, particularly differentiating his brand of Pan-Africanism from Garvey's version.[19]

Ultimately, Garvey ran afoul of the U.S. authorities, and was tried and convicted for mail fraud, spending time in federal prison before being deported unceremoniously. This led to the still resonant charge that Garvey's misfortunes were a product of the purported rivalry between him and Du Bois and their two organizations, respectively—a charge Du Bois rejected with contempt. "It is absolutely untrue that the NAACP is a rival organization to the UNIA or instigated the charges against Garvey," he contended. He conceded that *Crisis* had published articles about Garvey and his organization and that he "furnished" these to the Department of Justice. But, he maintained, three of the articles in his journal were simply "expository and on the whole friendly," though admittedly, the fourth was "severely condemnatory" but "was not published until after his conviction and because of the propaganda which he was sending out against our organization and against all Negroes in the United States who were standing up for their rights as American citizens." As Du Bois saw things, Garvey's troubles "originated in two ways. First because of suits brought against him by members of his own organization who had invested in the Black Star Line under false representation and secondly by the effort of the state and city of New York to make Garvey stop violating the law in his issuing and selling of stock. The prosecuting members," Du Bois emphasized, "in every single case were former members of Garvey's organization or officers of the law. Not a single member or officer of the NAACP appeared as witness against Garvey."[20]

This was no doubt true but this could not obscure the sharp differences that had arisen between the two, with Garvey commenting derisively more than once about the interracial nature of the NAACP and what he saw as the preponderance of light-skinned Negroes within their ranks. There was probably an ethnic component to the conflict, as well, as the controversy between the NAACP and UNIA erupted simultaneously as migrants from the Caribbean basin at times encountered conflict in integrating seamlessly into the boroughs of New York City.

Thus, in January 1922, Garvey was arrested by federal authorities and charged with using the mails to defraud, and it was at this point that his ideology began veering in a more conservative direction. He was tried in May 1923 before Judge Julian Mack, a contributor to the NAACP, which convinced many of his followers that the NAACP's hand in his conviction and imprisonment was not exactly benign or minor. Earlier, eight prominent African Americans—including William Pickens and Robert W. Bagnall of the NAACP—had petitioned the U.S. Attorney General to "push the government's case against Marcus Garvey."[21] Rather promptly Garvey was convicted and received a five-year prison term, although three codefendants were acquitted. President Calvin Coolidge commuted the sentence in 1927, and in December of that year, Garvey was deported to Jamaica, though this hardly ended the conflict between himself and Du Bois.

Given the circumstances, it was believed far and wide in black America that Du Bois helped to manipulate the prosecution and deportation of his political rival—an allegation that the NAACP leader was compelled to deny more than once. "I beg to say," he announced resolutely after the initial conviction, "I have never written any letters to the District Attorney or Judge Mack or anyone else in authority with regard to Marcus Garvey, nor have had anything whatsoever to do with the prosecution of the case against him."[22] But Du Bois's detractors were disbelieving. Among this proliferating group was Ida May Reynolds. Du Bois's presumed anti-Garvey posture, she said, was "unmanly and cowardly"; moreover, she insisted, "the methods used by you and your organization were . . . uncalled for," and "will always reflect to the discredit of you and your associates and cause everlasting enmity between the West Indian and the American Negroes which feeling will take a long time to eradicate."[23]

There was reason for Ms. Reynolds to be skeptical of Du Bois's rationalizations for what he had written in his journal about Garvey was quite lengthy—and pointed. Du Bois saw Garvey's movement as being expressive of the exploited peasantry of the Caribbean. Du Bois saw Garvey himself as "an honest and sincere man with a tremendous vision, great dynamic force, stubborn determination and unselfish desire to serve." Yet, Du Bois also perceived "very serious defects of temperament and training: he is dictatorial, domineering, inordinately vain and very suspicious." Moreover, "the great difficulty with him," said Du Bois of Garvey, "is that he has absolutely no business sense, no *flair* for real organization and his general objects are so shot through with

bombast and exaggeration that it is difficult to pin them down for careful examination." Yet, Du Bois was struck by the point that Garvey had
"become to thousands of people a sort of religion. He allows and en-
courages all sorts of personal adulation."[24]

Du Bois was also struck by the point that Garvey had "never published a complete statement" of the income and expenditures of his organization. Nevertheless, Du Bois was taken by the fact that Garvey had
"put vessels manned and owned by black men on the seas and they have
carried passengers and cargoes." Du Bois could hardly disagree with the
"main lines" of Garvey's program (since it mirrored his own): "American
Negroes can, by accumulating and ministering their own capital, organize industry, join the black centers of the South Atlantic by commercial enterprise and in this way ultimately redeem Africa as a fit and free
home for black men. This is true," said Du Bois.[25]

For Du Bois continued to be haunted by Garvey, even as his various
campaigns bore fruit. Thus, along with the *Crisis*, it was Garvey's newspaper, *Negro World*, that pioneered in providing a venue for the Harlem
Renaissance to flourish, and it was Garvey—despite his shortcomings—
who put forward the idea of closer relationships between African Americans and Liberia, which Du Bois saw fit to emulate.

But from Du Bois's viewpoint, it was not just that Garvey was not expert in the art of execution or that he saw fit to consort with the Ku Klux
Klan or express distaste for the lighter skinned—a tension that if pursued could have torn black America asunder. Du Bois recognized that
in some ways, Garvey—his emphasis on Africa notwithstanding—represented an update of the program of Booker T. Washington (the man
who brought the Jamaican to these shores in the first place), and, years
after the Wizard had left the scene, Du Bois remained concerned about
the impact of his ideas. As Du Bois saw things, both Garvey and Washington represented an evasion of the necessity to confront U.S. elites
on their home turf—the former by looking longingly toward Africa, the
latter by dint of his almost maniacal stress on building businesses in
black America.

It was in mid-1923 that Du Bois summed up his differences with Washington, asserting that his "weakness" was the "assumption that economic power can be won and maintained without political power," just as
Garvey too evaded the central question of political power in the United

States itself—even though this power could just as easily follow one to Africa, as the case of Liberia exemplified. "No Negro dreams today," stressed Du Bois, "that he can protect himself in industry and business without a vote and without a fighting aggressive organization."[26]

Still, it would be a mistake to view this conflict without a consideration of the context. That context was a sharp escalation of postwar racism, driven by apprehensions about the concomitant rise of the New Negro, that is, those who no longer saw the need to smile when nothing was funny, or shuffle when a confident stride would suffice, or confront white supremacy forcefully, if need be. On the one hand, the postwar era witnessed the ascendancy of the second iteration of the terrorist and racist Ku Klux Klan, which actually dominated the political scene in Indiana, among other states, during this rabid era. On the other hand, the Klan was confronted by the rise of the New Negro's own Harlem Renaissance, which was a remarkable flowering of artistic merit, symbolized by the creativity of figures such as Langston Hughes, Jesse Fauset, James Weldon Johnson, and others. Interestingly, Du Bois was at the center of this initiative since it was the journal he edited that gave many of these writers an opportunity to strut.

Actually, this efflorescence stretched far beyond Harlem, as exemplified by Leopold Senghor, who led independent Senegal and before that had established an estimable reputation as a poet writing in French, and Nicolas Guillen of Cuba, whose wonderful poetry in Spanish was translated by Hughes. This transnational effort was buoyed as well by Du Bois's continuing labor on behalf of the Pan-African Congress, which provided a rationale for these cross-border collaborations and linkages.[27] After the 1919 gathering in Paris, Du Bois convened yet another during the summer of 1921, this time in London (with the Labour Party participating) and Brussels (headquarters for, perhaps, colonialism at its most brutal: the Congo) with rapt attention paid to Paris (whose pretension to being a great power was based largely on its empire in Africa) and Lisbon (whose colonies, in Mozambique and Angola particularly, had contributed immeasurably to enslavement in the Americas).[28]

But even in this admirable effort, Du Bois revealed troubling signs that he may have been too busy peering over his shoulder at the presumed challenge from Garvey. For on the occasion of this congress, he informed Secretary of State Charles Evans Hughes—previously governor of

New York, later chief justice of the U.S. Supreme Court, and therefore a member in good standing of the U.S. ruling elite—that his Pan-African Congress "has nothing to do with the so-called Garvey movement." Du Bois sought to reassure the fretting that his own movement "contemplates neither force nor revolution in its program. We have had the cordial cooperation," he stressed, "of the French, Belgian and Portuguese governments" (though in a real sense this admission was discrediting in the eyes of many of the colonized).[29]

Nevertheless, it would be an oversimplification to dismiss Du Bois's handiwork peremptorily for to do so would mean dismissing the extraordinary "Manifesto [to] the League of Nations" that was submitted by him in the aftermath of this Pan-African Congress. His "three earnest requests" included the farsighted demand that the needs of African workers be made the concern of a special section of the International Bureau of Labor; that a person of African descent be appointed a member of the Mandates Commission, which had taken jurisdiction over Germany's former colonies in Africa; and that the League itself "take a firm stand on the absolute equality of races and that it suggest to the colonial powers" that there should be formed an "International Institute for the Study of the Negro Problems and for the Evolution and Protection of the Negro Race." That this manifesto was trumpeted in the mass circulation *Crisis* insured that it would receive wide dissemination.[30] Shortly thereafter, the attempt to have a special commission established by the International Bureau of Labor occurred.[31]

Moreover, Du Bois continued to persevere on behalf of Liberia, the West African state founded in the 19th century by repatriated African Americans, some of whom had been enslaved. Along with Ethiopia, Liberia stood as a lodestar among African Americans as African nations that had managed to escape colonialism. As 1923 dawned, Du Bois felt compelled to contact Secretary of State Hughes once more, this time because he was "alarmed at the failure of Congress to confirm the Liberian Loan." What was at play? It was "an open secret," argued Du Bois, "that the British and French governments have only been held back in their aggression on Liberian territory, by the interest of the United States and by the prospect of her active aid," and if Washington failed to follow through, this beacon of African hope would "practically become a British protectorate with complete absorption looming in the future." One alternative proposed by Du Bois, which, once more, mirrored ideas then propagated by Garvey, "would be to establish a direct commercial intercourse between America and Liberia under a small company in which colored people [U.S. Negroes] had representation." Again, in case the influential Hughes had not noticed, Du Bois chose once more to bring Garvey into this field of vision, reminding him that the Jamaican's similar plan failed since he "was not a business man and turned out to be a thoroughly impractical visionary, if not a criminal."[32]

Du Bois was referring to Garvey's most ambitious commercial plan, the creation of the Black Star Line: the burly Jamaican raised hundreds of thousands of dollars and four ships ultimately were obtained, though no business was ever actually conducted, at least not to any significant degree.

Unfortunately, the conflict with Garvey was not the sole relationship that rocked Du Bois's world. Walter Francis White, born in 1893, was a 1916 graduate of Atlanta University, whose family was well-known to Du Bois when he resided in Georgia. At Du Bois's recommendation and with his urging, White as a young man served alongside James Weldon Johnson, the chief administrator of the NAACP. White was to take the helm of the association in 1931 and remain until his premature death in the mid-1950s. He was a man of no small talent, having authored numerous articles and several books of both fiction and non-fiction.[33] Light skinned to the point where he was able to pass as white, he did so at times in order to investigate lynchings. White had a black belt in the dark arts of bureaucratic infighting, which allowed him to oust Du Bois from his NAACP position twice—first in 1934, then again in 1948. Their differences were stylistic but, as will be seen, also deeply political, and at their root as consequential as Du Bois's differences with Washington and Garvey.

NOTES

1. *Crisis*, 14 (October 1917): 286, and 15 (February 1918): 165.

2. W.E.B. Du Bois to NAACP Board of Directors, July 2, 1918, in Aptheker, *Correspondence, Volume I*, 227–228.

3. Bryon Gunner to W.E.B. Du Bois, circa 1918, in Aptheker, *Correspondence, Volume I*, 228.

4. *New York Post,* September 22, 1917.

5. *Crisis,* 17 (Number 4, February 1919).

6. *New York Evening Globe,* February 22, 1919.

7. *Crisis,* 17 (Number 5, March 1919).

8. *Crisis,* 18 (Number 1, May 1919).

9. Note the widely circulated response of the chief aide of Booker T. Washington, Emmett Scott: *Nashville Globe,* May 30, 1919.

10. *Crisis,* 18 (Number 1, May 1919): 7–11.

11. *Crisis,* 18 (Number 1, May 1919).

12. *Crisis,* 19 (n.s., September 1919): 231–232.

13. *Crisis,* 18 (Number 5, September 1919).

14. *New York World,* November 28, 1919.

15. Marcus Garvey to W.E.B. Du Bois, April 25, 1916, in Aptheker, *Correspondence, Volume I*, 214–215.

16. Marcus Garvey to W.E.B. Du Bois, July 16, 1920, in Aptheker, *Correspondence, Volume I*, 245.

17. W.E.B. Du Bois to Marcus Garvey, July 22, 1920, in Aptheker, *Correspondence, Volume I*, 245–246.

18. W.E.B. Du Bois, "Back to Africa," *Century,* 105 (February 1923): 539–548.

19. *New York Age,* June 25, 1921.

20. W.E.B. Du Bois to P. B. Young, August 25, 1925, in Aptheker, *Correspondence, Volume I*, 317–318. See also Du Bois's contribution to "A Symposium on Garvey," *Messenger,* 4 (December 1922): 551, and also *Crisis,* 21 (December 1920), 21 (January 1921), 24 (September 1922), and 28 (August 1924).

21. E. U. Essien-Udom, Introduction, *Philosophy and Opinions of Marcus Garvey,* edited by Amy Jacques Garvey, London: Cass, 1967, xxvi.

22. W.E.B. Du Bois, July 10, 1923, in Aptheker, *Correspondence, Volume I*, 271–272.

23. Ida May Reynolds to W.E.B. Du Bois, July 5, 1923, in Aptheker, *Correspondence, Volume I*, 271–272.

24. *Crisis,* 21 (Numbers 2, December 1920).

25. *Crisis,* 22 (Number 3, January 1921).

26. W.E.B. Du Bois to Walter White, June 12, 1923, in Aptheker, *Correspondence, Volume I*, 266–267.

27. *New York Age,* May 28, 1921.

28. *Manchester Guardian,* August 30, 1921.

29. W.E.B. Du Bois to Charles Evans Hughes, June 23, 1921, in Aptheker, *Correspondence, Volume I,* 250–251.

30. *Crisis,* 23 (Number 1, November 1921).

31. *Crisis,* 25 (Number 5, March 1923).

32. W.E.B. Du Bois to Charles Evans Hughes, January 5, 1923, in Aptheker, *Correspondence, Volume I,* 260–261.

33. See, for example, his autobiography, Walter White, *A Man Called White,* New York: Viking, 1948.

William Edward Burghardt Du Bois and his mother, Mary Silvina Burghardt Du Bois. (Department of Special Collections and University Archives, W.E.B. Du Bois Library, University of Massachusetts, Amherst)

W.E.B. Du Bois, his wife Nina, and their son Burghardt in 1897. (Department of Special Collections and University Archives, W.E.B. Du Bois Library, University of Massachusetts, Amherst)

W.E.B. Du Bois. (Department of Special Collections and University Archives, W.E.B. Du Bois Library, University of Massachusetts, Amherst)

Du Bois at Atlanta University. (Department of Special Collections and University Archives, W.E.B. Du Bois Library, University of Massachusetts, Amherst)

W.E.B. Du Bois chats with artist Pablo Picasso at the opening of the World Congress of Partisans of Peace, held in Paris in April 1949. (AP Photo/Jean-Jacques Levy)

Representing the National Council of Arts, Sciences, and Professions (ASP), Du Bois addresses the World Congress of Partisans of Peace, April 22, 1949. (AP Photo)

Shirley Graham Du Bois and President Kwame Nkrumah of Ghana. (Department of Special Collections and University Archives, W.E.B. Du Bois Library, University of Massachusetts, Amherst)

President Kwame Nkrumah (second from right) talks with Dr. Du Bois shortly before opening the World Peace Conference in Accra, Ghana, on June 21, 1962. Du Bois was then 94 years old. (AP Photo)

Chapter 7

TALENTED TENTHS

When Du Bois stepped off a ship at the dock in West Africa in 1924, he recognized instinctively the potent importance of his arrival. Finally, he had arrived on the continent that had electrified his dreams and whetted his imagination. After spending so many hours of musing about Africa, he had arrived—but this was a bittersweet moment.[1] "When shall I forget the night," he waxed, "I first set foot on African soil—I, the sixth generation in descent from my stolen forefathers." Yet the poverty and misery that greeted him was bracing during this 15,000 mile journey that took him to four African islands and five African colonies.[2]

This was part of Du Bois's largely successful attempt to escape the cloister that cocooned all too many scholars. For just before this punishing and lengthy tour, Du Bois had embarked on a lengthy lecture tour in the United States that took him from Massachusetts to Minnesota, Oklahoma, Louisiana, and back to his home in New York; all in all he spoke before over 20,000 people. His lectures were not only meant to enlighten but also to recruit for the NAACP, then in the midst of a membership drive.

These tours of Africa and the United States exemplified the contrasting aspects of Du Bois's life and career as he entered the second half of his life: a slashing indictment of white supremacy while in the United States, and a less forceful approach in Africa, which was a virtual precedent condition to gaining admission to a continent, admission to which was often denied to African Americans.

For as his minuet with U.S. military intelligence exemplified, Du Bois had difficulty in reconciling the apparently contrasting ideas that African Americans should be included at all levels of U.S. society—even if this meant representing a nation whose record abroad was considered questionable by some of his closest colleagues. Of course, when he accepted an offer by President Coolidge as special envoy to represent the United States at the inauguration of President C.D.B. King of Liberia in 1924, he had the added incentive—as noted—of seeking to block London's and Paris's incursions into this rare independent African nation. Certainly, traveling with the imprimatur of Washington gave Du Bois added credibility when he arrived in Monrovia (the capital named after U.S. President James Monroe), though in retrospect his journey illustrated once more that he and Garvey shared similar ideas when it came to Pan-Africanism.

For Du Bois insisted in language that could have been uttered by Garvey that Liberia "needs the aid of American Negro capital and colored technical experts to help Liberians in the development of agriculture, industry and commerce."[3] But, unlike Garvey, Du Bois had another agenda, which did not necessarily reflect well upon him: he was an emissary of Washington and, thus, was carrying his nation's portfolio in a way that the anticolonial Jamaican did not. Thus, Du Bois argued that Liberia should favor capital infusions from the United States—in contrast to, for example, capital from Britain and France—since "if white Americans invest in Liberia and if they do not treat Liberia fairly and they try and get the United States Government to back up their demands, the Negroes of America [unlike the Negroes of London and Paris] have enough political power to make the government go slowly"; thus, "as between these three great countries, Liberia should apprehend least danger from American capital." This argument was no doubt pleasing to those in Washington.[4]

The available menu of choices was decidedly unappetizing, Du Bois thought. After returning to the United States, he told Harvey Firestone, whose eponymous rubber company was to make a major fortune in Liberia, "I have seen parts of British and French colonial Africa and have come in close contact with those who know colonial conditions in other parts of Africa. In all these cases," he asserted, "with the exception of the French, the procedure has been to enter the black country with entirely white personnel, to use the natives as laborers with the lowest wage and to use imported whites as the personnel in control." He warned Firestone against replicating this distasteful pattern in Liberia by dispatching there "whites used to 'handling' colored laborers" who "get results by cruelty and brow-beating alternating with pandering to drunkenness, gambling and prostitution among the blacks." Du Bois also requested that Firestone recruit "American Negroes" for his enterprise, seemingly unaware that the pattern was to keep this group as far away as possible for fear they might influence Africans toward sedition.[5]

Certainly, this naïve approach was not Garvey's—but Du Bois's words, which the Jamaican would vilify, were a response to the abject weakness of Africans and African Americans at this moment. Garvey's approach, in a sense, ignored this weakness amid a farrago of verbiage about "up you mighty race!," while Du Bois—at this point—was seeking to leverage U.S. nationality in a positive manner, which was considered naïve (not only by the cynics). Moreover, Du Bois's position carried more nuance than that of Garvey. Thus, he argued, there was "only one power" that might prevent Firestone Rubber from repeating "in Liberia all the hell that white imperialism has perpetrated heretofore in Africa and Asia," and "that is the black American with his vote."[6] Du Bois was vainly seeking to play a weak hand strongly. Meanwhile, he reprinted in his journal an italicized letter from Ernest Lyon, Liberian consul general in the United States, who stated bluntly, "no person or persons leaving the United States under the auspices of the Garvey movement in the United States, will be allowed to land in the Republic of Liberia," a response to the perception that rather than seeking to assist this small West African nation, the UNIA was seeking to take it over.[7] This was a perception shared by Du Bois who observed that "Liberia discovered that the Garvey organization was practically setting up a government within a government"—though, to be fair, Garvey's aim seemed to be anticolonial in nature, which ruffled the feathers of London and Paris, forcing Monrovia to act.[8]

Yet, to Du Bois's credit, this African initiative was not his only approach. He sought to forge an alliance with Moscow, which too was interested in destabilizing colonialism in Africa, as a way to weaken a

formidable foe in Europe. Unlike Garvey, he also sought to build domestic alliances beyond the mainstream. This was the import of his attempt
over the years to ally with the Socialist Party. And, consequently, in 1924
he supported the third-party candidacy of Robert La Follette—the noted
and influential Wisconsin leader of the left—(as did, by the way, both the
NAACP and the American Federation of Labor). He issued an appeal
to his fellow Negro voters, urging them to do likewise,[9] though he lamented the fact that the graying orator with a lion's mane, despite his
positive platform, bowed to Jim Crow dictates and avoided any direct reference to the plight of African Americans.[10] On the other hand, La
Follette had condemned the Klan and promised "to free Haiti," and, after
all, a bit of a loaf was better than none at all.[11]

But this positive gesture illustrated the weakness that characterized Du
Bois's position because La Follette performed poorly at the ballot box in
a nation that had extended its bigotry from African Americans to European immigrants. About 2 million African Americans cast ballots, with—
most likely—about 1 million for Coolidge the Republican and half a million each for the Democrats and La Follette—which was something of a
breakthrough from the time that the great Frederick Douglass proclaimed
that the GOP was "the ship, all else is the sea." In Texas, the Negro vote
defeated the Klan candidate for governor—though the Klan won important victories in Indiana, Kansas, Oklahoma, and Colorado.[12] Du Bois
knew that as long as labor organizations were reluctant to embrace workers of all stripes, the most debilitated workers of all—African Americans—would be perpetually weak.[13]

Hence, when his fellow intellectual, Kelly Miller, convened a meeting of the best and the brightest to ponder the plight of the Negro, Du
Bois was disappointed with the outcome. For their denunciation of
unions and "economic radicalism" was "most pitiful," he thought. "Union
labor has given the modern worker . . . whatever he has of decent wages,
and hours and conditions of work" said Du Bois. As for "economic radicalism," now a live issue in light of events in Moscow, there "lies," said
Du Bois "the only hope of the black folk."[14] Nonetheless, Du Bois was
not naïve about the potential of these radicals since he knew that they
very often functioned without even being aware of the special and awful
oppression of over 12 million Negroes: radicals' willful ignorance meant,
whether they knew it or not, that their programs would remain stymied.

"It is absolutely certain," he pronounced, "that the future of liberal and radical thought in the United States is going to be made easy or impossible by the way in which American democracy treats American Negroes."[15]

As a result of such thinking, Du Bois hailed the organization into a union of the Pullman porters under the leadership of A. Philip Randolph, born in 1889; though they had had endured sharp differences in the past, Du Bois was elated with his success. For this union of mostly Negro men also served as a communications network as they traveled by rail from city to city, often transmitting news and dropping off bundles of journals that might be unwise to send through the mail—such as the *Crisis* itself.[16]

Still, Du Bois—above all—was an intellectual and (jaunts to West Africa aside) this was what had come to occupy a good deal of his waking activity. Thus, the year of his first visit to Africa, appropriately, witnessed the publication of his still worthy book, *The Gift of Black Folk: Negroes in the Making of America.* This book was copyrighted by the Knights of Columbus in 1924 and was written at the request of that predominantly Catholic organization. This otherwise staid grouping was moved to this effort because of the anti-Catholicism and nativism, which had reached a zenith during the 1924 election, spearheaded largely by the Ku Klux Klan, which had expanded its agenda beyond the traditional target— African Americans—to those who were Jewish and Catholic. A few years earlier in Georgia, Leo Frank, a Jewish factory manager, had been lynched in retaliation for his alleged killing of a young Christian woman; this outrage had spurred many Jewish Americans to join the NAACP on the accurate premise that anti-Semitism would rise or fall in the United States, depending on what fate befell African Americans. Many Catholics were arriving at a similar conclusion—hence the Knights of Columbus' sponsorship of Du Bois's new book. This book, carrying chapters on such matters as "Black Explorers," "Black Labor," "Black Soldiers," and, one of Du Bois's central preoccupations, "The Freedom of Womanhood," also carries reflections on music, art, and literature.[17]

Nevertheless, despite this collaboration with the Catholics, he was not blind to their liabilities, noting subsequently that "because Catholicism has so much that is splendid in its past and fine in its present, it is the greater shame that 'nigger' haters clothed in Episcopal robes should do to black Americans in exclusion, segregation and exclusion from opportunity all that the Ku Klux Klan ever asked."[18] In fact, he continued, "in over 400 years the Catholic Church has ordained less than a half dozen black Catholic priests either because they have sent us poor teachers or because American Catholics do not want to work beside black priests and sisters or because they think Negroes have neither brains nor morals enough to occupy positions open freely to Poles, Irishmen and Italians."[19] The Catholic Church was a powerful institution in Louisiana particularly, where Jim Crow seemed to have no bounds. This body, thought Du Bois, "stands for color separation and discrimination to a degree equaled by no other church in America, and that is saying a very great deal."[20] Lest any think that Du Bois was singling out the Catholics for a special critique, he went on to note that the mostly Protestant YMCA (Young Men's Christian Association) may have been worse, that "the Negro race" could "teach" the YMCA a "good deal about Christianity."[21]

So there it was: although the 1920s may have been roaring for some, African Americans faced a dull roar of lynchings, exclusion, and the like. With rare exception, radical organizations were not sufficiently radical to take up their cause, and religious bodies were not sufficiently divine to counter this exclusionary tendency. In response, Du Bois was reduced to approaching those who desired to exploit Africa—like Firestone—with modesty and deference. The NAACP continued to plod along, though there were already disturbing signals that like Villard before him, Walter White had severe doubts about the autonomy of their chief journal and its editor.

In short, things seemed rather bleak, which drastically circumscribed Du Bois's available options. One response he did develop was the notion of the Talented Tenth or a cadre of the "best and the brightest" who would, somewhat selflessly, serve African Americans. Du Bois was one of those rare individuals who did not become more conservative as he grew older, but more radical (most leaving radicalism behind with their departed youth), and, eventually, he was to discard the idea of the Talented Tenth as unreflective of the reality of how easily the United States could seduce the talented with various emoluments. But by the time the 1920s arrived, he was still smitten with this notion, which seemed to reach stunning heights with the advent of the Harlem Renaissance, the emergence of an incredibly talented array of artists and cultural workers.

As early as 1903 when Du Bois was beginning to think more deeply about his differences with Washington, he began to lay out more systematically what he meant by this concept. "The Negro race, like all races," he announced "is going to be saved by its exceptional men." Obviously, this notion was naïve about gender—and evasive about the class interests of the "exceptional." Still, Du Bois continued, "men we shall have only as we make manhood the object of the work of the schools—intelligence, broad sympathy, knowledge of the world that was and is, and of the relation of men to it . . . on this foundation we may build bread winning, skill of hand and quickness of brain, with never a fear lest the child and man mistake the means of living for the object of life." The character of past leadership is traced down to "the present—a day of cowardice and vacillation, of strident wide-voiced wrong and faint-hearted compromise; of double-faced dallying with Truth and Right." In this context, he emphasized, education must be stressed: "there must be teachers, and teachers of teachers and to attempt to establish any sort of a system of common and industrial school training, without *first* (and I say *first* advisedly) without *first* providing for the higher training of the very best teachers, is simply throwing your money to the winds."[22] The Harlem Renaissance, which featured the ascendancy of university trained intellectuals such as the paradigmatic figure, poet, and playwright Langston Hughes—of Columbia and Lincoln University in Pennsylvania—was, thus, emblematic of the rise of the Talented Tenth that Du Bois had envisioned. "I'm always proud of *The Crisis*," Hughes told Du Bois, "and proud when you print me there." Hughes's praise was understandable, since the poems that appeared there helped both to propel Hughes's career and the Renaissance that he symbolized.[23]

In short, Du Bois sought to bolster those with sufficient talent to aid a beleaguered African American community. Foremost among these was the novelist, Jesse Fauset, who, like Hughes, was university trained, in her case at Cornell, where she studied German and French among other subjects. Du Bois thought so highly of her that he invited her to join the staff of the *Crisis*, an invitation she accepted. The publication of her novel *There Is Confusion* and Jean Toomer's *Cane* were said by Du Bois to "mark an epoch." Enthusiastically, he pointed to the work of five poets—Hughes, Countee Cullen, Georgia Johnson, Gwendolyn Bennett, and Claude McKay—and two essayists and critics (Eric Walrond and Walter White) as being emblematic of the Renaissance then being bruited.[24]

Du Bois was also a critic of some of the work that emerged from this protean era. This included Claude McKay's novel *Home To Harlem*, which brought the demimonde and the underworld of black New York to a wider audience.[25] McKay, who was born in Jamaica, had migrated to the United States, where he attended college in Manhattan, Kansas, and became quite close to the Communist Party. Though he found the writing to be both "beautiful and fascinating," with "all the materials of a great piece of fiction," overall, Du Bois was less than impressed. Actually, Du Bois confessed, the book "nauseates me," as the NAACP leader felt McKay seemed to "set out to cater [to] the prurient demand on the part of white folk." As Du Bois saw it, a "number of New York publishers" were encouraging such fiction, work that was marked by an "utter absence of restraint." Predictably, McKay was displeased with Du Bois's evaluation. Writing from Barcelona—McKay was a habitual traveler and a veritable permanent exile—he took particular umbrage at the notion that Du Bois published his review in the same edition of the journal that carried some of McKay's poems. McKay was outraged, telling Du Bois, "I should think that a publication so holy-clean and righteous-pure as the 'Crisis' should hesitate about printing anything from the pen of a writer who wallows so much in 'dirt,' 'filth,' 'drunkenness,' 'fighting' and 'lascivious sexual promiscuity.'"[26]

McKay seemed to forget that Du Bois was of the view that all art was "propaganda" not in the pejorative sense of this phrase but in the sense that a beset population of Negroes had a special need for art that was uplifting, not degrading, just as this population desperately needed artists who spoke to and of their deepest and most heartfelt needs: a Talented Tenth, in other words. "All art is propaganda," Du Bois thundered, "and ever must be," adding angrily, "I do not care a damn for any art that is not used for propaganda." Again, what he meant was that art conveyed ideas—for better or for worse—and the oppressed were desperately in need of uplifting ideas.[27]

Du Bois also thought that the Negro had a peculiar contribution to make to the arts. The "Negro as a race," he announced "has always exhibited peculiar artistic ability." To flourish, he opined, this art requires freedom for the artist to perform and create and support from an audience that would allow the artist to produce. Their overarching theme—the black experience—provided these artists "an astonishingly fertile field," which was a positive way of evaluating the dialectic of oppression.[28]

Thus, Du Bois saw art and creativity not as trivial frivolity but an essential component of the uplift of an oppressed people, and to execute this important task, a Talented Tenth was absolutely necessary. The Harlem Renaissance, therefore, reflected a flowering of Du Bois's own vision. It is often difficult to conceptualize eras and epochs as they are unfolding, precisely because they are so close to one's own eyes. Despite this natural handicap, in 1926, as the Harlem Renaissance was still taking shape, Du Bois began to analyze this phenomenon, observing that beginning about 1910 there commenced "something that can be called a renaissance," and since then there had appeared a "more careful consideration of the Negro's social problems." In the field of history, he pointed to the trailblazing work of Benjamin Brawley and Carter G. Woodson. Yet, their eye-opening work notwithstanding, "the true renaissance," said Du Bois "has been a matter of spirit," which was manifested most effectively among the poets, dramatists, and novelists—not to mention musicians such as J. Rosamond Johnson.[29] Du Bois could well have added the development of blues and jazz, particularly the work of W. C. Handy, Scott Joplin, Louis Armstrong, Sidney Bechet, and Buddy Bolden.

Given his pivotal role in helping to give rise to a wildly riotous outpouring of creativity, it should not be overly surprising that Du Bois decided to try his hand at novel writing. It was in 1911—just after he had noticed a "renaissance" in creativity among Negroes—that his novel *The Quest of the Silver Fleece* was published. And it was in 1928 that his next effort in this realm appeared. *Dark Princess: A Romance* featured a worldwide conspiracy of the colored peoples—led by an Indian princess—to overthrow forcibly the evil machinations of white supremacy.[30] The conspiracy never reaches the point of actual attempt but in the process of developing the theme, Du Bois discusses the intricacies of Chicago politics and upper-class life among Negroes (though Du Bois personally was not affluent, his position with the NAACP and his intellectual candlepower meant that he became conversant with these circles). Still, it is working-class Negro life that Du Bois portrays with the utmost sympathy. This novel may have been prompted by his tours of Europe where he had met people from the colored world who had proposed—for example—a military attack on Europe via North Africa and through Spain (not unlike what had occurred hundreds of years ago at a time when Islam was spreading globally). Du Bois also had met Asian women, who bedazzled him with their pulchritude and brilliance. As World War I was winding down, San Francisco was the site of a lengthy trial—the so-called Ghadr conspiracy trial—of South Asian revolutionaries who had been plotting to overthrow the rule of the empire in what was referred to as British India. One can detect in these novels suggestions that this trial did not escape Du Bois's attention. In this "romance," he was seeking to signal to those who held white supremacy dear that there was a raging discontent against this praxis that soared far beyond the precincts of black America.

And by placing an Indian character at the center of his narrative, he was also paying homage to the crowning jewel in the British Empire—India—a nation to which he long had looked for inspiration. Early on he struck up a friendship with L. L. Rai of Lahore, a journalist, historian, and political activist—that is, a man not unlike Du Bois in profile—with whom he corresponded frequently and who he escorted during his journey to the United States.[31] As for the paramount leader, Mohandas K. Gandhi, he was effusive, speaking of him generously as a "a man who from sheer impeccability of character and extraordinary personality and from loftiness and originality of doctrine and ideas, takes rank at once among the great men of the world."[32]

But in addition to his crusade to mobilize art and creativity via the Talented Tenth on behalf of Black Liberation, Du Bois—as his novel demonstrated—also sought to take advantage of tumultuous events worldwide and in the 1920s that meant taking the measure of Moscow. Du Bois had his doubts to begin with. Claude McKay, an early proponent of the Bolshevik Revolution of November 1917, queried Du Bois in late 1921 as to why he seemed to neglect or sneer at the result of the Czar's overthrow. Taken aback, Du Bois replied that he did not wish to sneer at the Russian Revolution: "Russia is incredibly vast," he offered, and while he thought there were positive developments occurring, he was quick to observe that he had been "hearing of other things which frighten us." Du Bois was elated with the declaration emerging from Moscow that placed emphasis on freeing of Africa and Asia from colonial tyranny as a priority, which Du Bois as a Socialist could only applaud. But he rejected the "dictatorship of the proletariat," and observed dryly that he was "not prepared to dogmatize with Marx or Lenin." Though a professed Socialist himself, Du Bois was concerned about the applicability of this philosophy to the United States, since he was doubtful if the white working class in particular could ever be prevailed upon to overcome its racism. In any case, he informed McKay that the immediate program of the NAACP, focused on voting rights and antilynching, should not be ditched in favor of repatriating to Africa (yet another shot at Garvey) or joining a revolution that "we do not at present understand." At the same time, Du Bois noted, "as McKay says, it would be just as foolish for us to sneer or even seem to sneer at the blood-entwined writhing of hundreds of millions of our whiter human brothers."[33]

Overall, however, Du Bois had severe doubts for much of his lengthy life as to whether white workers could ever come to break from the grip of white elites and ally with laborers of the same class, yet of a different color. It was not just the Bolsheviks coming to power in Moscow; the fact was that unlike London, which featured a strong Labour Party, or France, Germany, and Japan, all of which had relatively strong political parties with substantial support from trade unions, the United States simply had no equivalent, and, as Du Bois saw things, racism was a major reason why. Du Bois was not purblind. He recognized the greatness of Eugene Debs, the Terre Haute–born U.S. socialist leader who was jailed for his antiwar views and who ran for president from a prison cell. At Debs's passing in 1926, Du Bois praised him since he "knew that no real emancipation of laboring classes in the United States can come as long as black laborers are in partial serfdom."[34]

Yet, just as there was a discontinuity between Du Bois's thunderbolts launched at white supremacy in the former slave South and his comparatively soft-spoken approach to the likes of Harvey Firestone, there was also a discontinuity between his relative pessimism about the prospects of socialism in the United States and his bright-eyed optimism elsewhere. This came clear most dramatically during his first trip to Russia in 1926. Alone and unaccompanied—once again leaving his spouse and daughter behind—the aging leader walked through a half dozen of the larger cities there. He was in the region at a time when Leon Trotsky, a Soviet founder, was under siege by the ultimate winner in their power struggle—Josef Stalin—as the nation writhed in turmoil in the face of a concatenation of unforced errors and hostile encirclement that followed the premature death of V. I. Lenin. But Du Bois, who was bent on finding an ally against his antagonists did not focus on this matter (just as the United States itself did not when it was seeking allies against Berlin and Tokyo a few years later). Instead, he seemed ecstatic at what he had witnessed, "I stand in astonishment and wonder," he enthused, "at the revelation of Russia that has come to me. I may be partially deceived," he conceded, "and half-informed. But if what I have seen with my eyes and heard with my ears in Russia is Bolshevism. I am a Bolshevik."[35] During this journey, the peripatetic Du Bois had passed through Antwerp—"to see Rubens," confessed this patron of the arts—before reaching Cologne, Frankfurt, and Berlin, past German haunts. But always the center of the journey was Soviet Russia.[36] This fascination was to bring him much grief during the early cold war when Moscow–Washington relations suffered a profound downturn, and Du Bois refused to repudiate his position.

Yet there were parallels between Du Bois's faith in the ability of a Talented Tenth to lead black America to the promised land and his abiding faith in what had been wrought in the Soviet Union, for similar to the Talented Tenth, the revolutionary vanguard was a slice of the population that had pledged to lead the nation; in the vanguard's case, they pledged to lead the nation beyond the merciless misery that had afflicted czarist times.

Du Bois also saw an intimate tie between the hysteria in the North Atlantic generated by the rise of communist parties and the possibility of pushing back vigorously against Jim Crow terrorism. When Moscow and their surrogates in the United States began making vigorous appeals to African Americans at a time when Washington itself was challenged by a nation whose territory spanned the richest and most populous continents (Europe and Asia), an opening was created that Du Bois rushed to exploit. Almost from the moment the Bolsheviks seized power, Washington began raising a clamor about real and imagined human rights violations that were besetting this vast land. But how could the United States credibly point the finger of accusation at Moscow about—for example—extrajudicial executions when there was a similar phenomenon in place in the United States (lynchings that Washington claimed there was nothing the federal government could do about because the regulation of justice was purportedly the province of the individual states)?

Moreover, when Du Bois began to look positively toward Moscow, he was both exemplifying a long-term trend in black America that often sought allies abroad and often found them in nations that had problems with Washington. Thus, just as more enslaved Africans fought with the British during the 18th-century war that led to U.S. independence than fought with the victors, thousands more Negroes fled to British lines during the War of 1812, many of whom decamped afterwards permanently to Bermuda, Trinidad, and elsewhere within the Empire.[37] London abolished slavery well before Washington did, which meant that the enslaved of North America often fled in droves to British soil, be it Canada or the Bahamas—all the while tensions between the Empire and the United States did not abate, with one reason being this draining capital loss in human "commodities."[38] As Japan began to rise as a power and sought leverage in North America, Tokyo too developed a robust relationship with African Americans—and vice versa.[39] This was nothing peculiar to African Americans and Washington: Palestinians in the Occupied Territories looked to Moscow during the Soviet era at a time when both were in conflict with Israel; the Quebecois in Canada often looked to Paris—such was the nature of diplomatic statecraft to which African Americans were not immune.

Thus, Du Bois was merely walking in the footsteps of those who came before; moreover, Du Bois's growing fascination with Moscow was not sui generis. In fact, a good deal of the Talented Tenth that Du Bois had helped in part to propel—including Hughes and McKay, the leading luminaries—had a similar orientation with both of these skilled artists spending considerable time in the Soviet Union. Even the NAACP, whose leadership was often at odds with its feisty editor, consented to allowing staff member William Pickens to sail to Belgium in order to participate in the International Congress of the Oppressed Nations, whose very title was a telling indication to Washington that Moscow was deeply imbedded in this campaign.[40] At a time when the official ideology of the United States was white supremacy—infused with apartheid—while the Soviet Union was proclaiming officially that it would provide material assistance for those fleeing from colonialism in Africa and moral support for opponents of Washington, it was not that difficult a choice for those of Du Bois's stripe to lend an ear.

Thus, during the same year that he visited the Soviet Union, the *New York Times* reported worriedly about "Communists Boring into Negro Labor." No less provocatively, Du Bois replied that if there was a true desire to stop Negro interest in communism, then more aggressive steps should be taken to halt racism.[41] This became a repetitive theme of his. Responding to the hysteria in the press about the purported rise of Bolshevism among Negroes, Du Bois pointed to the profusion of bigotry targeting them as a reason for their disenchantment with the United States.[42] This was during a time when the Communist-led American Negro Labor Congress was thought to be making gains in organizing, which generated no small amount of consternation. It was "unjust of white men and idiotic of colored men to criticize" such efforts, Du Bois concluded. As for their presumed patrons in Moscow, he argued with no less provocation that "we should stand before the astounding effort of Soviet Russia to reorganize the industrial world with open mind and listening ears."[43]

Moreover, when Du Bois and some within the Talented Tenth reached out to Moscow, this was part and parcel of a larger global initiative to place excruciating pressure upon Jim Crow. After the founding of the United Nations, Du Bois pioneered the search to place the plight of the Negro before this august body. After the founding of the League of Nations following World War I, Du Bois advocated that black Americans should seek permanent representation at their headquarters in Geneva, Switzerland. In the pages of Crisis he pondered the applicability of various international conventions to African Americans, although these were ostensibly designated with the colonized in mind.[44] Seeking solace in global bodies a fortiori meant seeking support from those who might not be bosom buddies with Washington—and, of course, that included Moscow.

It is worth noting that Du Bois's global initiatives, notably the outreach to Moscow, did not win him many friends even among liberal constituencies that may have been predisposed to back his cause. But this was only a reflection of a deeper dilemma faced by black Americans as a whole: descendants of slaves, largely stigmatized, they were reduced to seeking succor from Talented Tenths, at home and abroad.

NOTES

1. W.E.B. Du Bois, "The Primitive Black Man," The Nation, 119 (December 17, 1924): 675–676.

2. Crisis, 27 (Number 6, April 1924).

3. W.E.B. Du Bois to President C.D.B. King, January 21, 1924, in Aptheker, Correspondence, Volume I, 279–280.

4. W.E.B. Du Bois to President C.D.B. King, January 21, 1924, in Aptheker, *Correspondence, Volume I*, 279–280.

5. W.E.B. Du Bois to Harvey Firestone, October 26, 1915, in Aptheker, *Correspondence, Volume I*, 320–322.

6. W.E.B. Du Bois, "Liberia and Rubber," *New Republic*, 44 (November 18, 1925): 326–329.

7. *Crisis*, 28 (Number 4, August 1924).

8. W.E.B. Du Bois to P. B. Young, August 8, 1925, in Aptheker, *Correspondence, Volume I*, 317–318.

9. *New York Times*, October 21, 1924.

10. *Crisis*, 28 (Number 4, August 1924).

11. *Crisis*, 29 (Number 1, November 1924).

12. *Crisis*, 29 (Number 2, December 1924).

13. W.E.B. Du Bois, "Worlds of Color," in Alain Locke, ed., *The New Negro*, New York: Boni, 1925, 385–414.

14. *Crisis*, 28 (Number 1, May 1924).

15. *Crisis*, 29 (Number 5, March 1925).

16. *Crisis*, 31 (Number 2, December 1925). For more editorials by Du Bois urging support of Randolph's campaign, see *Crisis*, 33 (January 1927) and 34 (December 1927).

17. W.E.B. Du Bois, *The Gift of Black Folk: Negroes in the Making of America*, Boston: Stratford, 1924.

18. *Crisis*, 30 (Number 3, July 1925).

19. W.E.B. Du Bois to Joseph B. Glenn, March 18, 1925, in Aptheker, *Correspondence, Volume I*, 309.

20. W.E.B. Du Bois to Joseph B. Glenn, March 24, 1925, in Aptheker, *Correspondence, Volume I*, 311.

21. W.E.B. Du Bois to R. H. Athearn, April 2, 1925, in Aptheker, *Correspondence, Volume I*, 313.

22. W.E.B. Du Bois, "Talented Tenth," in Booker T. Washington, ed., *The Negro Problem: A Series of Articles by Representative American Negroes of Today*, New York: Pott, 1903, 33–75.

23. Langston Hughes to W.E.B. Du Bois, February 11, 1928, in Aptheker, *Correspondence, Volume I*, 374. Hughes's poetry in Du Bois's journal remains worth perusing: see, for example, "The Childhood of Jimmy" and "Song for a Dark Girl" in *Crisis* (May 1927); "Ma Lord" in *Crisis* (June 1927); "Tapestry" in *Crisis*, (July 1927); "Freedom Seeker" and "Being Old" in *Crisis* (October 1927); "Montmartre Beggar Woman" in *Crisis* (November 1927); "Johannesburg Mines" in *Crisis* (February 1927).

24. *Crisis*, 27 (Number 4, February 1924).

25. Claude McKay, *Home to Harlem*, New York: Harper and Bros., 1928. Du Bois's critical review appears in *Crisis*, June 1928.

26. Claude McKay to W.E.B. Du Bois, June 18, 1928, in Aptheker, *Correspondence, Volume I*, 374–375.

27. *Crisis*, 32 (Number 6, October 1926).

28. *Crisis*, 34 (Number 2, May 1927).

29. W.E.B. Du Bois, "Negro Literature," in *The Encyclopedia Britannica*, 13th edition, Volume 29, New York: Encyclopedia Britannica, 1926, 110–111.

30. W.E.B. Du Bois, *Dark Princess: A Romance*, New York: Harcourt, Brace & Co., 1928.

31. Gerald Horne, *The End of Empires: African-Americans and India*, Philadelphia: Temple University Press, 2008.

32. *Crisis*, 23 (Number 5, March 1922).

33. *Crisis*, 22 (Number 3, July 1921).

34. *Crisis*, 33 (Number 2, December 1926).

35. *Crisis*, 33 (Number 1, November 1926).

36. *Crisis*, 33 (Number 2, December 1926).

37. See, for example, Simon Schama, *Rough Crossings: Britain, the Slaves and the American Revolution*, New York: Ecco, 2006.

38. See, for example, Gerald Horne, *Negroes with Guns! African-Americans and the British Empire Confront the United States before the Civil War*, forthcoming.

39. See, for example, Gerald Horne, *The White Pacific: U.S. Imperialism and Black Slavery in the South Seas after the Civil War*, Honolulu: University of Hawaii Press, 2007; Gerald Horne, *Race War! White Supremacy and the Japanese Attack on the British Empire*, New York: New York University Press, 2004.

40. *Crisis*, 33 (Number 3, January 1927).

41. *New York Times*, January 17, 1926.

42. *Crisis*, 34 (Number 6, August 1927).

43. *Crisis*, 31 (Number 2, December 1925).

44. *Crisis*, 33 (Number 3, January 1927).

Chapter 8

DIVORCES

Though Du Bois hardly recognized it at the time, from the time of his journey to the Soviet Union in 1926 all the way to 1934, he was on a death march to being sacked by the organization he had helped to found, the NAACP. This was not inevitable, and it was not exclusively a product of Du Bois's stated sympathies toward Moscow; after all, at this juncture (and unlike his second sacking in 1948, after his 1944 return) the board of the organization was hardly a fortress of anticommunism. Some of it had to do with his perceived prickliness, which was a partial product of shyness and a direct outgrowth of being a proud man who was too often forced into awkward situations where he was rejected precisely because he was seen as a descendant of a class of slaves. Moreover, just as he had clashed with Oswald Villard, as his tenure was winding down with the NAACP, his relationship with Walter White was deteriorating at warp speed. But, looming above all these issues in explicating why Du Bois parted company with the NAACP in 1934 was—ironically— the question of whether he had come to embrace unduly the philosophy of a man with whom he had jousted so famously, Marcus Garvey.

This was not an ideal moment for this dustup to occur for the buildup to Du Bois's exit from the NAACP occurred simultaneously as a series of disasters bombarded black America. The Great Mississippi Flood of 1927 caused hundreds of deaths and mass destruction over an area of 27,000 square miles due to the failure of levees (not unlike the destruction caused by Hurricane Katrina along the Gulf Coast in 2005). That this catastrophe was centered near what was probably the epicenter of Jim Crow—Mississippi—only complicated the attempt by the NAACP to assist Negro victims. For example, shortly after the height of this tragedy, Du Bois was contacted by Tillman Jones of Hinds County, Mississippi. He felt compelled to send the letter "under a camouflaged address to avoid the consequences of racial hatred and mob violence." He added ominously, "it is dangerous for the name of Mr. Du Bois or the name of Mr. Spingarn to be seen in this section . . . the eternal danger is highly imminent"; he complained bitterly about a "reign of terror" and the "ceaseless toils of whitecap persecution."[1] Jones's language is probably too mild to capture the humdrum hounding of being forced to abandon the sidewalk for the gutter as a white person approached or not being able to try on shoes or clothes at stores before purchase (and being unable to return same if such did not fit) or the inability to visit restaurants or bathrooms while on a driving trip through the region— and far, far worse.

Then in October 1929 the stock market collapsed and soon to follow was the economy as a whole: unemployment lines stretched as far as the eye could see; once affluent stockbrokers were reduced to selling apples for coins; homeless hoboes stalked the land, riding the rails from town to town. Harlem, where Du Bois resided at 409 Edgecombe Avenue on a bluff overlooking Yankee Stadium in the Bronx (a baseball shrine where stellar African American stars like Josh Gibson and Jay "Cool Papa" Bell were routinely barred from making a living), was hit hard by this economic distress. As Du Bois strolled to the subway stop to ride the iron horse downtown to his Spartan office, he could not help but notice the growth in panhandling, which was a marker for a community that had been pushed to the edge of survival.

It was in this context of utter desperation that Du Bois—along with other African Americans—began to contemplate self-help regimes in the midst of conservative nostrums symbolized by the Republican Party many had supported to that point, which abjured any aggressive role for government in economic recovery. The dominant ethos nationally was "do for self" with government aid to the needy seen widely in the United States as worse than blasphemy. The movement led by Marcus Garvey had already demonstrated that it would be unwise for the NAACP leadership to ignore an underlying sentiment among their constituency that—apparently—hungered for approaches that called on Negroes themselves to help themselves. Garvey's relative success in attracting adherents was quickly followed by the rise of the organization that came to be known as the Nation of Islam, which had a similar outlook with the added fillip of devotion to a religion whose roots in Africa—including the regions from which many African Americans had sprung—ran deep.

Du Bois could hardly be immune to these trends. As a lifetime student, he was not above evolving or parsing ideas that were thought to be well-nigh eternal. Thus in 1927 he was queried about the possibility of constructing an all-Negro state somewhere within the bounds of the United States, an idea that had been broached decades earlier by President Thomas Jefferson and that had been adumbrated when Oklahoma was initiated—supposedly as a state for indigenes, many of whom were forced to move from the southeast. Now the official NAACP policy was to compel desegregation—if not, the analytically distinct category of integration—and Du Bois was a founder and most influential member of this organization. Yet, Du Bois—though hedging and hesitating—conceded that the idea of a state for the Negroes was "feasible."[2] In retrospect, it seems apparent that the ideological momentum created by Du Bois's insistent call for self-determination and self-reliance for Africans, as an antidote to colonialism, inexorably pushed Du Bois in a similar direction in his advocacy for African Americans. In 1928 Du Bois noted offhandedly that "Black America is going to have a voice in Black Africa's fate. Black Africa must and will do the same or die trying," suggesting the everlasting linkage between the two.[3] It was an ever delicate task to strike the appropriate balance between the rights of African Americans to voluntarily carve out their own path and the necessity to push for equal rights within a diverse polity. Du Bois was accused more than once of hewing too closely to the path of self-determination—as opposed to equal rights—which was ironic indeed in light of his clashes with Garvey, the embodiment of this purportedly heretical trend.

His failure to renounce such purported heresy led directly to his divorce from the organization he had toiled so long to build, at the none too tender age of 66. Yet instead of gracefully accepting being placed in the pasture, Du Bois instead went on to make some of the most important contributions in his extraordinarily lengthy career.

*   *   *

Du Bois was far from being the ideal father and husband. Like other renowned men—Nelson Mandela comes to mind—he seemed to be married to the struggle and more devoted to being father to a people. So, when his daughter, Yolande, chose to marry the famed poet, Countee Cullen, he pulled out all the stops, as if in compensation for his lengthy absences during her childhood and adolescence. It seemed to be a marriage made in Talented Tenth heaven with their union destined to produce progeny primed to engage fruitfully in uplift. Adopted at the age of 15 by an influential Harlem pastor, Cullen went on to become elected to Phi Beta Kappa while studying at New York University, then receiving an advanced degree at Du Bois's alma mater—Harvard—in 1926.[4] His blushing bride, born in 1900, had attended the elite British Preparatory Academy, the Bedales School, and later Fisk University, where she graduated with a degree in Fine Arts in 1924. While in school, her father acted the martinet, lecturing her repeatedly about the need to excel academically, sending her one stern letter after another on this topic. Though she was infatuated allegedly with the talented musician Jimmy Lunceford, a pioneer of swing music, this did not halt her rush to the altar on April 8, 1928, accompanied by Cullen as her groom.[5]

So, just as *Dark Princess*, Du Bois's self-proclaimed romance was published, he was presiding over an actual romance with potential similar to his fictional creation. Thus it was that the great and the good (hundreds in fact) came uptown to Harlem—the Salem Methodist Church, to be precise—to witness the betrothal: it was an affair to remember. Attending the groom were a virtual all-star team of the Talented Tenth: Arna Bontemps, whose literary contributions were to rival the man with whom he often collaborated, Langston Hughes; W. Alphaeus Hunton, from a prominent family himself, a budding scholar who, like Du Bois, eventually chose exile in Africa in order to escape persecution in the United States; and, among others, Hughes himself. Among those watching this spectacle were Du Bois's NAACP comrades, James Weldon Johnson and Mary White Ovington.

Two hundred white doves were released during this lavish ceremony that cost hundreds of dollars to produce—no small sum in a time of growing financial distress. The couple honeymooned in Philadelphia, then it was off to Paris where Cullen had received a fellowship. But like so many marriages before and since, this one did not last; it was exceedingly brief, as there were differences that at the time seemed irreconcilable, though—as so often happens—such were not readily evident. For groom Countee Cullen was a gay man with a lover all his own, a fact which raises severe questions as to why he chose to marry Du Bois's daughter.[6] This love triangle was not revealed immediately, and the notoriously private Du Bois betrayed his New England reserve by broadcasting widely his joy at his daughter's marriage to Cullen and the deep emotion that welled up inside him as a result.[7]

Thus, what seemed to be the crowning glory of Du Bois's ambitious plans to embellish in a lively fashion the Talented Tenth turned out to be something else altogether. Homosexuality in black America—as in the nation as a whole at the time—was not necessarily embraced, and the prolific Du Bois, who seemed to churn out articles, reviews, and essays as if he had a factory of elves toiling on his behalf, chose not to seize the occasion to expound on this fraught matter.

Unfortunately, this was not the only setback endured by Du Bois during what was a tumultuous decade. The alarming increase in lynching had not ceased, and, in response, Du Bois and the NAACP initiated a legislative response. After diligently collecting congressional support, Congressman L. C. Dyer of Missouri introduced antilynching legislation. Yet the bill quickly collided with the age-old shibboleth of states' rights (i.e., the notion that the Civil War and concomitant constitutional amendments were thought to have resolved, that states of the former Slave South were "sovereign" to the extent that they could block initiatives from Washington). As early as April 1922, Du Bois contended angrily that if the bill did not pass, it would "end the United States."[8] That the bill did not pass (and the United States did not end) maximized his frustration, causing him to turn his back on both Republicans and Democrats in the 1924 presidential election, and back La Follette, while escalating his ongoing effort to build a Talented Tenth.

Although Du Bois's failed attempt to augment the Talented Tenth via marriage of his daughter was daunting for Du Bois, it did not shake his belief in what was a bedrock belief for him. As noted, he had introduced this notion of the Talented Tenth as early as 1903, and he argued that he had not constructed this idea from whole cloth, observing that "talented tenthers" [sic] had arisen in the antebellum era in the form of abolitionists, such as Henry Highland Garnet, Sojourner Truth, Frederick Douglass, among others. The added plus he envisioned for this group was higher education.[9] Thus, one of the least discussed though most successful initiatives by the talented men—and women—who Du Bois had slated to lead black America toward progress was their desire for college degrees, a possession not so common in his day. Black Americans had been admitted to matriculate in colleges like Oberlin before the Civil War but the number of those who had received higher education by the 1920s was extremely meager. Indeed, what made Du Bois himself stand out—his worthy qualities aside— was the sterling education he had received at Fisk, Harvard, and Berlin. Du Bois was fortunate to have been born after the Civil War, when the newly freed slaves targeted education as one of their top priorities, and as a result, there was a proliferation of universities and colleges founded during this era, including Du Bois's original alma mater, Howard, and a number of others, particularly in the South, where the overwhelming preponderance of African Americans continued to reside.

Yet, as Du Bois's notorious confrontation with Booker T. Washington exemplified, there was fierce contestation about the actual role that colleges and universities should play, and this controversy did not die with his death. In one of the earliest editions of the *Crisis*, Du Bois had cited prominently to great effect the words of Governor Cole Blease of South Carolina who growled that "the greatest mistake the white race has ever made was in attempting to educate the free Negro."[10]

In fact, the 1920s witnessed an upsurge of student protest that prefigured a similar wave in the 1960s—inferentially confirming Blease's ominous words. Du Bois and the NAACP were central to the student protests of the 1920s, some of the more important protests of that period. Perhaps unsurprisingly, a particular target of Du Bois's ire was the college once known as Hampton Institute, located in easternmost Virginia, which happened to be the alma mater of Washington himself. The stress there on industrial education at the expense of the humanities and liberal arts, riled him to no end, and, he thought, education that did not embrace the humanities was a concession to the desires of Jim Crow. Thus, in the 1920s, Du Bois took up the cudgels against Hampton since it chose to segregate audience members at cultural performances there—yet continued to be the biggest recipient of white philanthropy. When students went on strike there in 1927, Du Bois became their loudest champion. These students seemed to be illustrating what a Talented Tenth should do and be—struggling to open doors for those other than themselves.[11]

As its most distinguished alumnus, Du Bois was keenly interested in the destiny of Fisk University. Though it was in the eastern region of the conservative state that was Tennessee, and though Nashville was known for its cosmopolitanism, as evidenced by the presence of Vanderbilt University, Fisk did not seem to benefit from this purportedly favorable location.

In 1912 Du Bois observed that the General Education Board, which aided Fisk, had made unusually harsh conditions for the receipt of a grant—but he thought that in its parlous condition, the school had no choice but to comply.[12] Du Bois cared deeply for his school since, he once said, "it was to me a place of sorrow, of infinite regret; a place where the dreams of great souls lay dusty and forgotten."[13]

But caring for Fisk and the wider cause of creating a Talented Tenth by means of higher education did not cause Du Bois to evade the flaws he espied. As student protests were heating up in October 1924, Du Bois tossed down the gauntlet charging that the university had failed in providing true education to African Americans—in the sense of failing to respect them, to seek to give them the best, to develop their self-knowledge and self-pride: no, charged Du Bois, Fisk had insulted them and, instead, curried favor with the racists who honeycombed Nashville and imposed a brutal Jim Crow that the school was bound to observe.[14]

A major source of information for Du Bois concerning events at his alma mater was James Ford. Born in Alabama in 1896, he too was an alumnus but had veered in a radical direction, founding the left-leaning American Negro Labor Congress in 1925 and joining the Communist Party in 1926, on whose platform he ran for Vice President of the United States in 1932, 1936, and 1940. He had left Birmingham in 1913 to enter Fisk, graduating with the class of 1918. He volunteered for service in the U.S. Army in the waning days of his senior year, and saw eight months service in France with the Signal Corps, an experience sufficient to radicalize even the least conscious. "I remember too," said Ford subsequently, "those more vital days of hell in France."

"Now that the exposure of conditions at Fisk has started we must not relent," Ford instructed Du Bois in early 1925. Waxing nostalgic, he recalled his years in Nashville and "the abrogation of the fundamental principles of education and the attempt at suppression of manhood and courage by [the college administration]." For Ford recalled bitterly a time when he had returned from the bloody battlefields of France to address Fisk students: "I sensed that the students were eager for experience and something of the practical contacts of war." Ford graciously complied and "told them something of these contacts; of hope for better conditions thru out the world; and most of all, of the contribution of black men from all parts of the world to this war. This said, I took my seat and to my surprise," said the still startled Ford, "I was followed by the President [of Fisk] who delayed chapel long enough to make, in a sarcastic manner, the statement that there was nothing to feel 'chesty' about; that we had contributed no more than anybody else." The next day Ford was asked to speak to a classroom of students and, again, he complied. "Again I found," said the dumbfounded alumnus, "the President's private secretary was in the rear of the room taking down everything I said." Ford—and he was far from being alone—was even more incensed in that this occurred at a "Negro University with a white president who had, previously, so willingly espoused the cause of democracy and urged Negro students to go to war."[15]

Consequently, the dramatic 1925 student strike at Fisk should have been a shock only to those not paying attention. For Du Bois, it seemed to be vindication of the faith he had placed in the Talented Tenth, the idea that this group could be the vanguard to lead black America to the promised land. The heart of the students' grievance was their charge that tyrannical racism was the accepted norm on campus. A delightedly heartened Du Bois announced dramatically, "Men and women of Black America: Let no decent Negro send his child to Fisk until Fayette McKenzie [the President] goes."[16] As things turned out, some of the students had to go, ousted as a result of their militancy. But the sparks from Nashville, ultimately helped in setting ablaze campuses far and wide.

Thus, Howard University, long regarded as the Capstone of Negro Education, was founded in Washington, D.C., in 1867, and quickly distinguished itself from the model provided by both Hampton and Tuskegee, which meant that it attracted the apt attention of Du Bois. Ralph Bunche, who like Du Bois was trained at Harvard (and eventually won a Nobel Peace Prize and served at the highest level at the United Nations), taught there, along with a number of others who fit the Du Bois mold, as did historian Rayford Logan: he too taught at Howard, collaborated with Du Bois on the Pan-African Congress movement (acting as the chief translator into French) and conducted pioneering research on United States–Haiti relations. When Fisk students in 1925 faced ouster due to their protests there, it was Du Bois who intervened on their behalf, requesting that Howard admit them.[17] Being in Washington, D.C., Howard's location meant that students were forced to endure the Jim Crow that was endemic there; such a hostile environment helped create a militant student culture that in some ways exceeded that obtaining at Fisk. Unsurprisingly, it was at Howard that one of the initial demands of Negro students—that mirrored subsequent demands in the 1960s for more black faculty—was met when the board capitulated and consented to name an African American, Mordecai Johnson, as president.[18]

It was early in 1929 that Du Bois chose to make a tour of campuses and—like a latter-day Johnny Appleseed—sprinkled seeds of dissent all along the way. The choices were in the heart of the Deep South: Virginia Normal in Petersburg; Palmer Institute in Sedalia, Shaw in Raleigh, State Normal at Fayetteville, and Johnson C. Smith in Charlotte, all in North Carolina; Allen (and Avery High School) in South Carolina; and Bethune-Cookman and Edward Waters College in Florida. The very act of launching this tour involved a leap of faith since an African American man attired in a suit and tie traveling through this benighted region then aroused suspicion automatically, and in some areas if Du Bois had been searched and the purportedly seditious *Crisis* had been found on his person, he might have become the guest of dishonor at his very own old-fashioned necktie party. Thus, friends arranged his transportation with great care and tact, as if he were being smuggled along an updated Underground Railroad. He often moved about surreptitiously, furtively stealing a glance over his shoulder as he ducked into an automobile or the odd train car. The latter was to be avoided, not least since they were segregated rigidly, and the "Negro cars" were often grimy and disgustingly unclean. In Georgia he spoke at the Haines Institute in Augusta. As for his once and future hometown, Atlanta, he was palpably unimpressed, finding it "taller and fiercer and richer" than ever—but with "no culture, no humanity, American in the crassest sense." After an absence of a quarter century, he entered the lion's den, visiting Tuskegee, and was disheartened with the regimentation he witnessed. He was pleased with the presence there of the National Veterans Hospital ("a miracle"), which employed a number of Negro professionals, but would have been outraged if he had lived to hear of the so-called Tuskegee Syphilis Experiment that was to be launched there soon after his departure, in which some of these very same professionals collaborated in a horrific experiment that left poor Negro men with a sexually transmitted disease untreated—though they were told otherwise—thus jeopardizing their lives and that of their families. If nothing else, knowledge of this episode would have shaken Du Bois's confidence in the beneficence of his beloved Talented Tenth.

What Du Bois did see at Tuskegee, on the other hand, was sufficiently noteworthy that later he observed that most of graduates of this university had not become artisans and farmers—contrary to Booker T. Washington's prognostications—but teachers, professionals, and small businessmen.[19]

His journey to Fisk was a kind of homecoming. He found it markedly improved from the time of his tenure there; the freedom of students was greater, not least due to the sacrifice of strikers a few years earlier and new buildings were desperately needed. Interestingly, only Fisk and Talladega in Alabama dared to select the more daring lecture topics Du Bois had offered (e.g., "The Russian Revolution"). Befitting the more vibrant atmosphere in Nashville—compared to, say, Tuskegee—students from adjacent white universities attended his lecture, as did some visitors from overseas.[20]

It was at Howard that Du Bois delivered one of his more important addresses on education, which anticipated his tenure-ending rift with the NAACP. It was June 1930, and the proud young graduates had gathered on a warm day on the hilltop where this lovely campus was sited. Du Bois did not disappoint those seeking intellectual nourishment for it was there that he argued that neither the industrial education ideas of Booker T. Washington nor his own more enlightened notions had succeeded in addressing the dire needs of Negroes. He therefore called for an agonizing reappraisal of what education for African Americans entailed, a reappraisal that would be driven by the specific needs of this community, rather than what the "American" state required.[21]

Nevertheless, Du Bois needs to be credited for doing well what he chose to do. Months before his daughter's ill-fated wedding, once again he convened what had come to be one of his crowning accomplishments: this version of the Pan-African Congress was better attended that the previous ones, as 5,000 attendees and 208 paid delegates descended on New York City, hailing from 22 states in the United States and the District of Columbia, not to mention the Caribbean, South America, much of West Africa, Germany, and India. Uplifting Africans and African Americans was central per usual but highlighted was "real national independence" for Egypt, China, and India, and the termination of Washington's interference in the internal affairs of the Americas—the occupation of Haiti that had begun in 1915 had plodded on murderously. Strikingly, Moscow was "thanked" for its "liberal attitude toward the colored races and for the help which it has extended to them from time to time."[22]

Though the NAACP Board was not as far to the left as Du Bois, his positions were not wholly incongruent with theirs—yet, it would be hard to see how this organization could lead African Americans into the mainstream, as long as it harbored radical views akin to those spouted routinely by its most prominent personality, Du Bois. Though differing views on Negro self-reliance were the ostensible reason for the messy divorce between the NAACP and its founder, the fact is there were fundamental differences that created the yawning chasm between Du Bois and the board that had controlled the organization, and a similar gap between Du Bois and the donors who had helped to generate some of the litigation successes that were beginning to accrue.

Actually, this idea of the differences between Du Bois and his organization were not as simple as suggested at first blush. In 1930, Du Bois placed side by side the programs of the NAACP and the American

Negro Labor Congress, "a Communistic organization." The parallels were obvious even to the dimmest of his readers in the *Crisis*: though the latter group stressed the needs of workers, his own group, he said irritably and tellingly, was the "potential leader of a class of small capitalists."[23]

Nevertheless, while the mainstream thought that Moscow was—to put it mildly—on the wrong side of history, in 1928 Du Bois took to the pages of a radical journal to proclaim that the Soviet Union was a "victim of a determined propaganda of lies," as he hailed what "it is trying to do."[24] Then in May 1933, the *Baltimore Afro-American* blared a headline that must have caused some of the NAACP's more affluent donors to wince, if not blanch: "U.S. Will Come to Communism, Du Bois Tells Conference." It was true that this was during the midst of a devastating economic depression with confidence in the future of capitalism diminishing rapidly, and it was equally true that in this maddening maelstrom, black Americans were suffering disproportionately— yet, some within the NAACP wondered how politic (or accurate) was their eminent founder's prediction. Still, these words were delivered by Du Bois at a gathering sponsored by the Rosenwald Fund, founded by an affluent Jewish American with a decided interest in Negro uplift, and there were no reports of shoes or chairs being hurled at Du Bois after he spoke for what he said was being said by many others. This is why the *Afro-American*, not known to be a Leninist newspaper, devoted 12 entire columns to Du Bois's speech, reprinting his remarks in full.

Du Bois insisted at this confab that production for private profit was wrong and disastrous and that African Americans in particular should undertake various forms of cooperative and collective efforts, thus helping to prepare the way for and preparing themselves to be an essential part of the coming revolutionary transformation.[25] Even the *New York Times* found this important meeting to be sufficiently newsworthy to devote 75 words to it.[26]

Du Bois was not above introducing these unconventional views to the readers of the NAACP's prime journal. Du Bois toasted Moscow on the 10th anniversary of the Bolshevik Revolution—and denounced the royal family that had been displaced in the process, a clan which he found notably despicable. Despite the denunciations, he exclaimed, "the Union of Soviet Socialist Republics is celebrating today its Tenth Anniversary and here's hoping that this is but the first decade towards its hundred years," one of many Du Bois wishes that wound up unfulfilled.[27]

Yet Du Bois's push towards radicalism was influenced not only by the imminent signs of the economic collapse of capitalism. What was occurring simultaneously was a wrenching political evolution by black America itself and when such a rare event occurs, it opens up all manner of alternative possibilities that were barely visible previously. In 1928, Republican Herbert Hoover challenged Democrat Al Smith for the right to occupy the White House. Hoover, a Stanford-trained engineer, if history was the guide, would receive the bulk of votes from those African Americans who could vote (which excluded the vast majority who were trapped in the former slave South). Yet Hoover seemed strangely indifferent to the distress inflicted upon black America, demonstrated most dramatically along the Gulf Coast in 1927 when the levees broke. In addition, he seemed embarrassed by the presence of Negroes in his party and did not seem overly concerned when a movement arose to purge them—a movement that claimed as an initial victim, Benjamin Davis, Sr., of Atlanta, whose son of the same name was a Harvard student who eventually became a comrade of Du Bois's in the Communist Party.[28] Governor Smith of New York, on the other hand, was a standard-bearer for a party that saw no problem with segregating African American delegates quite rudely at their quadrennial convention, and, perhaps worse, welcomed the Ku Klux Klan into its ranks.

Thus, weeks before the 1928 election, Du Bois argued that those black Americans who could vote should look towards a party other than the major two. Once that possibility was opened, it was only a short step to looking toward the Communist Party or their patron in Moscow.[29] The election, concluding with Hoover's victory after a noticeable bump in anti-Catholic sentiment generated by the prominence of Smith, repulsed Du Bois. This campaign, he said disgustedly, was "the most humiliating" ever experienced by African Americans, which was quite a statement given the opprobrium they routinely endured. Black people, he said, were flagrantly and intentionally ignored by both parties. The situation, again, demanded a search for options. Moreover, as events in the 1920s were beginning to shape the decades to come, Du Bois anticipated what occurred in 1941 when Washington itself found it opportune to ally with Moscow in order to confront Berlin and its allies. It was in 1928 that Du Bois noticed what was evident: he found it curious that the U.S. press, despite having been so critical of V. I. Lenin, was so favorable to the epigone of fascism, Benito Mussolini. Du Bois would have preferred the U.S. view of 1941, which reversed this tendency.[30]

Thus, when the bottom fell out and Wall Street collapsed, auguring even more woe, Du Bois saw it as "above all, a shaking of the faith of Americans in American industrial organization and in all private capitalistic enterprise"; exposed for all to ponder was "the fundamental weakness of our system."[31]

Too much can be made of this trend in Du Bois's thinking, however, for it does not explain how he could simultaneously be favorable toward the Soviet Union and critical of its domestic surrogate, the Communist Party. In 1931, for example, the case of the Scottsboro 9 erupted in Alabama; it involved nine Negro youth charged falsely with sexual molestation of two white women, with the death penalty looming for the defendants before the Communist Party-USA and their allies intervened, galvanizing a global crusade in their behalf. The NAACP too had sought to intervene in this case but were outmaneuvered by the Communist Party; yet, it was evident, that Du Bois's sentiments rested with his employer.[32]

Still, this apparent defense of his parent organization could not obscure the widening differences that separated the two. Finally, in May 1934, writing from Atlanta, Du Bois did the inevitable: he resigned. This was after his journal had opened its pages to criticisms of the NAACP's adamant opposition to segregation, something to which the board took strong exception. Du Bois was equally adamant, saying the journal "never was and never was intended to be an organ of the Association in the sense of simply reflecting its official opinion"—and this was the direction in which the Board was now pointing.[33] Differences over the rationale for segregation—or self-help, more precisely—was thought to be at issue also, but it was not the "main reason" for his resignation, said Du Bois. He recalled the World War I era when at first the NAACP protested the "colored camp" for soldiers in Des Moines, but upon losing this battle, the NAACP sought to make this facility as efficient as possible. There was no contradiction, said Du Bois, between struggling for desegregation of schools and seeking to make those schools (despite continued segregation) work smoothly. Du Bois had wanted to broach these matters in the journal but was forbidden, and now he let loose with full shotgun blasts, asserting that the NAACP "finds itself in a time of crisis and change, without a program, without effective organization."[34]

Du Bois's resignation left black America thunderstruck. It was like an otherwise responsible parent abandoning his child. Yet the reputably bristly Du Bois was known to be rather protective of a journal he had founded, and he revolted at any indication of invasion of his jurisdiction. Besides, he was ascending the scale of age and had reason to believe—given the average or median lifespan of Negro men—that he was already living on borrowed time and, perhaps, deserved more change in his life. Moreover, donors and board members were becoming increasingly exasperated with some of the stances of their illustrious founder, for example, his favoritism toward the Soviet Union. Still, Du Bois's divorce from the NAACP was as shocking and disconcerting to him as the divorce that split asunder the marriage of his daughter to Countee Cullen.

NOTES

1. Tillman Jones to the NAACP, April 26, 1927, in *Correspondence, Volume I*, 349–350.

2. W.E.B. Du Bois to James J. Jones, September 2, 1927, in Aptheker, *Correspondence, Volume I*, 359–360.

3. W.E.B. Du Bois, "Africa," *World Tomorrow*, 11 (October 1928): 420–421.

4. Scot Guenter, "Countee Cullen," in Gerald Horne and Mary Young, eds., *W.E.B. Du Bois: An Encyclopedia*, Westport, CT: Greenwood, 2001, 45–46.

5. Laura de Luca, "Yolande Du Bois," in Horne and Young, *Encyclopedia*, 63.

6. David Levering Lewis, *W.E.B. Du Bois: The Fight for Equality and the American Century, 1919–1963*, New York: Holt, 2000, 220–228.

7. *Crisis*, 35 (June 1928).

8. Courtney Young, "Dyer Anti-Lynching Bill," in Horne and Young, *Encyclopedia*, 67.

9. Malaika Horne, "Talented Tenth," in Gerald Horne and Mary Young, eds., *W.E.B. Du Bois: An Encyclopedia*, Westport, Connecticut: Greenwood, 2001, 203–204.

10. *Crisis*, 1 (Number 3, January 1911).

11. Jonathan Silverman, "Hampton Institute," in Horne and Young, *Encyclopedia*, 95–96. See also W.E.B. Du Bois, "The Hampton Strike," *The Nation*, 135 (November 2, 1927): 471–472. See also W.E.B. Du Bois, "Negroes in College," *The Nation*, 122 (March 3, 1926): 228–230.

12. *Crisis*, 3 (Number 6, April 1912).

13. *Crisis*, 28 (Number 5, September 1924).

14. *Crisis*, 28 (Number 6, October 1924).

15. James W. Ford to W.E.B. Du Bois, February 20, 1925, in Aptheker, *Correspondence, Volume I*, 306–307.

16. *Crisis*, 34 (Number 6, April 1925).

17. Amy Bowles, "Howard University," in Horne and Young, *Encyclopedia*, 104–105.

18. *Crisis*, 32 (Number 4, August 1926).

19. *Crisis*, 38 (Number 6, June 1931).

20. *Crisis*, 36 (Number 2, February 1929).

21. William M. King, "Journal of Negro Education," in Horne and Young, *Encyclopedia*, 117–118.

22. *Crisis*, 34 (Number 8, October 1927).

23. *Crisis*, 37 (Number 4, April 1930).

24. *Labor Defender*, November 1928.

25. *Baltimore Afro-American*, May 20, 1933.

26. *New York Times*, May 14, 1933.

27. *Crisis*, 34 (Number 10, December 1927).

28. See Gerald Horne, *Black Liberation/Red Scare: Ben Davis and the Communist Party*, Newark: University of Delaware Press, 1994.

29. *Crisis*, 35 (Number 10, October 1928).

30. *Crisis*, 35 (Number 12, December 1928).

31. *Crisis*, 37 (Number 1, January 1930).

32. *Crisis*, 38 (Number 9, September 1931).

33. W.E.B. Du Bois to Board of Directors, May 21, 1934, in Aptheker, *Correspondence, Volume I*, 478–479.

34. W.E.B. Du Bois to Board of Directors, June 26, 1934, in Aptheker, *Correspondence, Volume I*, 479–481.

Chapter 9

WARS

New York City was no prize for the Negro. As late as the onset of the Civil War, it was the metropolis that financed slavery and slave trade expeditions, and this profiting from the misery of Africans trickled down to influence day-to-day attitudes of the populace as a whole. It was no accident that African Americans were sited mostly in segregated neighborhoods, such as Harlem (where Du Bois chose to reside), and were subjected to systemic harassment by often trigger-happy police officers. Yet, with all of its problems, Gotham may have seemed like paradise to Du Bois, compared to the Atlanta to which he was returning. Though it prided itself on being the "city too busy to hate," this would have come as a rude surprise to those African Americans forced to endure the hateful Jim Crow that occupied every nodule of the city.

Yet, the job to which he was returning—professor at Atlanta University—was a symbolic aspect of the rift that had driven him from the NAACP. Du Bois was of the opinion that, yes, the University of Georgia should be desegregated, but in the meantime African Americans should not slacken in building a university that could train the Talented Tenth so necessary for liberation. In any case, the life of the mind was not alien to Du Bois, and beyond training the next generation, he had books percolating in his brain that were yearning to break free, and his job in Atlanta would provide the time and occasion for these to emerge.

Still, Du Bois was not just a thinker, he was also a man of action, and he held firmly to the belief that it was "painfully easy" for one living in a thickly populated city like New York to "mistake it for the nation," and he sought to avoid this error by regularly journeying at length throughout the continental-sized nation in which he resided. Thus, 1934 was not only a time of transition for him, it was also a time for exploration as he visited and lectured in a good deal of the South and the West. As ever, he shared his impressions with a wider audience, a service which allowed others to share his experiences. Interestingly, it was in Chicago that he debated with African Americans who were advocates of a separate 49th state for this community; just as interestingly, he opposed this scheme, while insisting that where segregation existed in fact one had the duty not only to fight it but also to improve whatever institution that was so segregated.[1] Allied with this idea was Du Bois arriving steadily at the conclusion that what was called racial "integration" actually meant an effort to make Negroes a subordinate part of a nation based on exploitation and class division, and he counseled in response more collective remedies for African Americans.[2] Though he was often at odds with U.S. Communists, tellingly his viewpoint was reflecting theirs, insofar as he too often spoke of black Americans as a "Negro Nation within the Nation."[3]

In line with U.S. Communists, Du Bois saw Karl Marx, the stern critic of capitalism and advocate of socialism, as a "colossal genius of infinite sacrifice and monumental industry and with a mind of extraordinary logical keenness and grasp." Yet, he added forlornly, "it seems to me [that] the Marxian philosophy is a true diagnosis of the situation in Europe in the middle of the 19th Century," and not necessarily applicable to the United States where a pike of racism divided the working class racially.[4] It was evident that at this juncture, Du Bois harbored a profound pessimism about the ability of Euro-Americans to overcome the obscenity that was racism, which inexorably pushed him toward a firmer advocacy of the notion of black solidarity.

For it should be understood that what has been interpreted as Du Bois's endorsement of segregation was actually a creative response to this dilemma sensed by African Americans, that is, the sense that they were bereft of allies, and, thus, there was hardly an alternative to trying to make the most out of a bad situation, that is, improving these segregated institutions. But even as Du Bois was formulating this notion, forces were at play that would cause him to downplay ideas that had caused him to depart from the NAACP. For the Great Depression had led to a rebirth of unions—the primary transmission belt bringing the dispossessed of all colors together, thus serving to undermine the racist segregation that Du Bois (in an ironic replay of Booker T. Washington) felt he had to accommodate himself to. Thus it was in the Bronx, New York, in the late summer of 1935 at the National Negro Baptist Convention attended by a massive crowd of 3,000 that Du Bois argued that the salutary impact of the New Deal of President Franklin D. Roosevelt lay in the emphasis it gave to the duty of government to provide for the needs of all its citizens.[5] The myrmidons of the former slave South had defeated the antilynching bill—and other progressive legislation—by asserting that the federal government's role should be limited, and it was the obligation of the states to take the initiative, which they inexorably chose not to do: this served as the foundation of conservatism and racism. But with the rise of the Great Depression the government began to feel that it needed to intervene in the economy and elsewhere forcefully. These policies at once served to erode segregation, the foundation of conservatism, and the need for Du Bois to make the best out of a bad situation.

Consequently, as the Depression marched on savagely, Du Bois continued to refine his thinking on fundamental matters, observing at one juncture that the so-called race problem was at root a socioeconomic problem and identical "with the labor problems of the world and with the whole question of the education, political power and economic position of the mass of men," who in some cases happened to be "colored."[6] The dilemma for Du Bois was that this kind of thinking seemed to lead him inevitably into the embrace of the Communist Party, which had been buoyed by economic devastation. Yet his dearth of faith in the feasibility of class-based coalitions across racial lines made him skeptical at best about the long-term prospects of this organization. Thus, despite the rise of unions—which seemed to erode his skepticism—he remained staunch in his advocacy of organizations and institutions rooted among African Americans, perhaps because he saw a benefit in providing them with skills that had eluded them in a segregated society. "We must have power," Du Bois insisted in 1933. "We must learn the secret of economic organization." And building cooperatives of various sorts was his preferred solution, since it would allow black Americans to circumvent the bonds of segregation and "stretch hands of strength and sinew and understanding to India and China and all of Asia," not to mention Africa and the Americas. Only with global freedom, Du Bois contended, could "we become in truth, free."[7]

In academia Du Bois was the epitome of the scholar as activist, the man of ideas as the man of action. As chairman of the Department of Sociology at Atlanta University, Du Bois approached his old friend university president John Hope with the idea of publishing a social science journal that would not shrink from publishing articles of literary merit and that would engage the types of issues he was debating in Chicago and elsewhere. Hope's untimely death meant that he was replaced by Rufus Clement, who was not enthusiastic about Du Bois's demarche. Thus, Du Bois queried the leader of his alma mater, Charles Johnson of Fisk, and he was more enthusiastic about initiating a quarterly journal that would rival Carter G. Woodson's *Journal of Negro History* and Charles Thompson's *Journal of Negro Education*. With a mere thousand dollars and the promise that more would be solicited, *Phylon: A Quarterly Review of Race and Culture* was launched. Johnson ultimately pulled back and the initial edition emerged in 1940 under Du Bois's leadership. Unlike the *Crisis*, this journal had more of a scholarly patina and was published less frequently. It was a throwback, a continuation of the Atlanta University Studies he presided over from 1897 to about 1914. In his opening words in the opening issue, Du Bois announced that *Phylon* (from the Greek, meaning "race") would "proceed from the point of view and the experience of black folk where we live and work in the wider world." In other words, the journal, under Du Bois's leadership, would specialize in publishing original scholarship on a broad array of matters relevant to the culture and life of peoples of African descent, especially African Americans. Yet, ultimately, the *Crisis* and *Phylon* shared commonalities as much as differences, for it was his stinging critiques of the Atlanta University administration—not unlike his opening the NAACP journal to criticism of its leadership—that led to his ouster from the school in 1944 at the age of 76 and his return to the NAACP, an organization that had been transformed by the antifascist war then in motion.[8]

But his return to the embrace of the organization he had helped to found was far from his mind in the 1930s, occupied as he was with the economic cataclysm that had descended. This was a complicated moment for Du Bois to return to the reflective groves of academe for if ever there was a moment that the frontlines of struggle needed a man of Du Bois's caliber, it was the 1930s when fascism was on the march, and financial distress and uncertainty were stalking the land. For African Americans like Du Bois, the fascist danger hit home most dramatically when Mussolini's Italy invaded Ethiopia in 1935. Now this East African nation had long been a bright lodestar for black Americans, given its independence—rare for a continent generally in thrall to colonialism—and its ability to beat back the previous attempt at European domination, besting the Italians in the late 19th century. Though tragically underdeveloped, Ethiopia also provided an outlet for some black American professionals, as some could flock to Addis Ababa to toil as pilots and doctors at a time when opportunities in the United States were distortedly circumscribed.

Du Bois knew better than most that the relationship between black America and Ethiopia was bilateral. It was during the time of the Italian occupation of this East African nation that he wrote affectingly about Malaku Bayen, who had been the personal physician of Ethiopia's deposed leader, Haile Selassie. Like so many from Africa and the diaspora, Bayen had been trained as a doctor at Howard University, and, like so many other students from abroad that had matriculated at such institutions, he too had married an African American, then went on to serve as a strong link in a sturdy chain of Pan-Africanism.[9]

As such, it should come as no great surprise that Du Bois—and African Americans as a whole—were extremely hostile to Mussolini's invasion.[10] This widespread sentiment was manifested most directly at New York's Madison Square Garden in the early autumn of 1935. A positive aspect of this gathering and the entire movement against Rome's brigandage was how it helped to bridge the chasm that in the previous decade had pitted African Americans against those of African descent from the Caribbean: Ethiopia provided a common platform on which all could unite. Thus, 10,000 chanting protesters—overwhelmingly with African roots from varying points on the globe—applauded and cheered the stirring words of a range of speakers, including Du Bois's fellow Fisk alumnus, communist leader James Ford; Walter White of the NAACP; and representatives of Garvey's movement and from the Brotherhood of Sleeping Car Porters. In this context Du Bois was asked why public opinion was so alarmed by this invasion, when Europeans overrunning Africa seemed to be a normative event. Du Bois's response revealed that just as the New Deal had eroded the necessity to make the best out of segregation—which had driven him from the ranks of the NAACP—the complicated global situation was having a similar effect. For he asserted that "the World War has taught most of Europe and America that the continuing conquest, exploitation and oppression of colored peoples by white[s] is unreasonable and impossible and if persisted will overthrow civilization." Colonialism, which was complemented by segregation, was finding it difficult to survive in these altered conditions.[11]

That the locus for the central problem confronting the world was headquartered in Berlin, provided Du Bois with a special challenge since he had long been a close student of Germany and had spent some of his most fruitful days there. It was in 1936 that he applied for a grant from the Oberlaender Trust—part of the Carl Schurz Memorial—to study developments in education in Germany. He won this grant and sailed for Germany in June. On this lengthy journey Du Bois also visited England, Austria, the Soviet Union, China, and Japan. He returned to his professorial perch in Atlanta in early 1937. It was an enlightening adventure, as he found time in London to dine with the famed novelist and futurist H. G. Wells and the celebrated anthropologist Bronislaw Malinowski; his other ports of call were just as intriguing.[12]

One reason that Du Bois spent so much time abroad was precisely because he felt that generally black Americans were treated better abroad than at home; however, there were signs of increasing racism in England, as he recounted saddening stories of what had befallen Paul Robeson, his fellow African American and noted actor and activist, who had decamped to London some years earlier in order to escape bigotry at home. Yet, Du Bois acknowledged, what befell black Americans overseas was small potatoes compared to what they encountered at home.[13]

As he wandered the streets of Berlin, Du Bois found himself appalled by what he saw. Adolf Hitler had come to power a few years earlier, and it was unclear to some—particularly governments in the North Atlantic—what devastation would be wrought by his rule. Du Bois, on the other hand, was not fooled: he reported that Hitler's party, the Nazis, had constructed a tyrannical state of breathtaking proportion replete with storm troopers, devious spies, brutal police, and a bloodthirsty military. He saw in Hitler's petit bourgeois German Austrian background the basis for his personal appeal, and suggested that this leader's ordinary experiences as an artisan (Hitler thought of himself as a painter of note), war veteran, and worker who—supposedly—had to confront the economic interests of those who were Jewish made him a leader with whom many Germans identified, which was then translated into votes.[14]

Du Bois's harrowing experience in Germany helped to solidify his appreciation for the travails of Jewish Americans, who had played such a pivotal role in the founding of the NAACP and the struggle for equality generally. This tie eventually led him to be in the vanguard of those who endorsed the idea of a Jewish state, which came to fruition in 1947–1948. Thus, when he sought to justify his ideological conflict with the NAACP, he resorted to pointing to the formation of the United Hebrew Trades of the late 19th century, which was seen widely at the time as a form of so-called self-segregation but whose aim was to break down the anti-Semitism that prevailed in the trade union movement as a whole.[15]

Du Bois was received in Germany with proper courtesy, which obviously contrasted sharply with how those who were Jewish were then being treated. This was a reflection of larger phenomena: as their brutal colonial past in the nation now known as Namibia suggested all too accurately, Berlin was not necessarily gentle to those who appeared to hail from Africa. The point was, however, that those like Du Bois were not central to Nazi racism at home in Germany in the same way that those who were Jewish tended to be. Thus, the tremendous African American athlete, Jesse Owens, had a similar experience during the Berlin Olympics of 1936. In fact, Owens confessed that while in Germany, his hosts "bent [over] backward in making things comfortable," which included inviting him to "the smartest hotels and restaurants."

This was a reflection of another reality with which Du Bois was all too familiar, the operation of which served preponderantly in eroding Jim Crow: that is, those nations with seemingly insoluble problems with Washington, saw an advantage in not maltreating those thought to have their own grievances with the United States (i.e., African Americans).[16] In any case (and bizarrely enough), if by some stroke of fate—or catastrophe—Berlin had been able to defeat Washington in war, waiting in the wings to rule this nation on Germany's behalf was a man who was born as an African American, Lawrence Dennis.[17]

Despite being treated relatively well, Du Bois had good reason to be concerned with the scenes he witnessed in Europe. Like others, he was overwhelmed by the tragedy that was befalling Spain, a reality that was difficult to ignore on the continent, as refugees from there were pouring into various capitals. The duly-elected republican government in Madrid was under siege by fascist elements backed avidly by Berlin and Rome in a precursor of what was to overcome the entire continent rather shortly. The Spanish Civil War attracted Langston Hughes, Ernest Hemingway, and hundreds of volunteers from the United States who went to fight, arms in hand, under the rubric of the Abraham Lincoln Brigade. "There is no working class in the world," Du Bois advised correctly, "that is not intimately and definitely interested in the outcome of this battle."[18]

His presence in Berlin provided Du Bois with an inkling of what would occur to others—those in Spain not least—if Hitler's minions were to prevail. It was true that Du Bois was treated courteously (which was more that could be said about what he experienced in the states of the Old Confederacy), but while he was in Berlin, his mail was opened, and he was subjected to other forms of espionage. Yet, despite the obvious tragedy that was ensnaring the Jewish population, Du Bois had reason to believe that many Germans were supportive of Hitler. "And yet," he added, "in direct and contradictory paradox to all this, Germany is silent, nervous, suppressed." He could not help but notice that "there is a campaign of race prejudice carried on, openly, continuously, and determinedly against all non-Nordic races but specifically against the Jews, which surpasses in vindictive cruelty and public insult anything I have ever seen and I have seen much," said this man who then resided in Jim Crow Georgia.[19] Particularly disturbing to Du Bois was the perception that what had propelled the Nazis forward—bigotry and hatred of Moscow—was achingly present in his own nation.[20]

Perhaps because he thought that the logic of Germany's xenophobia—extermination—could conceivably be followed in his own nation, Du Bois did not stint in limning the disastrous consequences of what came to be known as the Holocaust or Shoah, and, in that regard, was one of the more far-sighted, visionary, and perspicacious of U.S. nationals who were witnessing this catastrophe. "There has been no tragedy in modern times," he cried, "equal in its awful effects to the fight on the Jew in Germany. It is an attack on civilization, comparable only to such horrors as the Spanish Inquisition and the African Slave Trade." Du Bois, fluent in German, was outraged by the bile and vitriol spewed by certain newspapers; such attacks echoed with his own experience. One journal he observed was "the most shameless, lying advocate of race hate in the world," and "it could not sell a copy without Hitler's consent," meaning that this racism was sanctioned officially and was no accident.[21] As early as 1933, not long after Hitler's ascension, when the full import of his rise had not been recognized by many, Du Bois was launching thunderbolts across the Atlantic in the direction of Berlin. "Race prejudice," charged Du Bois, "is an ugly, dirty thing. It feeds on envy and hate," of which Germany then had a surplus. "One has only to think of a hundred names like Mendelssohn, Heine and Einstein, to remember but partially what the Jew has done for German civilization."[22]

This rigid opposition to anti-Semitism was not wholly selfless since Du Bois knew that this poison was of a piece with anti-Negro racism, with which it enjoyed a symbiotic relationship. "The Nazis made a mistake in beginning their propaganda in New York," he said in late 1933, since "they should have started in Richmond or New Orleans. Their whole philosophy of race hate [has] been so evolved in our own South," he added sardonically, "that Hitler himself could learn a beautiful technique by visiting us."[23]

Nevertheless, as riveting as his journey to Europe might have been, it was his first journey to China that enchanted him; it was "inconceivable," he said wondrously. "Never before has [a] land so affected me," not even Africa: he found the vastness, the hundreds of millions of people, its venerable civilization, all remarkable.[24] In Shanghai he was struck by the pervasive influence of European colonialists, who had carved out their own sectors where they ruled supreme in the heart of this populous city, amidst a terrible differentiation in terms of the how the rich and poor lived (with the colonialists disproportionately among the former, while the poverty among the latter was overwhelming). Aghast and disgusted, Du Bois's pungent remarks captured why revolution was erupting in this Asian giant even as his eyes were overpowered by what he saw. He observed that "three things attract white Europe to China: cheap women; cheap child-labor; cheap men."[25] His journey to China acquainted him with a land that he visited again more than two decades later after the Communists came to power (which they did in 1949) precisely because of the misery that moved him so.

Yet, perhaps more than Germany or China, it was his first trip to Japan that may have been the most controversial—and most enlightening—part of his long journey. In the period before World War II, there was little doubt that Japan was the nation most admired by black Americans, not least since its very existence exploded the convenient fiction that only those of European descent could construct an advanced society: if Japanese could do so, why not Africans, was the weighty question that was posed. In return, like any other nation that endured tensions and conflict with Washington—Moscow comes to mind—Tokyo painstakingly cultivated African Americans, a task that was reciprocated.[26] Hence, Du Bois found Manchuria—Chinese territory seized and colonized by Japan—to be exceptional as a form of colonialism purportedly devoid of racism, a conclusion reached by few other observers who denounced Tokyo's aggression. Du Bois was moved by the hospitality shown him in Japan, which he saw as a diplomatic gesture from one colored people to another and "for this reason," he added gratefully, "my visit is not to be forgotten."[27]

Traveling to Nagasaki, Yokohama, Kobe, Kyoto, and Tokyo, his admiration for Japan seemed to increase with each mile traversed, as he was treated like a visiting dignitary. At a well-attended press conference in Tokyo he speculated that it was white racism in the United States in the form of anti-Japanese immigration sentiment that helped politicians in the U.S. West and South strike a deal to squash anti-lynching legislation that he championed. He also had the opportunity to meet the young author who was translating *The Souls of Black*

Folk into Japanese. Upon departing this nation that was about the geographical size of California (though today it has a population of 110 million), he informed his African American audience back home, "it is above all a country of colored people run by colored people for colored people . . . Without exception, Japanese with whom I talked classed themselves with the Chinese, Indians and Negroes as folk standing against the white world."[28]

His fondness for Japan extended to the point where it seemed that he wanted China to renounce its anticolonial struggle against Tokyo. During his time in Shanghai, he recalled "sitting with a group of Chinese leaders at lunch." Rather "tentatively," he told them that he could "well understand the Chinese attitude toward Japan, its bitterness and determined opposition to the substitution of Asiatic for an European imperialism." Yet what he "could not quite understand was the seemingly placid attitude of the Chinese toward Britain." Indeed, he thought "the fundamental source" of Sino-Japanese enmity resided in China's "'submission to white aggression and Japanese resistance to it.'" The Chinese, he concluded acerbically, were "Asian Uncle Toms of the same spirit that animates the 'white folks' nigger' in the United States." With a dismissive wave of the hand, Du Bois dismissed concerns about violations of Chinese sovereignty by Japan. "In 1841," he argued, "the English seized Hong Kong, China with far less right than the Japanese had in seizing [Manchuria]."[29]

It is difficult to comprehend Du Bois's apparent dearth of solicitude for the travails of the Chinese languishing under the heavy hand of Japanese colonialism without an acknowledgment of his suspicion of those in the corridors of power in Washington and London who railed against Tokyo while remaining deathly silent about European misdeeds. These elites, he charged, were creating "quite a dither" about China but that was only because they wanted to feast exclusively on this Asian carcass.[30] Moreover, Du Bois was alarmed when a movement seemed to be forming around the dangerous ideas of Charles Lindbergh, the famed pilot who in 1927 had defined celebrity when he flew an airplane unaided across the Atlantic. Lucky Lindy, as he was called, was among a "number of voices," Du Bois warned, who were calling for the so-called white nations to stop fighting each other and to join hands in war against the colored peoples of the world.[31]

Nevertheless, it would be mistaken to see Du Bois's fondness for Tokyo as wholly and purely blind. He was impressed with its modernization but was not as enthusiastic about the capitalism that had produced this result. By this juncture, Tokyo feared London, and this was driving her toward expansionism as a way to counter the latter's strength in Hong Kong, Singapore, and other critical nodes. But "worst of all," lamented Du Bois, "this alliance of Japan with fascism sets her down as an enemy of Russia," whose assistance to anticolonial fighters in Africa he admired most of all.[32]

Du Bois worried endlessly about the fate of the Soviet Union. Ultimately, Moscow was to be driven into an alliance with London and Washington in order to confront Berlin, Tokyo, and Rome: this anti-fascist alliance both saved the planet from the Nazi scourge and carried the seeds of the cold war that was to follow quickly after the conclusion of World War II. Since visiting Moscow a decade earlier, Du Bois had developed a deeper analysis of this self-proclaimed socialist state. He viewed Josef Stalin as a "tyrant," but coupled this denunciation with the idea that he "expected" the Soviet Union to "stagger on in blood and tears toward their magnificent goal with many a stumble and re-treat." Thus, he announced even before the antifascist alliance made such statements less controversial, "I still believe in Russia."[33] Articu-lating views that have become no less controversial decades hence, Du Bois asserted, "I believe that the Russian Revolution in its essence and depth of real meaning was greater than the French Revolution, with more vivid promise of healing the ills of mankind than any movement of our day; and [I] believe this despite the murder of [Leon] Trotsky and dozens of great Russians who dared to disagree with Stalin."[34]

Yet the complexity of this global conflict that was unfolding before his very eyes as he traipsed from Europe to Asia confounded Du Bois. As he put it, "if Hitler wins," this means "down with the blacks!" But "if the democracies win," well, "the blacks are already down."[35]

Du Bois returned to the United States traveling eastward via Ha-waii and arriving after President Roosevelt's smashing victory over the Republicans in the 1936 election, which extended his New Deal's lease on life. Roosevelt's victory also meant a continuing revival of an upsurge of growth in unions, particularly in the industrial heartland where a number of African Americans resided (in cities like Detroit,

Gary, Cleveland, Chicago, and St. Louis); the growth in unions had the effect of increasing their incomes, just as their political clout was growing likewise, as black America jumped ship from the GOP and cast their fate with FDR. This brought them face to face with the Dixiecrats who theretofore had dominated this party and hastened the day when their influence would be eroded. For Du Bois this was part of a gradual process that served to give him reason to believe that, perhaps, the white working class was not hopelessly deluded, and, therefore, the reason for his departure from the NAACP—the felt desire to strengthen rather than dismantle automatically all-Negro entities—began to lose its original rationale.

Thus, it was a transformed Du Bois that returned to the classroom in Atlanta. He was approaching the age of 70, a time when lesser mortals would have chosen retirement but for Du Bois, in many ways, his best years were ahead of him. For it was after he had departed the NAACP and while he was ensconced in Georgia that he published, perhaps, his most significant historical work. *Black Reconstruction in America: An Essay Toward a History of the Part which Black Folk Played in the Attempt to Reconstruct Democracy in America, 1860–1880*, befitting its lengthy title, was his magnum opus, his landmark on a major topic. This profoundly thoughtful book forced readers of that era—and this one too—to rethink fundamentally what they had thought about one of the more contentious eras in U.S. history, the period following the Civil War. Theretofore, as represented in the shockingly popular Hollywood blockbuster *The Birth of a Nation*, this fecund era was seen as a disaster, an orgy of Negro misrule visited upon their beset former masters. Through diligent research and a visceral rejection of the racist stereotypes that too often characterized the writing of U.S. history, Du Bois emblazoned a new trail of scholarship that continues to reverberate, and, in some ways, his efforts have revolutionized the historical profession itself. Though acknowledging the earlier contributions of Carter G. Woodson, John R. Lynch, Frederic Bancroft, and a raft of other historians, Du Bois undoubtedly made a great leap forward in the historiography.

This book also stands as a document of another time when many major libraries and archives in the South particularly were closed to African Americans, and, as an unfortunate result, there were numerous documents that Du Bois was unable to examine: sadly, this lacunae hindered his ability to construct a timeless narrative.

On the other hand, *Black Reconstruction* stands as an outline, leaving plenty of room for other scholars to fill in the blanks, which has happened in succeeding generations, thereby vindicating his original insights. The emphasis in this book, as in much of his work, is on the agency or active engagement of ordinary people, mostly African Americans, in the face of racist violence (much of it spearheaded by the Ku Klux Klan), fraud, and the like. The monumental final chapter, "The Propaganda of History," continues to be a classic denunciation of the rampant chauvinism that to that point had been hegemonic, and, to a degree, has not dissipated altogether.

Despite the strain and time consumption of teaching, Du Bois also found time to publish while in Atlanta yet another classic, *Black Folk Then and Now: An Essay in the History and Sociology of the Negro Race*, which was—in a sense—an update of what he had written in his justly praised book, *The Negro*, which had been published over two decades earlier. The later book contains 16 chapters and an extensive bibliography with the first nine offering a history of Africa and its early civilizations, the coming of modern slavery and the slave trade, and the movement for the abolition of both. Two chapters treat those of African origin in the United States and Europe contemporaneously, while four chapters treat Africa, particularly landownership, the plight of subalterns, and systems of political control and of education. Here again he repeats his archetypal phrase that the problem of the century is the "problem of the color line."

Finally, it was in Atlanta that Du Bois completed his insightful, *Dusk of Dawn: Essay Toward an Autobiography of a Race Concept*. While *Souls* and *Darkwater* "were written in tears and blood," Du Bois wrote that while *Dusk of Dawn* was "set down no less determinedly," it was written with "wider hope and some more benign fluid," hence the title, which he saw as optimistic. Until the publication of his more official autobiography, published posthumously, this book was the most basic source for biographical data about him. Also displayed here—and quite typically—was a luscious and affecting writing style of a type that is all too rare nowadays. Herein is likewise revealed his positive attitude towards Moscow and his skeptical attitude toward domestic Communists.

This attitude received a stern and stiff challenge once Nazi Germany attacked the Soviet Union in 1941, quickly followed by Japan's bombing of Pearl Harbor, Hawaii. "Again the tragedy of the Negro American soldier festers," he lamented, "as it did in the Revolution, the Civil War, the Spanish War and the first World War. The sore will never heal," he moaned, "so long as we fight for a Freedom and Democracy which we dare not practice."[36]

What Du Bois came to see was that the dynamic unleashed by the antifascist war served to erode the encrusted bigotry of Jim Crow that had ruined the life chances of so many African Americans and the colonialism that had handcuffed Africa. That is, it became difficult for Western Europe to argue that it did not merit domination by Germany, while continuing to dominate Africa. African and African American soldiers shed blood in buckets (as they had throughout World War I) providing them with a further rationale to demand justice. Washington's alliance with Moscow served to undermine biases that associated the left—of which Du Bois was a constituent member—with a demonized Soviet Union, which led to an undermining of numerous Jim Crow barriers that he had railed against for decades.

It was in this radically altered atmosphere that a reconciliation took place between Du Bois and the organization he had helped to found, the NAACP. Their leader, Walter White, recognized more than most how the changing global environment could radically determine the fortunes of African Americans and with this idea firmly in mind, he invited Du Bois to return to Manhattan in 1944 as a kind of "Minister of Foreign Affairs" not just for the NAACP but black America as a whole.

NOTES

1. *Afro-American*, May 5, 1934.

2. *New York Herald-Tribune*, November 18, 1934.

3. W.E.B. Du Bois, "A Negro Nation within the Nation," *Current History*, 42 (June 1935): 265–270; see also *New York Times*, May 21, 1935. See also W.E.B. Du Bois, "Does the Negro Need Separate Schools?" *Journal of Negro Education*, 4 (July 1935): 328–335.

4. *Crisis*, 40 (Number 5, May 1933).

5. *New York Times*, September 7, 1935.

6. *Pittsburgh Courier*, November 14, 1936.

7. W.E.B. Du Bois, "The Right to Work," *Crisis*, 40 (Number 4, April 1933): 93–94.

8. Catherine M. Lewis, "Phylon" in Horne and Young, eds., *Encyclopedia*, 165–166.

9. *New York Amsterdam News*, June 1, 1940.

10. W.E.B. Du Bois, "Inter-Racial Implications of the Ethiopian Crisis: A Negro View," *Foreign Affairs*, 14 (October 1935): 82–92.

11. *New York Amsterdam News*, September 28, 1935.

12. *Pittsburgh Courier*, September 26, 1936.

13. *Pittsburgh Courier*, September 5, 1936.

14. Robert Fikes, Jr., "Adolf Hitler," in Horne and Young, *Encyclopedia*, 100–102.

15. *New York Amsterdam News*, November 25, 1939.

16. Gerald Horne, *Race War! White Supremacy and the Japanese Attack on the British Empire*, New York: New York University Press, 2004.

17. Gerald Horne, *The Color of Fascism: Lawrence Dennis, Racial Passing and the Rise of Right-Wing Extremism in the U.S.*, New York: New York University Press, 2007.

18. *Pittsburgh Courier*, October 24, 1936.

19. *Pittsburgh Courier*, December 5, 1936.

20. *Pittsburgh Courier*, December 12, 1936.

21. *Pittsburgh Courier*, December 19, 1936.

22. *Crisis*, 40 (Number 5, May 1933).

23. *Crisis*, 40 (Number 12, December 1933).

24. *Pittsburgh Courier*, February 20, 1937.

25. *Pittsburgh Courier*, March 6, 1937.

26. Gerald Horne, *Race War!*

27. *Pittsburgh Courier*, March 20, 1937.

28. Robert Fikes, Jr., "Japan," in Horne and Young, eds., *Encyclopedia*, 111–113.

29. Gerald Horne, *Race War!*, 110–111.

30. *New York Amsterdam News*, December 23, 1939.

31. *New York Amsterdam News*, February 3, 1940.

32. *Pittsburgh Courier*, 27 March 1937.

33. *New York Amsterdam News*, 24 February 1940.

34. *New York Amsterdam News*, 4 October 1941.

35. *New York Amsterdam News*, 31 May 1941.

36. *New York Amsterdam News*, 13 September 1941.

Chapter 10

TURNING POINT

Du Bois had departed from the NAACP in 1934 because of a dispute with the group's leadership. This led to his return to Atlanta University from whence he had departed a quarter century earlier to play a leading role in Manhattan in the NAACP. But like a human yo-yo, he departed Atlanta University in 1944 to return to Gotham—again, to play a leading role in the organization he had helped to found, the NAACP.[1]

Why would Du Bois return to an organization with whose leadership he had feuded quite famously? The short answer is that there were both push and pull factors. By 1944 Du Bois was 76 years old and given actuarial projections for African American men was thought to be soon headed to the nearest mortuary; moreover, he had come into sharp conflict with the administration of Atlanta University—a contretemps that was in some ways fiercer than his previous dustup with the NAACP leadership—and returning to New York City seemed suddenly to be more attractive than enduring the routine indignities of Jim Crow that Atlanta offered.

But why would the NAACP leadership see fit to ask him to return, since their top leader—Walter White—was still in office and continued to be decidedly immune to Du Bois's charms? White was responding to a global climate in the midst of a war against fascism and militarism that was profoundly different from the environment that obtained in 1934 when he and Du Bois had last feuded. For after Nazi Germany invaded Soviet Russia in June 1941, followed swiftly by militarist Japan bombing Pearl Harbor, Hawaii, in December of that same tumultuous year, the United States felt compelled to ally with its former antagonist in Moscow, a decision that substantively altered the situation inside the United States. For now that Washington was allied with a nation that many had seen theretofore as the embodiment of an "evil empire," there was a felt desire to reduce the intensity of anticommunism, which was now seen as an impediment to prosecuting successfully a war for survival. Thus, Hollywood—partially at the behest of President Franklin D. Roosevelt—began shifting from its previous portrayal of the Soviet Union as an "evil empire" to more benign portraits.[2] Inexorably, this climate influenced how Du Bois—a man with socialist convictions who was not unfriendly to Moscow—was perceived. This changing climate heightened the need for the NAACP to have on staff someone with expert knowledge about the state of the world. More pointedly, in seeking someone to fill a post that amounted to black America's "Minister of Foreign Affairs," White and the NAACP were hard-pressed to find someone more qualified than Du Bois, a man who did not require intensive study to get up to speed on the intricacies of the international situation and the politics of Russia, China, Europe, and the African and Caribbean nations whose independence was deemed a high priority emerging from the war.

Such circumstances led to the NAACP offering and Du Bois accepting a job with the organization that he had helped to build. The association itself was in a growth spurt, affording it the increased dues payments—and the concomitant increased budget and ambitions — that would allow it to turn its sights more intently on a world at war in which (once more) African American soldiers were being forced to shed blood and treasure. In 1940 the NAACP had about 40,000 members, by the time Du Bois came on board, membership had grown tenfold. Part of this phenomenal expansion was driven by the tireless labor of two women on the NAACP's staff—Ella Baker and Shirley Graham—the latter of which Du Bois was to come to know quite well.

Explicating this growth also sheds light on how and why Du Bois would be invited to return to the NAACP: again, those with whom the United States was now in a battle to the death—principally Nazi Germany with their insidious nostrums of racial superiority—seemed all too similar to those who stood as the major proponents of Jim Crow. The idea was growing that unless the NAACP took a more active role in combating bigotry abroad, it would be disadvantageous to the anti-racist struggle at home. Moreover, in recent decades, Japan had made pointed overtures to black America, playing adroitly upon their bruised racial feelings and assuring one and all that if Tokyo prevailed, African Americans could be assured that the hated Jim Crow would simultaneously suffer a death blow.[3] In short, racism was very much at issue during this war, and the U.S. authorities had little choice but to retreat from the more egregious aspects of white supremacy. It was in such an environment that for the first time since the end of Reconstruction—a period of which Du Bois had written so eloquently—minority voting rights were expanded during the war. An indication of the growth of the left that accompanied this retreat of ossified racism—which made Du Bois's return to Manhattan possible—was the election in 1943 of a black Communist to the New York City Council. Ben Davis, Jr., yet another son of Atlanta who had moved north to secure a niche, succeeded his good friend Adam Clayton Powell, Jr., when this Harlem minister was elected to Congress.[4] In sum, the period from 1941 to 1945, an era suffused with massive bloodletting and untold agony, also marked a sharp break from the recent past, creating an opening for the left, for African Americans, and, not least, for Du Bois.

Du Bois's journey northward was no simple matter; in fact, it was a major logistical exercise to move the 883 miles that separated Atlanta from Manhattan. For over the years he had accumulated thousands of volumes that needed to be moved and a number of file cabinets bulging with files and letters that stretched back to his teenage years. Naturally, his personal library was especially strong when it came to the most neglected of continents, Africa; but he also was a fan of the Welsh writer Dylan Thomas and the British novelist Agatha Christie. He had to cart away numerous musical albums—his favorite was Beethoven's Ninth Symphony, though he was also a devotee of Vivaldi and Tchaikovsky. Naturally, he had a deep appreciation of the old Negro spirituals, as even a casual glance at his classic *The Souls of Black Folk* would reveal. He was a subscriber to numerous publications, particularly those concerning colonized Africa, though he also kept a close eye on publications from the Caribbean (a region he visited repeatedly over the years, particularly his homeland of Haiti and its neighbors, Jamaica and Cuba). Naturally, he read carefully the numerous newspapers that covered black America, notably the *Pittsburgh Courier,* where his good friend P. L. Prattis served as editor. He subscribed to the *New York Times* and the Communist *Daily Worker,* indicative of his open-mindedness and ecumenical approach. Yet somehow, he was able to move this intellectual fortress that accompanied him from south-to-north and quickly settled into what he saw correctly as a major task: helping to shape black America's position on a major issue of the war, that is, how to bring freedom to a world that remained largely colonized. In brief, Du Bois had to convince the major powers why it was wrong and irrational to assert that it was unjustifiable for them to be ruled from Berlin and Tokyo but it was justifiable for Africa, the Caribbean, and a good deal of Asia to languish under a colonial system administered principally from London and Paris.

Being a man of action and a man of thought, Du Bois chose to pursue this exalted goal on two major fronts. Shortly after his arrival at the NAACP, he published a thoughtful book that provided an intellectual and political framework for his newly minted activism. *Color and Democracy: Colonies and Peace* was a tour de force, at once an indictment of the white supremacy that had buoyed Berlin and had provided Tokyo with a basis for appeal.[5] Suggestive of the importance of this topic to him was the fact that he placed the title of this book as an emblem on his stationery. This small planet, Du Bois contended, was simply unsustainable as long as the multitudes of Africa and Asia were doomed to be colonial appendages of the major powers. In some ways, this book-length essay was an extension of his famed essay on the African roots of war that sought to explain the explosion that was World War I as flowing from jousting and contestation by the major powers—in this case, Germany—for their various places in the colonial sun, their share of colonial booty. Yet suggestive of the changed atmosphere brought by the antifascist war was the fact that the U.S. Navy alone brought a hefty 2,400 copies of this militant anticolonial tract for distribution within its ranks, as this now controversial book was viewed widely as reflecting common sense rather than the grinding of a political axe.

Rarely one to allow intellectual endeavors—no matter how laudable—to become the alpha and omega of his labor, upon arriving at the NAACP Du Bois immediately began to organize the Fifth Pan-African Congress, to be held in Manchester, England. This European metropolis was an appropriate site for serious planning for an anticolonial world. Its looms had once been fueled by cotton from the former slave South of the United States, which in turn had been picked by legions of enslaved Africans. Now in August 1945 just as the war was arriving at an exclamation point with the atomic bombings of Hiroshima and Nagasaki, the elderly Du Bois—the Father of Pan-Africanism—arrived in Britain, a nation that had been devastated by this bloody conflict and contained numerous subjects who were now yearning for a path that diverged sharply from the empire that had brought so much misery to so many.

Because of his towering intellectual accomplishments, it is sometimes forgotten that Du Bois was an organizer of no small talent. Surely, his approach to this Manchester gathering dispelled any doubts that may have existed. Though his fracases with the leadership at Atlanta University and the NAACP may have led the unsuspecting to conclude that he was hopelessly cantankerous, his skill and efficiency in building consensus for what amounted to a global conference belied this easy notion. In plotting his course, he brought on board the actor-activist Paul Robeson; Amy Jacques Garvey (spouse of the late Jamaican born leader); and Max Yergan, the North Carolinian born activist, who had lived in South Africa and served alongside Robeson as leader of the Council on African Affairs. Also essential to this effort was George Padmore; born as Malcolm Nurse in Trinidad, he had attended Howard University before decamping to London, where he became a principal contact point for African and Caribbean anticolonial leaders as the date for the congress approached. Du Bois also wasted no time in briefing the NAACP leadership, though already he had detected that they were not as enthusiastic about this gathering as he was.

Contradicting the commonly accepted idea that with age comes a slowdown in energy, Du Bois took it upon himself to organize an anticolonial conference in Harlem to complement the Manchester meeting.

It was at the Schomburg Library at 135th Street in the midst of a neighborhood whose very congestion and deterioration spoke loudly as to why the racism that underpinned colonialism had to be defeated that scores of delegates from India, Burma, Africa, and elsewhere met to debate the nature of the postwar world. Kwame Nkrumah, the future leader of Ghana who was to invite Du Bois to reside in his homeland, was generally pleased with this gathering at which he played such a prominent role—though he insisted that it should have been more insistent in its call for anticolonial independence, for many at the meeting were reluctant to part with the increasingly antiquated idea that envisioned a continuing role for the major powers in colonized lands.

As impressive as this Harlem gathering was, it proved to be a mere dress rehearsal for the impressive opening of the Pan-African Congress in Manchester in August 1945, the culmination of a series of gatherings that had begun decades earlier. With the battering absorbed by fascism and militarism, it was recognized by one and all that a momentous turning point had been reached in the epic battle against racism and colonialism, and that Du Bois's pronouncement that the century's problem was the "color line" was more accurate than once supposed.

Present at the Manchester congress were nearly 200 delegates from 60 different nations. Du Bois was one of seven elected to chair sessions and was ultimately chosen as permanent chairman of the entire body, suggestive of the esteem in which he was held. The man with whom he was to be linked in coming years—Nkrumah—set the tone by stressing militant action: strikes, boycotts, and the like, a course of action that was realized in Africa most notably as the war concluded, which paved the way for the retreat of the colonial powers. This congress differed sharply from previous efforts in that it was dominated not as much by intellectuals like Du Bois but more by trade union advocates. It was at Manchester that Du Bois first met Jomo Kenyatta, who was to lead Kenya to independence in 1963.

Yet amidst the self-congratulation and celebration there were somber notes. There was reluctance at the highest levels of the NAACP to endorse this gathering, a fact that stunned Du Bois since it seemed to be consistent with the organization's mandate. As a result, when he returned from Manchester, he found obstruction when he sought to organize a follow-up meeting and publish pamphlets about anticolonial struggles in Africa. Even though the antifascist war was just ending, a new era was beginning—the cold war—and militant anticolonialism was rapidly being seen by some as no more than a front for the soon-to-be primary foe, Communists.

Undeterred, Du Bois pressed on; 1945 was also the year that the United Nations was organized, and, as Du Bois saw it, forging a group that purported to bring under one roof all of the nations of the planet, when a good deal of the world was colonized, was not only unsustainable but deeply flawed. Thus, Du Bois the organizer took it upon himself to organize an African American delegation to intervene in this process and contacted the National Council of Negro Women, the National Bar Association, and many other groups in this vein.

Du Bois and White arrived in San Francisco where the United Nations was being planned and raised the prickly matter of including in this body's charter specific provisions concerning human rights. To that end, Du Bois sought to make alliances with delegates from Moscow and New Delhi but he also did not neglect rallying his base, for it was during this jaunt to the West Coast that he spoke to clamorous and cheering throngs of supporters in Oakland, Los Angeles, and the city by the bay, San Francisco. Suitably impressed with his effort, the NAACP Board voted to send a copy of his favorably received *Color and Democracy* to every member of the U.S. delegation in San Francisco.

Returning home from this triumphal journey, Du Bois detoured to Washington, D.C., for an appearance before the Senate Foreign Relations Committee, where he provided measured praise for the UN Charter that emerged in California—though he expressed reservations about the body's approach to colonialism.

Yet despite—or perhaps because of—this stellar debut, the tension between Du Bois and White, which had seemed to dissipate due to the necessity of war, was now rearing its head again as this conflict receded in the rearview mirror. Du Bois saw White as a narrowly educated manager. White saw Du Bois as overbearing and arrogant. Ideologically, Du Bois was a Socialist on a path toward the Communist Party. White was a pragmatist, unafraid to join the gathering anticommunist crusade.

As so often happens, their initial disputes were about nothing so high-minded as ideology; their disputes were about matters mundane—office space. Du Bois complained that his 12' x 20' office housed three workers, 2,500 books, two desks, a typing table, a balky Dictaphone contraption, and six four-drawer file cabinets. He wondered if cattle in rail cars were entitled to more space. There were also questions about whether he was allowed to attend the board meetings of the NAACP (where policy was crafted). To not be invited to attend the meetings of the organization he had helped found was quite a setback.

For their part, White and his deputy, Roy Wilkins, thought Du Bois operated as if he were an independent agency, a reprise of his previous experience with the *Crisis*. They could not understand why Du Bois balked at having his mail opened centrally, along with that of other leaders of the NAACP. Actually, the NAACP—perhaps because of the tense atmosphere in which it had to operate, filled with Jim Crow, lynchings, and the like—was a seething cauldron of tension as leaders bickered endlessly, irrespective of ideological clashes. Thus, the group's leading lawyer—Thurgood Marshall—feuded with White, while the board itself was split by various conflicts. The NAACP structure, which featured considerable power invested in White's post and, according to critics, insufficient power accorded to the branches and annual convention, may have exacerbated these conflicts. On top of all these rifts was a fractious drive to organize the group's staff into a union, a battle in which Du Bois stood with the workers, while his internal opponents did not: this too did not lead to an era of good feelings.

Similarly, the changing political climate in the United States did little to assuage internal tensions for—not coincidentally—external ructions intruded. For Du Bois's return to the NAACP not only coincided with the war, it also overlapped that conflict's end and the resultant cold war. As tensions rose between Washington and Moscow, almost in metronomic fashion, tensions correspondingly rose between the NAACP leadership symbolized by White and Du Bois. White and Wilkins did not take kindly to Du Bois's growing friendship with Paul Robeson, the actor and activist, who saw fit to launch a movement against lynching that was quite embarrassing to Washington as it sought to focus the world on human rights violations in Moscow.

At this time Robeson was probably closer to the Communist Party than Du Bois. In any case, when the leadership of this group was placed on trial in 1948, supposedly for teaching and advocating revolution,

Du Bois joined Robeson in rising to their defense—but the NAACP chose not to do so. During this same fateful year, a new political grouping came into being, the Progressive Party, which launched a stiff challenge that threatened the Democratic Party of President Harry Truman, who had become quite close to the NAACP leadership, White in particular.

This political cum ideological rift was a token of yet another rift: the NAACP was involved in more than litigation, but, as symbolized by the critical role played by Thurgood Marshall and other attorneys of note, the organization certainly tended to privilege litigation over mass mobilization. This was understandable at a time when repression reigned supreme in the South, where most African Americans continued to reside and was accelerating in the North and West as civil liberties began to fall victim to anticommunism. Yet Robeson, as symbolized by his crusade against lynching, and Du Bois, who joined him, thought that lawsuits could only take flight when buoyed by a mass movement—a lesson later exemplified by Dr. Martin Luther King, Jr., who too had his differences with the NAACP leadership. Du Bois took exception to what he saw as the overly centralized structure of the NAACP, which did not create favorable conditions for the ascension of grassroots activism.

This setup facilitated the rise of a Faustian bargain that was to define black America for decades to come: Truman spearheaded certain concessions on the civil rights front (e.g., the retreat from a racially segregated army in 1948), and in return the black leadership backed his anticommunism, including the prosecution of Communist Party leaders (e.g., the Harlem City Councilman Ben Davis, Jr.) and the decision to involve the nation in 1950 in the civil war in Korea.

When the NAACP began to purge its ranks of real and imagined Communists, it was inevitable that their attention would be diverted to the suspected Red on their staff, Du Bois.

A catalyst for this process occurred when Du Bois led in filing a petition at the United Nations charging the United States with human rights violations against African Americans. At a time when Washington was seeking to indict Moscow on similar charges, this petition was not accepted with equanimity in the Oval Office—or the inner sanctums of the NAACP. Actually, Du Bois had laid the foundation for this initiative in his book, *Color and Democracy*, which suggested that a wide audience existed for indictments of white supremacy. It was in August 1946 that Du Bois formally proposed to White that a petition be submitted. Strikingly, this effort was sanctioned, as the import of the rising cold war had yet to be comprehended altogether by the NAACP leadership.

With typically efficient haste, Du Bois moved swiftly to set this petition in motion, conferring with the UN leadership in Manhattan, enlisting the editorial aid of such luminaries as the future Nobel Laureate, Ralph Bunche; the scholar Rayford Logan; the attorney Earl Dickerson; and many others. Soon the international community was mulling over Du Bois's handiwork. Despite its lengthy title—*An Appeal to the World: A Statement on the Denial of Human Rights to Minorities in the Case of Citizens of Negro Descent in the United States of America and an Appeal to the United Nations for Redress*—this work was a tightly written 94-page indictment covering history, law, politics, economics, and related topics.

Like the Fifth Pan-African Congress and the San Francisco meeting that founded the United Nations itself, Du Bois again displayed his formidable organizing skills, as hundreds of organizations endorsed this petition, including the leading fraternity Kappa Alpha Psi and the National Medical Association. Remarkably, this indictment of the rulers of the United States was not only endorsed by mainstream organizations, signaling a growing disaffection at home with Washington's Jim Crow but similarly notable was the deafening response abroad, particularly in Africa and the Caribbean. Such an indictment gave momentum to their own anticolonial efforts and raised severe questions about whether millions would align with Washington—or Moscow—as cold war tensions waxed. Unavoidable was the fact that it was the Soviet Union that brought the petition before the United Nations. Candidly, Attorney General Tom Clark, who hailed from Jim Crow Texas, confessed that he was "humiliated" by the Du Bois–Moscow collaboration. Yet, his concrete response was to enlarge and strengthen the Civil Rights Division of the Justice Department, reinforcing the notion that this kind of collaboration was eminently useful.

Unsettled by this turn of events was the NAACP's own leadership, which included Eleanor Roosevelt, who was a member of the powerful Board of Directors, as well as the UN's Economic and Social Council. She was not pleased with this petition and rather quickly her attitude became the consensus within the NAACP leadership.

When this petition was then followed by Du Bois's support for the left-leaning Progressive Party challenge to Truman in 1948, the NAACP leadership came to believe that his left-wing initiatives were inconsistent with the organization's attempt to seek mainstream backing for civil rights concessions. The Progressive Party, which was led by former U.S. Vice President Henry Wallace, challenged Jim Crow in the South directly, which prodded the Democrats to act similarly, rather than run the risk of defection of droves of African American voters from their ranks. For the Progressive Party placed the largest number of black candidates ever selected to run for an office on a single ticket since the days of Reconstruction, as this group nominated proportionately more black candidates than did the other parties. The Progressive Party launched a form of guerilla warfare against Jim Crow, refusing to hold racially segregated rallies, defying the law in the process, thereby hastening apartheid's end and serving as a harbinger of the 1960s upsurge.

As the November 1948 election approached, it was evident that Du Bois was not operating in sync with the NAACP leadership. For though he never missed an opportunity to utter high praise for Wallace and the Progressive Party, his NAACP comrades acted similarly on behalf of Truman and the Democrats. The problem was that the latter party was in thrall to a Dixiecrat wing in the South that considered Jim Crow laws to be holy writ, and thus the Democrats were highly vulnerable to Du Bois's charge that they countenanced segregation.

As things turned out, the 1948 election witnessed the greatest turn out of black voters to that point. Sensing that the African American vote, which they had come to rely on, might be slipping away, the Democrats borrowed liberally from the Progressive platform, particularly as it concerned civil rights.

Yet the battling between these two parties was dwarfed in animosity and intensity by the internal wrangling that engulfed the NAACP in the dueling personalities of Du Bois and White. Ultimately, the 1948 election, a significant turning point in the struggle for equality, also was the prompting factor that led to yet another turning point in the torturous history of black America: the ouster of Du Bois from the organization he had re-joined only four years earlier.

Ignoring their constant drumbeat of support for Truman, the NAACP leadership accused Du Bois of violating the group's ban on partisan political activity by backing Wallace so avidly. So, he was fired. This personnel decision proved to be of monumental significance. It lubricated the path for black America's tightened alliance with the Democratic Party and the liquidation of nascent attempts to build a left-wing alternative to this party that had such a strong Dixiecrat wing. Ultimately, the Dixiecrats were to bolt from this party in the 1960s and join the ranks of the GOP, giving this party a stranglehold on the votes of the white South that was to endure for decades to come and providing the GOP with an automatic advantage in presidential elections. In the short term, when black America's leading organization—the NAACP—embraced the Democrats so wholeheartedly, they also felt compelled to swallow their foreign policy agenda, favoring the waging of hot wars in Korea and Vietnam and a cold war globally, which not only demonized anticolonial movements as "Communist" but also drained the federal budget that could have addressed pressing needs in housing, health, and education. As Du Bois was sacked, the NAACP launched simultaneously an internal witch-hunt for real and suspected Communists that weakened the organization and settled the dispute over whether the organization would favor litigation or mass mobilization in favor of the former. This slowed down the struggle for equality and dissipated the energies unleashed by the 1948 election—a struggle that did not regain momentum until the arrival on the national stage of Dr. Martin Luther King, Jr., who too found himself in conflict with the NAACP and who too was accused of being all too close to the dreaded Communists. Nevertheless, despite the weighty significance of the foregoing, perhaps the most profound aspect of the sacking of Du Bois was the fact that a triggering factor—beyond the 1948 election—was the petition to the United Nations: taking black America off the global agenda was certainly a victory for Washington though it was not as certain that it was a victory for the constituency that the NAACP was sworn to protect.

Sensing the deeper meaning of the routing of Du Bois, a committee of his supporters was formed in an attempt to reverse this decision—though to no avail. It included such dignitaries as Robeson, and glittering intellectuals like E. Franklin Frazier, Alain Locke, and Horace Mann Bond (whose son, Julian, was to serve as NAACP Chairman in the late 20th and early 21st century). This committee was to take this dispute to the pages of the press—particularly the African American press—and to the broader left; the latter sensed correctly that the purging of Du Bois was a loud signal foretelling a wider ouster from influence of all those who refused to toe the anticommunist line. They recognized that if a man of Du Bois's importance could be barred from an organization he had helped to found simply because of a political dispute, then the entire nation was headed in a conservative direction that would make life quite uncomfortable for those unwilling to go along.

A bruised Du Bois, now an octogenarian, was forced to move his many books and file cabinets once more, this time to the office of the Council on African Affairs (CAA), another Manhattan-based organization. Founded in 1937 as a vehicle through which U.S. citizens could intervene more directly in the thorny matter of colonialism in Africa, it was seen in the public mind as the lengthened shadow of one of its founders, Robeson. This was not altogether accurate and Du Bois's arrival on the scene as vice chairman, indicated that the NAACP's loss was CAA's gain. The CAA was not a mass membership organization but more of a lobby that concentrated on producing newsletters and educational materials. The intellectual firepower that graced this group's leadership was formidable: the Los Angeles–based journalist and publisher Charlotta Bass; the famed music producer John Hammond, who like another CAA leader, Frederick Field, was the scion of a major fortune; the leading academics Ralph Bunche and Mordecai Johnson; and the jurist Hubert Delany rounded out this lineup. The key staff person was W. Alphaeus Hunton, who held a doctorate in English literature.

Yet it seemed that Du Bois had departed the frying pan only to land in the fire for it was not long before the CAA was torn by a left-right split not unlike that which had occasioned his hasty and unceremonious departure from the NAACP. In this case, the role of Walter White was played by Max Yergan. Yergan had toiled for years in South Africa on behalf of the YMCA. Like White, he too had a dalliance with the left but, if anything, his associations were deeper and more far-reaching, as he was suspected widely of being a Communist.

But like the NAACP, some within the CAA—notably Yergan—quickly sensed that the U.S. alliance with the Soviet Union, compelled by the exigencies of global war, would become inoperative once this titanic conflict ended. Also like the NAACP, the Yergan-induced split of the CAA, which caused a number of its leaders to depart for greener pastures, severely weakened the attempt to build anticolonial solidarity within the United States. For his part Yergan executed a dizzying transition from left to right, quickly becoming a favorite anticommunist witness before Congress and an avid supporter of apartheid in South Africa, while leaving a terribly weakened CAA in his wake.

As for Du Bois, he faced a real dilemma: with every political dispute in which he became ensnared, it became painfully more evident that the political course that had governed his life and career to that point—left of center with a tilt toward socialism—had become incongruent, inconsistent, and incompatible with the dominant course now being followed by the place of his birth. His options were few: he could tack to the prevailing winds and live a more comfortable life at the expense of his deeply held principles, or he could continue to sail fearlessly into the teeth of the bitter gales that now buffeted him. For a man who never had accumulated considerable income and was now elderly, this was no small matter—yet he opted for the latter course.

He chose a global stage on which to make an implicit announcement of this decision. The Cultural and Scientific Conference for World Peace was convened at the posh Waldorf-Astoria Hotel in late March 1949. Du Bois, the adroit organizer, helped to plan this meeting that brought progressive and left-leaning forces from around the world to midtown Manhattan to raise grave alarms about the growing tensions between Moscow and Washington that had frightening nuclear overtones. In the face of scurrilous attacks from the U.S. press, 2,800 people gathered with thousands turned away because of a lack of space. Appearing alongside Du Bois was a sparkling array of leading artists and intellectuals, including the physicist Albert Einstein; the actor Marlon Brando; the playwright Arthur Miller; the musician Leonard Bernstein; the writer Lillian Hellman; the architect Frank Lloyd Wright. Messages of solidarity were received from the actor Charles Chaplin; the poet Pablo Neruda; the novelist Alan Paton; and artists Diego Rivera and David Siquieros.

The zenith of this gathering occurred when 20,000 people congregated in Madison Square Garden in Manhattan to hear Du Bois speak about the ominous clouds of war that had descended. Du Bois had long sought to yoke the ostensibly domestic matter of civil rights for African Americans to a larger Pan-African and global agenda of liberation of Africa. His ouster from the NAACP and the split in the CAA that greeted his arrival had hampered materially this ambitious agenda. Now with the deterioration in relations between Moscow and Washington that spelled the possibility of a nuclear war that could mean the extinction of humankind, he shifted ground to stress the necessity for détente between and among the great powers, as this liberalization would at once disarm the conservative hawks who were the major impediment to world peace, anticolonialism, and equality. From standing on a civil rights platform and reaching out to the world, he was now standing on a world platform and reaching back to his homeland.

This came clear when he cochaired the World Congress for Peace, which convened in Paris weeks after he spoke to cheering throngs in Manhattan. Present were over 2,000 delegates from 70 nations representing 700 million people. Yet what overshadowed press coverage of this historic gathering in the United States were controversial remarks made by Du Bois's good friend and frequent collaborator, Paul Robeson, who cast doubt on whether African Americans would fight on behalf of the United States in a war with the Soviet Union. When Du Bois actually traveled to Moscow to reiterate the calls for peace and disarmament that had become an essential component of his rhetorical armament, angry accusations erupted in his homeland suggesting that he had become a traitor—or worse.

Yet the travails that Du Bois had to endure during 1949 and early 1950 point paled into insignificance when war erupted on the Korean peninsula in June 1950 in a conflict that ostensibly pitted Communists against their foes—the latter of which were backed avidly by Washington. Increasingly, anticommunists were wondering why the United States should travel thousands of miles to fight Communists abroad, when suspected Communists like Du Bois continually and repeatedly challenged Washington's foreign policy. The result was predictable and inevitable: Du Bois was indicted, put on trial, and slated for a lengthy prison term, which, at his advanced age, would be the equivalent of a death sentence.

NOTES

1. Substantiation for the following pages can be found in Gerald Horne, *Black and Red: W.E.B. Du Bois and the Afro-American Response to the Cold War, 1944–1963*, Albany: State University of New York Press, 1986.

2. See, for example, Gerald Horne, *The Final Victim of the Blacklist: John Howard Lawson, Dean of the Hollywood Ten*, Berkeley: University of California Press, 2005.

3. Gerald Horne, *Race War! White Supremacy and the Japanese Attack on the British Empire*, New York: New York University Press, 2003.

4. Gerald Horne, *Black Liberation/Red Scare: Ben Davis and the Communist Party*, Newark: University of Delaware Press, 1994.

5. W.E.B. Du Bois, *Color and Democracy: Colonies and Peace*, New York: Harcourt, Brace, 1945.

Chapter 11

TRIALS

A familiar nostrum nowadays is that with age comes conservatism, a dismissal of past radicalism as so much youthful posturing. This did not hold true for W.E.B. Du Bois. During the cold war, the United States—a nation then approaching its second century of maturation—moved to the right and away from previous positions. Du Bois, almost half as old as the nation in which he lived, either moved to the left or adhered to his previous positions. This was bound to create friction, and it did, to the point where Du Bois faced the distinct possibility of spending his remaining days in a dank prison cell.

The immediate cause for many of his troubles was his crusading against nuclear weapons. The dropping of atomic bombs on Japan in August 1945, which instantly incinerated tens of thousands of civilians horrified many, including Du Bois, but unlike others he decided to try to do something about this menacing weaponry; hence his 1949 trip to Moscow, which was thought to be a likely target for nuclear detonation if obtaining trends persisted. His antinuclear stance sheds light on why he organized the World Congress of Partisans for World Peace and invited Pablo Picasso to the United States to confer about what steps to take to ban the bomb. Washington responded by denying this acclaimed artist and activist a visa.

His campaign against atomic weapons was further evidence—if any were needed—that Du Bois remained intellectually nimble, able to pivot and attack new menaces that arose. But Du Bois also was able to remain true and consistent, for as his move to the headquarters of the Council on African Affairs suggested, his devotion to the beleaguered continent continued unabated. One of his principal duties there was as an intellectual resource, a fount of information for those interested in news from Africa at a time when U.S. newspapers and diplomats often routinely paid little or no attention to the poorest continent. Thus, in his early days there he analyzed in depth the onset of apartheid in South Africa (which had been proclaimed formally only in 1948) and the vexing matter of Ethiopia and its troublesome province (Eritrea), and above all, he hammered home a point that was his trademark: as long as Africa was colonized, it contained the seeds of war as the major powers jousted to take advantage of its vast wealth.[1]

But the hallmark of Du Bois's last years was clear: as he continued to lean to the left—which had been the key characteristic of his entire career—the nation in which he resided shifted sharply to the right during this same period, and with that Du Bois found himself increasingly isolated. The cold war conflict with Moscow compelled Washington to adopt positions that were to hamper the nation for some years to come; thus, as the Soviet Union stressed the control by the state of the commanding heights (if not the entirety) of the economy, the United States felt compelled (in contrast to many of its European allies) to emphasize the primacy of private enterprise, even in spheres where a leading role for government seemed reasonable (e.g., health care). This was just one more indication of the political and emotional investment that had been made in the cold war; and, as a result, when Du Bois began to raise his insistent voice against a course of action that seemed normative and positive to most, the backlash against him became all the more fierce.

As ever, there was a silver lining in the cloud of vexation that had descended upon Du Bois as the second half of the 20th century began to unfold. As Washington began to point the finger of accusation at Moscow for human rights violations of various types, it was forced to respond forcefully to its own weaknesses in this realm—Jim Crow most of all. Remarkably, African Americans came to learn that they could escape the most egregious aspects of Jim Crow if they simply steered clear of the left wing that Du Bois had come to symbolize. But, as the saying went, Negroes gained the right to eat at restaurants and check into hotels but not the wherewithal to pay the bill, for as civil rights were in the process of being expanded, unions (which black Americans, a mostly working-class population, had come to rely upon) were being pulverized; simultaneously, the right to association generally—be it in unions or political parties or, in some cases, even civil rights organizations—was being constricted.

Du Bois was one of the few individuals who in oracle-like fashion was able to foresee this course of events, but as early as 1950, his was a voice that many were coming to ignore. As a man of thought and action, Du Bois not only articulated an alternative course of action but proceeded to embody and actualize it. In this he became a leading—and lonely—symbol of opposition to the cold war. The cold war was a project that would eventually cost his homeland trillions of dollars and countless lives; it also gave rise in Afghanistan to a form of religious fundamentalism that was to bedevil the United States indefinitely.

The utter seriousness of the cold war was to come clear in 1950 when war erupted forcefully and terribly on the north-south divide of the Korean peninsula. That same year saw the efflorescence of the Peace Information Center, which Du Bois had helped to bring into existence; its first meeting was held at his office, with Shirley Graham and Paul Robeson present. Their first activity was sponsoring the Stockholm Peace Petition, known colloquially as the "ban the bomb" initiative.

Perhaps signed by more individuals globally than any other petition before or since, this campaign also was able to garner significant support from African Americans, which was no easy matter at a time when signing one's name to such a document was known to bring—minimally—added scrutiny from the government. Charlie "Yardbird" Parker, the innovative saxophonist from Kansas City, and Pearl Primus, the talented dancer and anthropologist. were among those who affixed their signatures to this petition.

When war exploded in Korea in late June 1950, Du Bois sought to galvanize the antiwar sentiment evident among African Americans, which lurked beneath the surface as this community was being asked to give their lives purportedly for freedoms that they most certainly did not enjoy.

As Paul Robeson's comments in Paris suggested, raising disconcerting issues about whether black Americans would stand by the United States during a war was guaranteed to bring a forceful response. And so it was that on July 13, 1950, that Secretary of State Dean Acheson bitterly denounced Du Bois's Peace Information Center. Du Bois responded with a reciprocal asperity in the *New York Times* as the infant industry of network television besieged him for interviews—but the more typical response was that the Manhattan landlord of the Peace Information Center demanded that they vacate the premises. Undeterred, Du Bois called on Acheson to promise that the United States would "never be first to use [the] bomb"—a request greeted with stony silence in Foggy Bottom.[2] Shortly thereafter, the Department of Justice demanded that the Peace Information Center register as agents of a foreign power. Who this power might be was left unsaid but the impression was left that it was Moscow; in other words, to favor banning nuclear weapons meant you were either a Communist or a dupe of same.

So prompted, petitioners were subjected to a reign of terror and violence, battered from coast to coast for their activism. In the midst of this vortex of fury, the elderly Du Bois—at a time when most of his venerability had chosen a comfortable retirement—decided to run for the U.S. Senate seat from New York held by the powerful and affluent Herbert Lehman. Only the dire circumstances that the nation and world faced in 1950 could compel the aging Du Bois to cast the state of his health to the winds and take on the responsibility of a grueling election campaign. He received a formidable dose of the abuse heaped on candidates who veered beyond the realm of Democrats and Republicans when he campaigned ceaselessly for the Progressive Party in 1948. New York was one of the bastions of left-leaning thinking generally in the United States and, as a result, a local affiliate of the Progressive Party had arisen—the American Labor Party—which had sunk deep roots in New York City particularly. Though Du Bois knew that his chances of prevailing in this race were slim, at least a campaign platform provided an opportunity to raise certain issues concerning peace and civil rights that might otherwise be downplayed or ignored.[3]

This bold maneuver was made more complicated by Du Bois's abject refusal to endorse the reigning notion that the Soviet Union was
the "evil empire." In 1949 he made his third visit to this vast land (he
had been there in 1926 and 1936) and though he was critical of what he
saw, he left once more with a fundamental admiration, not least since
he saw this nation as one of the few that chose to assist Africans struggling against colonialism rather than providing tortured rationalizations
as to why African protests were supposedly premature or moving too
rapidly.[4] "The Dark World is moving towards its destiny much faster
than we in this country now realize," he said shortly after his return to
these shores.[5]

Such heretical ideas became the trademark of Du Bois's uphill climb
to the Senate. Early in October 1950 found him in old haunts in Harlem,
telling a cheering crowd of 1,500 that they should speedily enlist in his
antiwar army.[6] Withdrawal from Korea, banning nuclear weapons, liberating Africa, and barring Jim Crow were his call to arms. In the early days
of this battleground race, the *New York Times* echoed the sentiments of
many when it proclaimed that "Dr. Du Bois is expected to add strength
to the Labor Party ticket in Harlem and other Negro sections of the city
and state."[7]

At that juncture, this journal may have been selling Du Bois a bit
short, since he was expected to add strength to the ticket in college towns
like Ithaca and Hamilton and Syracuse too. In this period before the
ouster of dissident voices from the airwaves, Du Bois was regularly inter-
viewed on the radio declaiming about peace and civil rights. In turn,
Senator Lehman unleashed a barrage of commercial advertisements on
black-oriented radio stations in New York City especially, perhaps to
erode what was thought to be Du Bois's continuing base of support in this
community.

This election race was a hinge moment in black America, as it pitted
a traditional liberal—the incumbent, Senator Lehman—against a man
decidedly to his left: Du Bois. One course led away from the cold war
with Moscow and the hot war in Korea and toward peace, and the other
in an opposing direction. But many Negro leaders felt that they could
hardly move in the same direction as an increasingly marginalized left
wing, even if led by Du Bois; as they saw it, backing Lehman was a step
toward long promised civil rights concessions. Consequently, Mary

McLeod Bethune (the leading African American activist, who served alongside Du Bois at the founding of the United Nations) and Channing Tobias, who knew Du Bois well since he served on the NAACP board, were among the leading lights in black America who supported Senator Lehman avidly. Strikingly, those who turned against Du Bois often raised the question of his real and imagined ties to Communists and how this was thought to be "un-American."

Yet, perhaps, even more than these ties, there were unsettling and blasphemous notions that Du Bois had latched on to, that in its breadth and daring surpassed virtually everything his capacious intellect had devised to that point. The words he enunciated in November 1950—the month of his defeat for the Senate—seem radical more than a half century since they were pronounced: "Social control of production and distribution of wealth is coming as sure as the rolling stars. The whole concept of property is changing and must change. Not even a Harvard School of Business can make greed into a science, nor can the unscrupulous ambition of a Secretary of State use atomic energy forever for death instead of life."[8]

Unsurprisingly, given the political climate and the disparity in campaign funds raised by the various candidates, Du Bois went down to defeat in November 1950. On the other hand, he received 12.6 percent of the total vote in Harlem, not unrespectable given the obtaining hysteria about Communists that prevailed. Moreover, while the GOP spent $600,000 in this race and the Democrats spent $500,000, Du Bois's party spent a relatively meager $35,000. In other words, the major parties spent one dollar per vote, while the Labor Party spent considerably less.

Yet Du Bois's stirring race for higher office was not greeted unanimously with equanimity. The Peace Information Center, which he had helped to bring into being and which spearheaded the landmark crusade against nuclear weapons, was operative from April 3, 1950, until October 12, 1950, when, in response to economic and governmental pressures, it went out of existence. Moreover, it proved more than daunting for Du Bois to—simultaneously—run a Senate campaign and an antiwar office. Yet, perhaps stung by Du Bois's gumption in confronting the cold war consensus, his adversaries chose not to accept this challenge supinely. On February 9, 1951, he was indicted, along with his coworkers, as an unregistered foreign agent. This dramatic indictment, which threatened to insure that his last days would be spent in a prison cell, instigated an equally dramatic move on his part: his marriage, which had been drained of emotional content certainly since the death of his first born, ended when Nina Gomer Du Bois passed away, and shortly thereafter he married the celebrated intellectual Shirley Graham, not least so that she could have easy access to him because of spousal privilege if he became a prisoner. He was to be acquitted but the signal sent was clear, as one had to beat only one slave to keep the entire plantation in line.

In some ways, the woman who was to become Shirley Graham Du Bois brought many of the qualities to marriage with Du Bois that were wanting in his first betrothal. First of all, she was an intellectual, perhaps the leading black woman thinker of her era (or any era) and, also like her spouse, a highly motivated political activist.[9] Born in 1896, the daughter of a preacher, she had a peripatetic upbringing, spending time in Louisiana, Washington State, Colorado, and elsewhere. Like many daughters of this era, she was forced into a maternal role at an early age, helping to raise her siblings, and, it seemed, she sought to escape this drudgery by marrying early. This led quickly to two children and, perhaps, seeing her future fade away before her very eyes, she departed her marriage and her children (leaving them with her parents) and decamped to Paris for a lengthy sojourn, where she studied at the Sorbonne and perfected her French, one of the many languages she came to speak.

She returned to the United States by the 1930s and enrolled at Oberlin College, which had been in the vanguard of enrolling African American students for decades, and there developed real skill as a musician. Eventually, she enrolled at the Yale School of Drama and quickly developed a sterling reputation as a brilliant playwright. It was in the 1930s that she first struck up a surreptitious romance with Du Bois that had difficulty gaining traction given his preexisting marriage.

As World War II was dawning, she moved to Arizona to work with Negro troops, soon to be dispatched to fight for freedoms that they did not enjoy. Here she spoke up repeatedly against racist discrimination and justifiably gained an image as an effective and militant organizer, which led her to the NAACP, where during the 1940s she presided over

the largest spurt in membership this organization has ever enjoyed—
before or since. This move to New York City was serendipitous—but
not exactly accidental—in that she managed to find herself in the same
metropolis to which Du Bois himself had moved in 1944. There their
romance heated up once more and when Nina Gomer Du Bois passed
away, followed swiftly by Du Bois's indictment, he came to rely upon her
even more, as their relationship deepened.

It was in July 1950 that Du Bois's spouse of 55 years died after a prolonged illness. She was buried in his hometown of Great Barrington,
Massachusetts. He had feared that he might die before she did and, consequently, would have been bereft of proper care. He paid tribute to her
"singularly honest character" and recounted what might have been the
singularly tragic aspect of their marriage, which had shaped it for decades, the tragic death of their first born.[10]

But, as the saying goes, when a window closes often a door is opened,
and that is precisely what happened when Du Bois's first wife died: a
widower, he was free to marry a woman to which he was, by all accounts,
better suited. But this marriage also brought its unique issues, for Shirley
Graham was reputed to be a member of the Communist Party, which was
not that unusual for African American intellectuals at the time but was
a factor rapidly being deemed to be radioactive. Thus, the myth quickly
developed that the younger Graham—like Eve in the Garden—was
leading Du Bois astray down the primrose path toward the Communist
Party. Left unsaid was that the feisty Du Bois had a mind of his own, and,
in any case, reacted negatively to the rightward drift of the nation by
clinging even more fiercely to bedrock notions, which for decades had
included an appreciation for socialism.

Du Bois and Shirley Graham were brought closer together as a result of their collaboration with the Peace Information Center. Ultimately, 2.5 million individuals signed the Stockholm Peace Appeal in
the United States, no small feat in a nation then in the throes of cold
war hysteria. Atomic bombs were viewed as the "winning weapon," the
"game changer," that placed Moscow at a decided disadvantage, and the
idea that it was U.S. nationals who were in the forefront of a campaign
for their demise was difficult for Washington to swallow. Hence, the indictment pointed to the idea—but did not say explicitly—that Du Bois
and his crusaders should have registered as agents of Moscow.

Du Bois was among those stunned by the prospect of imprisonment. After all, despite his politics increasingly being out of step with that of his homeland, he remained an icon, at least in black America; but that was precisely the problem; for Du Bois's popularity was thought to be incongruent with the notion that black America in the process of gaining civil rights concessions had to be wrested away from any identification with the left. Putting him on trial, then, was consistent with the political zeitgeist.

The year of his trial, 1951, was not propitious. The nation was bogged down in war in Korea and the newly installed Communist regime in China was making noises about intervening if the forces allied with Washington strayed too close to their borders—and interests. Increasingly gaining popularity was a quaint idea: why should the United States fight Reds abroad and let them gambol at home? This did not bode well for Du Bois's ability to escape the hoosegow.

But as pessimistic as Du Bois had reason to be, even he may have been surprised by being handcuffed when reporting to court. Since he was now a venerable 83 years old and hardly a danger to the authorities—at least physically—this manacling of the patriarch of the civil rights movement was sending a loud signal to those who might be so bold (or adventurous) to trod in his footsteps.

Yet like the operation of a principle in the physical world, the action taken against Du Bois generated an opposite—and perhaps larger—counterreaction. For the United States was bombarded by a deluge of protests from around the world, particularly Africa, where he was still viewed popularly and benignly as the Father of Pan-Africanism. Moreover, the beleaguered continent was now straining on the leash of colonialism, and it was clear even to the dimmest that this form of exploitation was not long for this world. And Washington had to wonder what would be the reaction in this cold war prize if Du Bois were to be accorded a lengthy prison term. This was not only the case for Africa since Du Bois had for the longest paid critical attention to the Caribbean, traveling frequently to Haiti, Cuba, and Jamaica, particularly, and this attention paid multiple dividends when he went on trial, and his tormentors were deluged with an avalanche of protests. The same held true for parts of Europe: in the east of this continent, there was a predisposition—given cold war norms—to lend him support, while in

Western Europe there remained strong socialist and communist parties (e.g., in France and Italy particularly) that too were inclined to lend Du Bois's defense a willing hand.

But there was also a spirited protest against the proposed imprisonment of Du Bois from many African Americans—though certainly not all. Nonetheless, many had long memories, and they had yet to forget his yeoman service over the decades from challenging Booker T. Washington, to founding the NAACP, to birthing Pan-Africanism, to publishing books for the ages. Nevertheless, Du Bois was taken aback when those he had touted—the Talented Tenth—generally headed for the exits when they were asked to support him. Thus was imploded one of his earliest theses, that the touting of this well-educated sliver of the population would be the savior for black Americans generally. What Du Bois did find was that trade unions, particularly unions with sizeable black memberships, formed the bulwark of his support. The International Longshore and Warehouse Union, (the San Francisco–based stevedores); the Marine Cooks and Stewards, and Detroit's Local 600 of the United Autoworkers union all were among those who rallied to his defense. Certainly the fact that the working class did not stray from his side unlike the middle-class elements he had hailed in devising the Talented Tenth notion—this played a critical role in shaping his thinking as he surveyed the political landscape.

In his unjustly neglected book, *In Battle for Peace*, Du Bois details his cold war travail of the early 1950s.[11] In telling this gripping story of how a symbol of black America's struggles almost became a jailbird, he seems most distressed in sketching the role of the NAACP leadership who spread damaging rumors of his "guilt" as the justification for their refusal to aid his defense, which may have been the most graphic rebuke of his previous hailing of the creation of a Talented Tenth.

Actually, there were some among the Talented Tenth who did not turn their back on Du Bois. Primary among these was Paul Robeson—with degrees from Rutgers and Columbia—whose newspaper *Freedom* became an echo chamber singing the praises of Du Bois. Lorraine Hansberry, who went on to challenge Shirley Graham Du Bois's role as the preeminent Negro playwright of the 20th century, was among this journal's contributors, as well as John Oliver Killens, whose subsequent novels were among the more revealing of black life ever devised. In their

March 1951 edition *Freedom's* banner headline exclaimed, "Southern Students Defend Du Bois."

Shirley Graham's father was a pastor, and, as such, had a network of ministerial contacts that proved effective in mobilizing for Du Bois's defense. These pastors were among those who spearheaded the National Committee to Defend Dr. Du Bois and Associates in the Peace Information Center. Of course, Robeson was essential in this effort but he was joined by former Minnesota governor Elmer Benson, then a firm advocate of the Progressive Party; and the prominent novelists Dashiell Hammett (whose detective stories including the "Maltese Falcon" helped to create the genre) and Howard Fast. Also helpful to Du Bois and his codefendants were sectors of the African American press, including the *Pittsburgh Courier*, the *Philadelphia Tribune*, the *Afro-American* (which was headquartered in Baltimore), the *Oklahoma Black Dispatch*, the *Chicago Defender*, and other organs that may have been owned by the Talented Tenth but who depended for their daily bread upon readers who were more likely than not part of this grouping.

Also reflective of the fact that the Talented Tenth did not turn its back wholly upon Du Bois was the support that he received from African American attorneys. There was a trio from Washington who were critical to defense efforts—George Hayes, James Cobb, and George Parker—and since this was where the case was tried, in some ways they were more important than the quartet from New York who traveled southward for this case: Congressman Vito Marcantonio, Bernard Jaffe, Stanley Faulkner, and Gloria Agrin. Like good lawyers should, they engaged in extensive pre-trial preparation, exhaustively examining every bit of evidence. But they also knew that this was not an ordinary trial, given the political climate and the public persona of the leading defendant.

One major hurdle to leap was the apostasy of one O. John Rogge, who had become active and well-known in Du Bois's inner circle but chose to become a chief prosecution witness. Born in rural Illinois in 1903, this wunderkind had graduated from Harvard Law School at the tender age of 21 and then rocketed to further prominence when in the 1940s he was among the first to draw a link between Nazi Germany and leading conservative circles in the United States.[12] Then as chief of the Criminal Division of the U.S. Justice Department he launched fusillade after fusillade at the gathering Red Scare, lambasting the so-called loyalty program of Truman's White House, which had led to a purge from the post office to important governmental agencies. Eventually, he was to become a sharp critic not only of Du Bois but also of the doomed alleged atomic spies, Julius and Ethel Rosenberg, and other cherished figures of a rapidly diminishing left-wing movement. It was Rogge who was supposed to carry the weight of the prosecution's case, demonstrating that the Peace Information Center was little more than a Trojan Horse on Moscow's behalf but he proved to be a wholly ineffective witness.

A liability for many federal prosecutions brought in Washington was the demography of this capital, which features a significant black population that often was not in accord with the rightward drift of the nation, and this may have been even more the case in 1951, since the Jim Crow the denizens of this city had to endure put few in the mood to accept that a man they had been taught was a hero—Dr. Du Bois—was now a despised figure. Thus, the jury of 12 featured 8 African Americans, overwhelmingly from the working class, which disproportionately leaned away from conservatism.

This prosecution also was something of a test case, a controlled experiment that would shed light on the ongoing controversy that had led to a profound rift between Du Bois and the NAACP leadership in the first place. For the former had come to believe that courtroom legerdemain—or histrionics as the case might be—was the key to civil rights advance; the outsized role played on the staff by the admittedly brilliant Thurgood Marshall seemed to justify this predisposition. But Du Bois thought otherwise. First of all, as he saw it, justice was hard to find in a legal system where the deck was stacked automatically against black American defendants—not to mention defendants of the left—and, consequently, something more than legal skill was required to prevail. As Du Bois saw it, legal cases were political—just as federal prosecutors were political appointees by the party in power—and, thus, political mobilization was the critical factor in prevailing in court.

It is one thing to argue this important point in a conference room at NAACP headquarters or in a seminar room at Atlanta University but it was quite another to have a dramatization of this otherwise abstract debate in a courtroom with life and liberty on the line. As things turned out, Du Bois prevailed. After six days of hearing testimony about Du Bois and his comrades being agents of an unnamed foreign power, the judge directed a verdict in favor of the defendants, ruling in essence that the jury would not be allowed, as the saying goes, to "speculate on a speculation."

As things turned out, this was one of the few victories that obtained as the Red Scare juggernaut gathered steam. It seemed that Du Bois's preexisting celebrity, the international renown that attached to him, his spouse's multifaceted contacts among pastors, his connections to the African American press, and the fact that McCarthyism was still in its infancy in 1951, all combined to save him from a prison term, though the same destiny was not enjoyed by others (e.g., Ben Davis, the Communist City Councilman from Harlem, who found himself imprisoned in the same year that Du Bois was allowed to escape this fate).

Still, Du Bois was not sufficiently chastened by this narrow escape, for instead of retreating into a cocoon of passivity or at least lowering his voice of opposition, he returned to his small but comfortable office at the Council on African Affairs and resumed the activism on world peace and African liberation that had brought him to the brink of disaster quite recently.

There in his office in Manhattan, just north of Greenwich Village then in the throes of a cultural upsurge that was to rock the nation subsequently, he wrote lectures and articles, and carried on a wide correspondence with a broad array of figures across the world. He taught classes at the currently defunct Jefferson School of Social Science, a socialist-oriented independent school that enrolled numerous students, including the inquisitive and eager young journalist Lorraine Hansberry.

A primary task for Du Bois was raising funds for the numerous anti-colonial movements in Africa, though he tended to give priority to Kenya and South Africa. Not long after Du Bois escaped imprisonment, the British authorities then ruling in Nairobi, imposed a state of emergency against an insurgent movement known colloquially as Mau Mau, which led to mass incarceration of Africans and an increase in their mortality rates. In South Africa, in 1948—the year Du Bois was ousted from the NAACP—the authorities imposed a system of apartheid, or turbo-charged racial segregation that bordered on slavery. As in Kenya, this crackdown only led to an escalation of the insurgency, requiring more funds to be funneled abroad by Du Bois.

In his dotage, some may have viewed Du Bois as ineffectual, isolated from the main currents of his homeland, alienated from the NAACP. Yet this perception hardly coincided with the ruckus that ensued when in May 1952, Du Bois sought to cross the border into Canada for a peace conference. Ordinarily, this was a simple matter with Ottawa and Washington regularly hailing the fact that this was the longest undefended border in the world. But these were not ordinary times. So, when he and Shirley Graham arrived in Toronto they were brusquely refused entry.[13] Ultimately, the passports of Du Bois and his spouse and comrades like Robeson were snatched so that the authorities would not have to worry about being embarrassed abroad. For the global peace movement this was a real setback as they were deprived of some of their more intelligent voices. Not only did the United States not want the peace activist's voices to be heard abroad, but Washington also denied visas for international campaigners visiting America (e.g., in the case of Pablo Picasso).

Nevertheless, Du Bois was not sufficiently cowed by his indictment or such harassment to steer clear of knotty matters of foreign policy, which is why on Independence Day in July 1952 he was in sweltering and sweaty Chicago providing the keynote address at the Progressive Party convention. His remarks were spare and simple: "The platform of the Progressive Party," he exclaimed, "may be reduced to these planks: Stop the Korean War; Offer Friendship to the Soviet Union and China; Restore and Rebuild the United States."[14]

In addition to the Progressive Party, much of Du Bois's activism concerning world peace was channeled through the American Peace Crusade. As the authorities saw it, this was like the snake shedding its skin; in other words, the Peace Information Center was forced into dissolution and taking its place was the American Peace Crusade, pursuing a similar agenda. It was not long before the American Peace Crusade also began to feel the heat from Washington. In between traveling to Chicago and seeking to enter Canada, Du Bois had to take the time to respond to an incredibly detailed interrogatory from the U.S. Justice Department, which seemed as a predicate for yet another prosecution. As Washington saw it, the American Peace Crusade was just another "front" for the Communist Party, and, akin to an associative law of mathematics, this meant that it was also a "front" for Moscow, which made it a threat to national security. Demanded were the names and addresses of virtually anyone who could have been connected with the American Peace Crusade; the government's surveillance of the group was certainly a deterrent to many wanting to associate with the American Peace Crusade, because it was clear that to join the group could mean undergoing scrutiny under a government microscope. Not reassuring was the fact that the government seemed most interested in the activities of Robeson, Howard Fast, and Du Bois. Stiffening its spine, the American Peace Crusade responded stoutly that it would not respond to these inquiries, and, instead, forwarded all its public statements, resolutions, and the like. The Justice Department was not assuaged and given that the CAA was under similar pressure, it seemed that the government decided if it could not jail Du Bois, at least it could eliminate his base of operations, rendering him less effective.[15]

Du Bois found it hard to accept that in the United States in the 1950s championing peace was akin to championing Communism. This contrasted sharply with the situation elsewhere, particularly in Europe, where memories of the ravages of war remained acute, or in Japan, the first and only victim of nuclear attack, or China, where clashes with the U.S. military on the Korean peninsula were sharp. Of course, there were internal problems in this peace movement—such as it was—that government harassment could not obscure. Shirley Graham was one of the few women in the top leadership, and there was only one representative west of Iowa.

Still, when the American Peace Crusade and the CAA were driven into extinction in the mid-1950s, it was not simply the struggle for peace and the campaign against colonialism that fell victim, nor was it Du Bois only who suffered as a result. Ultimately, a message was sent that dissent was dangerous and in such an atmosphere it became easier to hatch ill-considered schemes like the war in Vietnam—which a revivified peace movement and anticolonial movement could have forestalled, thereby saving millions of lives. Unbowed, Du Bois soldiered on as the 1950s unfolded.

NOTES

1. *New Africa*, January 1949, February 1949, March 1949.
2. *New York Times*, June 17, 1950.
3. *Chicago Globe*, October 28, 1950.
4. *Soviet Russia Today*, November 1949.
5. *New York Times*, June 2, 1949.
6. *New York Times*, October 6, 1950.

7. *New York Times*, September 11, 1950.

8. *Chicago Globe*, November 25, 1950.

9. The following is based substantively on: Gerald Horne, *Race Woman: The Lives of Shirley Graham Du Bois*, New York: New York University Press, 2000.

10. *Chicago Globe*, July 15, 1950.

11. See W.E.B. Du Bois, *In Battle for Peace: The Story of My 83rd Birthday, with Comment by Shirley Graham*, New York: Masses & Mainstream, 1952.

12. See, for example, Gerald Horne, *The Color of Fascism: Lawrence Dennis, Racial Passing and the Rise of Right-Wing Extremism in the United States*, New York: New York University Press, 2007.

13. Gerald Horne, *Black & Red*, 193.

14. *National Guardian*, July 10, 1952.

15. Gerald Horne, *Black & Red*, 197.

Chapter 12

REDEMPTION

In the 1950s Du Bois could look back fruitfully on a life well spent. He had been present at the creation of the NAACP, widely hailed as the locomotive behind the epic May 17, 1954, decision by the U.S. Supreme Court in *Brown v. Board of Education* to overturn racist segregation in public education—and, by implication, in society as a whole. This was a bittersweet moment for Du Bois since it was the culmination of a lifelong dream to which he had contributed copious amounts of sweat and tears, yet, the ebullient NAACP leadership that held a press conference to hail this epochal decision dared not mention Du Bois's name for fear of being enveloped by the nation's latest custom, Red-baiting or the fear of being associated with the reviled Communists. The historic decision of *Brown v. Board* came in the midst of a cold war struggle, and the high court judges were reminded repeatedly that the nation could hardly compete effectively for hearts and minds in Africa, Asia, and Latin America as long as their descendants and relatives in this nation were being treated so atrociously: Jim Crow had to go—and it did.

Du Bois was equally ecstatic when this decision was rendered. "Many will say complete freedom and equality between black and white Americans is impossible," he said. "Perhaps; but I have seen the Impossible happen. It did happen on May 17, 1954."[1] Du Bois may have been taken aback by this decision, for just weeks before it was handed down he was addressing a New York conference where his theme was "Colonialism in Africa Means Color Line in USA." But with separate but equal legislation effectively nullified in the United States, the implication, which proved to be accurate, was that colonialism was next on the chopping block.[2]

Like a wrangler whose horse had been shot out from under him, Du Bois had to stumble along as his base of support in the CAA and APC were removed from the scene. He seemed particularly aggrieved by the liquidation of the CAA. It seemed ironic that at a time when those of African descent in the United States were celebrating a new birth of freedom, their attempt to buoy their brethren in Africa was under siege. Du Bois thought he knew why. He found it curious that the African American press did not cover African struggles more assiduously and thought it to be part of an understanding with the rulers of the United States that if they—and other Negroes—acquiesced in the exploitation of Africa, they would be rewarded accordingly.[3] Actually, at the time Du Bois was drafting these weighty words, Washington was in the process of dispatching abroad leading Negro personalities such as the journalist Carl Rowan to ports of call in India particularly to reassure that the United States was not as bad as resistance to desegregation made it seem.[4]

Du Bois had become a regular columnist for the now defunct weekly, the *National Guardian*, which was tied closely to the Progressive Party and in the wake of the profound high court decision, he may have felt that Africa, wallowing in colonial misery merited more of his attention. Thus, readers were told regularly of the difficulties faced in Ethiopia, one of the continent's few independent states;[5] the problems of Uganda;[6] the difficulties in Ghana and Nigeria;[7] the exploitation of the Congo (which has the dubious honor of being the nation that has probably suffered more than any other in the 20th century);[8] and Kenya, whose anticolonial leader, Jomo Kenyatta, he knew well.[9]

One redeeming factor was the comfortable house he now shared with his new bride, Shirley Graham. Once it had belonged to the prizewinning playwright Arthur Miller, but now this lovely Brooklyn Heights abode housed the Du Bois family. A frequent visitor was Graham's son, who took the name David Du Bois in honor of his new stepfather, and his avid interest in Africa matched that of his parents. This guaranteed that a steady stream of visitors crossed the Brooklyn Bridge from Manhattan, after campaigning at the United Nations, to seek succor at the Du Bois home. It was also at the Du Bois home that the two young children of the slain accused-then-executed atomic spies, Julius and Ethel Rosenberg, came to be enveloped in a warm embrace of friends and supporters before moving to their new home.

The Rosenberg sons recalled later the joy of espying a large Christmas tree when entering the Du Bois's home, festooned with all manner of lights and a huge mound of presents eyed expectantly by many other children. This is where they met their adoptive parents, Abe and Ann Meeropol, as no one from their mother's or father's family would dare take them in for fear of further persecution. Robert Meeropol, the Rosenbergs' son, recalled the vases and other artifacts from places like China and the Soviet Union that caught the eye in the Du Bois home.

In Brooklyn the loving couple quickly developed a comfortable routine. He arose every morning shortly before eight o'clock, shaved (he continued to maintain a lush mustache and pointed Van Dyke to his dying days), took a leisurely bath allowing his thoughts to unwind, and ambled downstairs to breakfast by nine o'clock. Despite Du Bois's feminist inclinations, Graham did almost all the cooking, and she was the one who would fix him a bourbon and ginger ale, a quite tall one with Ritz crackers and blue cheese, as the evening wound down.

It was at their Brooklyn abode that the first issue of a quarterly magazine, *Freedomways*, which was to have enormous impact on the emerging freedom movement, was unveiled. Joining them in celebration were John Oliver Killens, Ossie Davis, Alice Childress, and other artistic luminaries.

It was not good news that Du Bois's organizational anchors—groups focusing on Africa and peace—had been driven out of business. It was even less fortuitous that this had occurred when he had reached an advanced age. Yet, there was an upside to what was otherwise a dilemma for he now had considerable time to devote to writing and though the venues for his writing were often limited to precincts of the left—even some Negro organs were reluctant to share a printed page with him—he still had the opportunity to avoid total censorship and quashing of his distinct voice.

A tangible result of his prodigious labor during this difficult period was *The Black Flame: A Trilogy*.[10] Published in seriatim as *The Ordeal of Mansart, Mansart Builds a School*, and *Worlds of Color*, these often insightful volumes present Du Bois's own view of what it meant to be an African American man in the United States from 1876 to 1956. Parading across the pages are legendary figures, many of whom he knew well, appearing under their under own names: from Booker T. Washington to Franklin Delano Roosevelt; from William Monroe Trotter to Harry Hopkins (FDR's top aide); from the noted reformer Florence Kelley to Kwame Nkrumah.

Actual quotations from books, newspapers, speeches, and the likes make these three volumes an underutilized resource for those seeking to comprehend this tumultuous era. All of this is imbedded within the life of Manuel Mansart, who in many ways is a stand-in for Du Bois himself. In some ways, these volumes are just as revealing about Du Bois as it is about the era of which he writes; it tells of what Du Bois thought about himself and the world in which he lived in a more free-flowing, revealing way than his autobiographies. The first draft of these 1,100 pages was produced initially in 1955, when he was 87 years old, and, thus, provides a summary of his life and thought to that point. By the mid-1950s, Du Bois was more frail than usual, and besides, though many in this nation did not desert him, by this point his organizational base in the CAA had withered, and many had absorbed the message that to be against nuclear weapons, to advocate for world peace, was to send the message that one favored the despised foe in Moscow.

Though Du Bois remained far from wealthy, he would have enjoyed renewing his acquaintance with his ancestral homeland of Haiti or even the developing anticolonial movements in Africa. The problem was that the government had deprived him of a passport. Yet liberalizing forces were beginning to emerge that would lead to his passport being renewed by 1958. Thus, the advent of the burgeoning civil rights movement embodied by the youthful Alabama pastor, Dr. Martin Luther King, Jr., had pointed to the incipient demise of Jim Crow and resultant liberalization. In order to accuse Moscow more effectively of human rights violations, Washington had to make sure its own hands were clean—or in the process of being cleaned, more precisely. On the international scene—and not coincidentally—the death of Soviet leader, Josef Stalin helped to contribute to a developing thaw between the two superpowers, which too was a liberalizing force.

This led directly to Du Bois regaining his passport. This atmosphere also led to a sentimental journey for Du Bois that preceded his globe-trotting. For it was in 1958 that his alma mater, Fisk University, chose to honor him. But suggestive of the fact that the Red Scare had not left Fisk unaffected, it was at this same time that his alma mater—over Du Bois's stout objections—chose to dismiss a young professor of mathematics, Lee Lorch, with little pretense of due process, because of his alleged ties to the Communist Party.[11]

Thus, when Du Bois and his spouse departed by ship for Europe in 1958, it was akin to an escape, as much as a well-deserved vacation.[12] In London they encountered the impact of the Afro-Caribbean immigration on Britain when they witnessed the Nottingham Riots, an uprising against maltreatment. They stayed at the home of Paul Robeson and spent considerable time with Claudia Jones, of Trinidadian extraction, who had been deported to England after serving time in prison in the United States because of her leadership of the U.S. Communist Party.

In Holland they were besieged by reporters and photographers eager to get a close-up view of the man heralded abroad as the Father of Pan-Africanism but hounded at home for similar reasons. They arrived in Paris just in time for the pivotal 1958 elections and had a ringside seat as the bitter conflict over the colonial occupation of Algeria unfolded.

But it was in Moscow that their reception seemed boundless. They arrived in the wake of the Soviets sending Sputnik into outer space, which was a landmark for humanity but a fear-inducing event in the United States, which thought it had reason to fear a military assault from the heavens. While Du Bois had been persecuted and prosecuted by his own government, in Moscow they met for two hours with the top Soviet leader, Nikita Khrushchev. The subject of their intense discussions were the principal concerns of Du Bois—the peace movement and the movement against colonialism. The concrete result of this meeting was Moscow's decision to establish an Institute on Africa, which continues to specialize in various topics of urgent interest to the still beleaguered continent. The royal treatment they received there, compared to what they had left behind at home, contributed to the gathering idea that, perhaps, living abroad should be considered seriously.

They stayed in a charming dacha about 50 miles from Moscow in a pine forest near a lake. On New Year's Eve in 1958, Cuban revolutionaries were preparing to seize Havana. Meanwhile in Moscow, their future patrons were feting Du Bois, his spouse, and their friend, Robeson. As the clock reached midnight, the orchestra played lustily, lights blazed, and a small army of butlers approached bearing large silver trays groaning with culinary delights. World-class dancers from the Bolshoi Ballet pranced to the tunes laid down by globally recognized musicians.

Du Bois was now approaching the age of 90, and though he was still sprightly for such an advanced age, he was far from being in the best of health, and his condition did not improve when his spouse —and increasingly, his helpmate—chose to leave him in Moscow as she departed for Ghana for an important Pan-African conference. Thus, though she was gone for less than two weeks, she returned to find that Du Bois was slightly depressed and lonely. This was something new for Du Bois, whose previous marriage had been marked by lengthy periods apart but he had changed, he had evolved, and, beyond that, he was in love and alone in a strange and distant land.

Thus, from the Soviet Union they traveled together to China. Du Bois had traveled there in the 1930s but that had hardly prepared him for what he witnessed in what remains the planet's most populous nation. It was in 1949 that the Communist Party had come to power, and it was not long before this regime clashed with U.S. forces on the Korean peninsula. But now the mood was changing in the capital that came to be known as Beijing, and, ironically, the Communists there were coming into ever sharper conflict with Communists in Moscow— tensions that would be exploited adroitly by U.S. President Richard M. Nixon.

Du Bois and his spouse found time to confer with the top Chinese leader, Mao Zedong, in his lakeside villa. China was undergoing wrenching change at that precise moment as a result of Chairman Mao's purges and policies that had contributed to mass famine and massive dislocation. They visited Wuhan, a center of heavy industry, and, per usual, were feted. Du Bois was provided with a skilled nurse round-the-clock, just one aspect of how he was venerated.

Apparently, this veneration in China did not impress back home for while they were gone, their Brooklyn home was burglarized, with desks pried open, papers searched and scattered—as there was a thorough and exhaustive scrutiny of their humble abode.

But back in China even this violation seemed tolerable in light of the intoxicating treatment that he received. It seemed that Beijing, which was to compete with Moscow, in various venues over coming decades, was vying with its competitor as to who could treat Du Bois the best.

They returned to the United States but it was clear at this juncture that it made little sense to reside in a nation where the political climate was frequently hostile and unforgiving when they could be feted abroad. Thus on June 25, 1960, Du Bois and his spouse boarded a Sabena Airlines flight from New York City to Brussels, with Prague being their destination, before heading to what was the become their eventual home—Accra, Ghana.

Again, the red carpet was rolled out when Du Bois and his wife landed in Prague. They were rushed to their hotel in a comfortable automobile, and he bathed and rested for an hour, before dressing, at which point he was chauffeured to a stadium filled with cheering throngs where after being presented to Czechoslovakia's president, they witnessed an extraordinary sports festival. There were 16,000 girls in colorful attire wielding white hoops dexterously as rhythmic music blared. Their five days and nights in Prague—a city of magnificent medieval architecture, fortunately unwounded grievously by wartime bombing—was a dizzying succession of such festivities, followed by banquets, state receptions, more sport sessions, and an array of convivial gatherings.

Then it was on to Rome, then Ghana, and with every passing moment it was evident that it no longer made sense for Du Bois to continue residing in the United States. Not only was it the exquisite treatment he received, but allied to that was the kind of medical treatment he would be accorded abroad at little or no cost—no small matter for a man of his advanced age.

But for Du Bois, his departure was punctuated by a grand and dramatic gesture. For it was in 1961 that he chose to join the Communist Party, which his detractors saw as simply the validation of a continuing reality. Of course, Du Bois long had been an advocate of socialism; on the other hand, he long had looked askance at the possibility of constructing such a system in the United States—the major aim of the

Communist Party-USA—because of his skepticism as to whether white workers could ever be won over to this cause. Yet, ironically and contradictorily, when he came under assault, culminating with his handcuffing and trial in 1951, he became progressively isolated, but standing resolutely by his side were Communists, like his Brooklyn neighbors, James and Esther Cooper Jackson. She had collaborated with Du Bois's spouse in the founding of the journal, *Freedomways*, while he was a Communist Party-USA leader, who had been seeking to recruit Du Bois to his ranks for years.

Finally, in 1961 Jackson succeeded, though Du Bois then upped and moved thousands of miles away, signaling that this new affiliation was intended as abject defiance of his political foes, as much as anything else. Moreover, impending decisions by the U.S. Supreme Court made many—including Du Bois—suspect that a new era of repression was in the works: this not only made him want to move far away but to signal that there were some who would not retreat from the ranks of those who were being demonized, that is, the Communists. This was not minor for if this suspicion of repression were to materialize in a difficult reality, again Du Bois's passport could be revoked, and, again, he could find himself bereft of the expert medical treatment he could come to enjoy abroad, and which, arguably, had extended his lifespan. Above all, in discussions with Nkrumah he had agreed to embark on the crowning achievement of his lengthy life: chief editor in the production of a proposed *Encyclopedia Africana*, a definitive reference work that was designed to transform not only the view of Africans but, perhaps more importantly, how Africans viewed themselves.

It did not take an expert accountant to recognize that the ledger of assets and liabilities seemed to be in Accra's—and not New York's—favor. The scale was tipped even further when Du Bois heard that the court ruling he feared was in the pipeline. He had planned to move to Ghana in the spring of 1962 but this turn of events caused him to accelerate his timetable.

Thus, Du Bois and his wife sold their comfortable Brooklyn Heights home for a handsome $69,000—receiving about $20,500 in cash—and so armed departed in early October 1961 for their new home in Ghana.

Ghana had invited Du Bois to Accra to witness this now independent nation's accession to the Commonwealth as a republic. After land-ing in Accra, an official came on board seeking, he said, "Dr. Du Bois." Acknowledging his name, the elderly U.S. national and his spouse were then escorted from the plane, as if they were arriving dignitaries and upon poking their heads beyond the plane noticed a full military guard. Then a band began to play, officials stood waiting, and behind barricades straining as hundreds sought to get closer to the visiting couple, Du Bois was hailed as the Father of Pan-Africanism, and, in many ways, the architect of Ghana's long-awaited independence.

Du Bois was invigorated by this "rock star" treatment with his wife concluding sagely that "years . . . literally dropped" from him as a result. It was clear that self-imposed exile in Africa was the luminous destiny of this elderly couple.

Du Bois attended the opening of the first session of the Ghanaian Parliament, and looked on in awe as an African carried the mace of power in the presence of 104 parliamentarians, and drums pounded out an ancient call, as a paramount chief gowned and crowned in gold poured libations. Women danced in solemn rhythm—then, like the Red Sea parting, President Nkrumah entered robed and alone. The symbolic Golden Stool of power was unveiled, and the national anthem was sung lustily.[13]

The journey featured a festive dinner in honor of Du Bois organized by the Ghana Academy of Learning and attended by the new nation's leaders and leading academics from the Americas, including St. Clair Drake of Chicago and C.L.R. James of Trinidad and Tobago.

Du Bois did not pull punches in instructing the Ghanaians that, like himself, they should not follow Washington's cold war policies and, instead, should accept aid from any who offered—and this should not exclude, therefore, Moscow and Beijing. He may have been preaching to the converted, since stormy applause greeted every word. With every passing moment, it seemed to Du Bois that exile appeared ever more attractive.

This was nothing new for African Americans. The novelist Richard Wright had moved to Paris in the late 1940s where he spent the rest of his life. He was preceded by the chanteuse Josephine Baker, whose attachment to her new homeland was affixed when she became an honored member of the anti-Nazi resistance during World War II. The novelist James Baldwin chose exile in France and Turkey. Robeson spent years in London. The ravages of Jim Crow had chased away African American too numerous to mention, and Du Bois was no exception to this trend.

Certainly the Du Boises did not seem to suffer a precipitous drop in their standard of living, thanks in no small part to Nkrumah, who treated the couple like honored guests. They were provided a beautiful seven-room residence in Accra with many windows, situated high on a hill in the center of an acre of land. The grounds were divided, like a British estate, by hedges and blooming trees. Two scarlet flamingo trees guarded the entrance. The house had a library, a living room, a dining room, two bedrooms with private baths, a study room for Graham Du Bois, and a screened porch with netting. They had a steward, a cook, a driver, and night watchman. They had two cars, one a Soviet model and the other an English make, preferred by Du Bois's spouse, who was often seen about town chauffeuring him about. On the walls of their lovely home were richly and prettily wrought red hangings of Chinese silk and a few similarly fetching paintings. Placed strategically about their home were busts of Marx, Lenin, and Mao.

Needless to say, by Ghanaian standards, this was all quite plush. The former Gold Coast, as was typical of an African colony, had been veritably looted by the former British colonizer, and in the countryside, numerous Africans resided in mud huts with no electricity and no indoor plumbing.

The Du Bois home, perhaps because it offered amenities that even many in the United States did not enjoy, became a beacon attracting to West Africa numerous African American visitors, who—in any case—felt that a trip to this Accra estate was akin to a pilgrimage. The list quickly widened to include Southern African exiles, who knew Du Bois's name from his days with the CAA and had read about him in dusty tomes about Pan-Africanism, and Chinese diplomats who knew of him because of his many publications and his visits to their homeland.

While in Ghana, Du Bois felt compelled to make another fateful decision. He had been driven to the U.S. legation in Accra in order to have his passport renewed—but instead was subjected to a surprise decision. The authorities refused to renew his passport because under legislation, then in force, it was a crime subject to 10 years' imprisonment for a member of the Communist Party to have a passport. Du Bois faced the distinct possibility of statelessness, a man without a country. This was no superficial matter for a man whose ability to travel from underdeveloped Ghana to other nations for medical treatment was more than a theoretical concern. Consequently, Du Bois, the Father of Pan-Africanism, the man who had done more than most to paint a more realistic picture of this diverse and multifaceted continent, chose in his last days to become a citizen of an African nation: Ghana.

Thus, becoming a national of an African nation, while supervising an encyclopedia important to its future development was like a dream come true for Du Bois. He had considered the idea of developing such an encyclopedia as early as 1909, simultaneous with the formulation of the NAACP, but that commitment and a dearth of funding compelled him to drop this estimable project. Then in 1934, after departing from the NAACP, he sought to revive this admirable initiative, but, once more, it was aborted because of an ability to raise the requisite support that was needed. In 1947, back at the NAACP, he expressed further interest in launching this enterprise but—again—he failed.

Underlining the importance of liberating Africa from colonialism, it was Ghanaian independence that reanimated the idea to bring this laudable idea to fruition. Du Bois was not sufficiently spindly to be kept from drawing up an ambitious scheme to bring this project to completion. His proposed encyclopedia was focused on Africans, since at this juncture knowledge of them and their accomplishments were either shrouded or distorted, whereas virtually all European explorers, missionaries, colonial officials, and so on were to be excluded, simply because this information could be found in abundance elsewhere. The estimated length was to be a bountiful 10 million words and was to touch on arts, politics, economics, and agriculture from prehistory to the present. With his usual optimism, the 93-year-old Du Bois acknowledged that he was embarking on a mission that would last at least a decade—if not longer—but undeterred, he pushed on. The budget called for a then hefty $43,000 to be expended in the first year with a sharp rise to $74,600 by the fourth. Du Bois fully intended to have the first volume in hand by 1970.

Du Bois's final burst of inventiveness and ingenuity was to be done in conjunction with the University of Ghana. He reached out to scholars across the globe. Early on he contacted Eric Williams, the leading historian and founding father of modern Trinidad and Tobago; eventual

Nobel laureate and favorite son of St. Lucia, W. Arthur Lewis; noted Kenyan paleontologist L.B.S. Leakey; progressive scholar-journalist Cedric Belfrage; British philosopher Bertrand Russell; and the Academy of Sciences in the major European powers, including Lisbon, Rome, and Madrid. The leading Africanist Kenneth Dike of the university at Ibadan, Nigeria, signed on, as did Jamal Mohammad Ahmed, Sudan's Ambassador in Ethiopia, and various other academics from Ivory Coast, France, and Germany.

A zenith in transnational intellectual cooperation occurred in late December 1962 when over 500 participants gathered at the University of Ghana in support of the encyclopedia's aims. There were participants from China, Brazil, Australia, and, of course, Africa. Press coverage was substantial, and Du Bois's own unique role was highlighted. But the fact was that his energy was ebbing rapidly, and, it is possible that the often intense heat of Accra was notably enervating.

For even before this important meeting at the University of Ghana, medical specialists from the Soviet Union and Romania traveled to Accra to provide treatment to him. Then he was transported to University College Hospital in London because of a prostate problem and remained there and in Switzerland for a considerable period convalescing as his doctors prescribed. It was there that he had time to confer with Charles Chaplin, the famed actor who too was in exile because of reasons not unlike that which had driven Du Bois away from the United States

Yet, Du Bois's time was up. As the heralded March on Washington was launched in late August 1963—a manifestation that was to emblazon Martin Luther King's name into history for all time—symbolically, his predecessor as leader of black America, expired in Accra, Ghana. Du Bois was accorded the equivalent of a state funeral, with soldiers at attention and masses weeping. As he was lowered into his final resting place in Accra—now the site of one of his adopted nation's top tourist attractions—his widow wobbled visibly as the tears she shed seemed to weaken her composure.

He had lived a fruitful 95 years in a life that had spanned the zenith of Reconstruction to the onset of Jim Crow's demise. Throughout this time, he had pursued various paths and utilized various tools— scholarship, political activism, Pan-Africanism, Black Nationalism,

Marxism—on behalf of the liberation of Africa and African Americans. Though by the time he passed away, he was hardly hailed in the land of his birth, it is no accident that today he is recognized as one of the most prolific and protean intellectuals and skilled political activists that this nation as a whole and black America in particular has produced. Yet, sadly, as happens all too often, Du Bois's redemption has arrived long since he was placed in his grave.

NOTES

1. *National Guardian*, May 31, 1954.

2. *Freedom*, April-May 1954.

3. *National Guardian*, February 14, 1955.

4. Gerald Horne, *The End of Empires: African-Americans and India*, Philadelphia: Temple University Press, 2008.

5. *National Guardian*, February 21, 1955.

6. *National Guardian*, March 14, 1955.

7. *National Guardian*, March 21, 1955.

8. *National Guardian*, March 28, 1955.

9. *National Guardian*, 4 April 1955.

10. W.E.B. Du Bois, *The Black Flame: A Trilogy*, New York: Mainstream, 1957–1961.

11. Gerald Horne, *Black & Red*, 218–219.

12. The following pages are based upon the account presented in Gerald Horne, *Race Woman*, passim.

13. This description and much of what follows is taken from Gerald Horne, *Black & Red*, passim.

SELECTED BIBLIOGRAPHY

Alridge, Derrick P., *The Educational Thought of W.E.B. Du Bois: An Intellectual History*, New York: Teachers College Press, 2008.

Andrews, William L., ed., *Critical Essays on W.E.B. Du Bois*, Boston: G. K. Hall, 1985.

Aptheker, Herbert, compiler. *Annotated Bibliography of the Published Writings of W.E.B. Du Bois*. Millwood, NY: Kraus-Thomson, 1973.

Aptheker, Herbert, ed., *The Correspondence of W.E.B. Du Bois, Volume I, Selections, 1877–1934*, Amherst: University of Massachusetts Press, 1973.

Aptheker, Herbert, ed., *The Correspondence of W.E.B. Du Bois, Volume II, Selections, 1934–1944*, Amherst: University of Massachusetts Press, 1976.

Aptheker, Herbert, ed., *The Correspondence of W.E.B. Du Bois, Volume III, Selections, 1944–1963*, Amherst: University of Massachusetts Press, 1978.

Aptheker, Herbert, ed., *Selections from Phylon* (Writings of W.E.B. Du Bois), Millwood, NY: Kraus-Thomson, 1980.

Aptheker, Herbert, ed., *Contributions by W.E.B. Du Bois in Government Publications and Proceedings*, Millwood, NY: Kraus-Thomson, 1980.

Aptheker, Herbert, ed., *Prayers for Dark People* (Writings of W.E.B. Du Bois), Amherst: University of Massachusetts Press, 1980.

Aptheker, Herbert, ed., *Selections from the Brownies' Book* (Writings of W.E.B. Du Bois), Millwood, NY: Kraus-Thomson, 1980.

Aptheker, Herbert, ed., *Writings by W.E.B. Du Bois in Non-Periodical Literature Edited by Others*, Millwood, NY: Kraus-Thomson, 1982.

Aptheker, Herbert, ed., *Writings by W.E.B. Du Bois in Periodicals Edited by Others*, Millwood, NY: Kraus-Thomson, 1982.

Aptheker, Herbert, ed., *Selections from the Crisis* (Writings of W.E.B. Du Bois), Millwood, NY: Kraus-Thomson, 1983.

Aptheker, Herbert, ed., *Against Racism: Unpublished Essays, Papers, Addresses, 1887–1961* (Writings of W.E.B. Du Bois), Amherst: University of Massachusetts Press, 1985.

Aptheker, Herbert, ed., *Creative Writings by W.E.B. Du Bois: A Pageant, Poems, Short Stories and Playlets*, White Plains, NY: Kraus-Thomson, 1985.

Aptheker, Herbert, ed., *Selections from the Horizon,* (Writings of W.E.B. Du Bois), White Plains, NY: Kraus-Thomson, 1985.

Aptheker, Herbert, ed., *Pamphlets and Leaflets* (Writings of W.E.B. Du Bois), White Plains, NY: Kraus-Thomson, 1986.

Aptheker, Herbert, ed., *Newspapers Columns* (Writings of W.E.B. Du Bois), White Plains, NY: Kraus-Thomson, 1986.

Aptheker, Herbert, *The Literary Legacy of W.E.B. Du Bois*, White Plains, NY: Kraus International, 1989.

Aptheker, Herbert, ed., *The Education of Black People: Ten Critiques, 1906–1960,* (Writings of W.E.B. Du Bois), New York: Monthly Review Press, 2001.

Balaji, Murali, *The Professor and the Pupil: The Politics of W.E.B. Du Bois and Paul Robeson*, New York: Nation Books, 2007.

Bell, Bernard, et al., eds., *W.E.B. Du Bois on Race and Culture: Philosophy, Politics and Poetics*, New York: Routledge, 1996.

Benjamin, Playthell, et al., *Reconsidering "The Souls of Black Folk": Thoughts on the Groundbreaking Classic Work of W.E.B. Du Bois*, Philadelphia: Running Press, 2002.

Blum, Edward J., *W.E.B. Du Bois: American Prophet*, Philadelphia: University of Pennsylvania Press, 2007.

Byerman, Keith, *Seizing the Word: History, Art and Self in the Work of W.E.B. Du Bois*, Athens: University of Georgia Press, 1994.

Carroll, Rebecca, *Saving the Race: Conversations about Du Bois from a Collective Memoir of Souls*, New York: Broadway, 2004.

Clarke, John Henrik, et al., eds., *Black Titan: W.E.B. Du Bois*, Boston: Beacon Press, 1970.

Conyers, James, ed., *Reevaluating the Pan-Africanism of W.E.B. Du Bois and Marcus Garvey: Escapist Fantasy or Relevant Reality*, Lewiston, NY: Edwin Mellen, 2005.

Dennis, Rutledge M., ed., *W.E.B. Du Bois: The Scholar as Activist*, Greenwich, CT: JAI Press, 1996.

Dickerson, Vanessa D., *Dark Victorians*, Urbana: University of Illinois Press, 2008.

Driver, Edwin D. and Green, Dan S., ed., *W.E.B. Du Bois on Sociology and the Black Community*, Chicago: University of Chicago Press, 1978.

Du Bois, Shirley Graham, *His Day is Marching On: A Memoir of W.E.B. Du Bois*, Philadelphia: Lippincott, 1971.

Du Bois, W.E.B., *The Suppression of the African Slave Trade to the United States of America, 1638–1870; Harvard Historical Series Number 1*, New York: Longmans, 1896; reissued, New York: The Social Science Press, 1954.

Du Bois, W.E.B., *The Philadelphia Negro: A Social Study: Publications of the University of Pennsylvania: Series In Political Economy and Public Law*, New York: Shocken, 1967.

Du Bois, W.E.B., *The Souls of Black Folk: Essays and Sketches*, Chicago: A. C. McClurg, 1903.

Du Bois, W.E.B., *John Brown*, Philadelphia: Jacobs, 1909.

Du Bois, W.E.B., *The Quest of the Silver Fleece: A Novel*, Chicago: A. C. McClurg, 1911.

Du Bois, W.E.B., *The Negro*, New York: Henry Holt, 1915.

Du Bois, W.E.B., *Darkwater: Voices from Within the Veil*, New York: Harcourt, Brace, 1921.

Du Bois, W.E.B., *The Gift of Black Folk: Negroes in the Making of America*, Boston: Stratford, 1924.

Du Bois, W.E.B., *Dark Princess: A Romance*, New York: Harcourt, Brace, 1928.

Du Bois, W.E.B., *Africa, Its Geography, People and Products*, Girard, KS: Haldeman-Julius, 1930.

Du Bois, W.E.B., *Africa—Its Place in Modern History*, Girard, KS: Haldeman-Julius, 1930.

Du Bois, W.E.B., *Black Reconstruction in America: An Essay Toward a History of the Part which Black Folk Played in the Attempt to Reconstruct Democracy in America, 1860–1880*, New York: Harcourt, Brace, 1935.

Du Bois, W.E.B., *Black Folk Then and Now: An Essay in the History and Sociology of the Negro Race*, New York: Henry Holt, 1939.

Du Bois, W.E.B., *Dusk of Dawn: An Essay Toward an Autobiography of a Race Concept*, New York: Harcourt, Brace, 1940.

Du Bois, W.E.B., *Color and Democracy: Colonies and Peace*, New York: Harcourt, Brace, 1945.

Du Bois, W.E.B., *The World and Africa: An Inquiry into the Part which Africa has Played in World History*, New York: Viking, 1947.

Du Bois, W.E.B., *In Battle for Peace: The Story of my 83rd Birthday, with Comment by Shirley Graham*, New York: Masses & Mainstream, 1952.

Du Bois, W.E.B., *The Black Flame: A Trilogy: Book One: The Ordeal of Mansart*, New York: Mainstream, 1957; *Book Two: Mansart Builds a School*, New York: Mainstream, 1959; *Book Three: Worlds of Color*, New York: Mainstream, 1961.

Du Bois, W.E.B., *An ABC of Color: Selections from Over a Half Century of the Writings of W.E.B. Du Bois*, Berlin: Seven Seas, 1963.

Du Bois, W.E.B., *The Autobiography of W.E.B. Du Bois: A Soliloquy on Viewing My Life from the Last Decade of Its First Century*, New York: International, 1968.

Fontenot, Chester J., and Keller, Mary, eds., *Recognizing W.E.B. Du Bois in the Twenty-first Century: Essays on W.E.B. Du Bois*, Macon, GA: Mercer University Press, 2007.

Gabbidon, Shaun L., *W.E.B. Du Bois and Crime and Justice: Laying the Foundations of Sociological Criminology*, Aldershot, England: Ashgate, 2007.

Gillman, Susan, and Weinbaum, Alys, eds., *Next to the Color Line: Gender, Sexuality and W.E.B. Du Bois*, Minneapolis: University of Minnesota Press, 2007.

Golden, L. O., et al., eds., *William Du Bois: Scholar, Humanitarian, Freedom Fighter*, Moscow: Novotsi, 1971.

Guterl, Matthew, *The Color of Race in America, 1900–1940*, Cambridge, MA: Harvard University Press, 2001.

Horne, Gerald, *Black and Red: W.E.B. Du Bois and the Afro-American Response to the Cold War, 1944–1963*, Albany: State University of New York Press, 1986.

Horne, Gerald, *Communist Front? The Civil Rights Congress, 1946–1956*, London: Associated University Presses, 1988.

Horne, Gerald, *Black Liberation/Red Scare: Ben Davis and the Communist Party*, Newark: University of Delaware Press, 1994.

Horne, Gerald, *Race Woman: The Lives of Shirley Graham Du Bois*, New York: New York University Press, 2000.

Horne, Gerald, ed., *W.E.B. Du Bois: An Encyclopedia*, Westport, CT: Greenwood, 2001.

Horne, Gerald, *Race War! White Supremacy and the Japanese Attack on the British Empire*, New York: New York University Press, 2003.

Horne, Gerald, *Black and Brown: African-Americans and the Mexican Revolution, 1910–1920*, New York: New York University Press, 2005.

Horne, Gerald, *The End of Empires: African-Americans and India*, Philadelphia: Temple University Press, 2008.

Hubbard, Dolan, ed., *"The Souls of Black Folk" One Hundred Years Later*, Columbia: University of Missouri Press, 2003.

Johnson, Brian, *W.E.B. Du Bois: Toward Agnosticism*, Lanham, MD: Rowman & Littlefield, 2008.

Juguo, Zhang, *W.E.B. Du Bois: The Quest for the Abolition of the Color Line*, New York: Routledge, 2001.

Kirschke, Amy Helene, *Art in Crisis: W.E.B. Du Bois and the Struggle for African-American Identity and Memory*, Bloomington: Indiana University Press, 2007.

Kostelanetz, Richard, *Politics in the African-American Novel: James Weldon Johnson, W.E.B. Du Bois, Richard Wright and Ralph Ellison*, New York: Greenwood, 1991.

Levander, Caroline Field, *Cradle of Liberty: Race, the Child and National Belonging from Thomas Jefferson to W.E.B. Du Bois*, Durham, NC: Duke University Press, 2006.

Lewis, David Levering, *W.E.B. Du Bois: Biography of a Race, 1868–1919*, New York: Henry Holt, 1993.

Lewis, David Levering, ed., *W.E.B. Du Bois: A Reader*, New York: Henry Holt, 1995.

Lewis, David Levering, *W.E.B. Du Bois: The Fight for Equality and the American Century, 1919–1963*, New York: Henry Holt, 2000.

Logan, Rayford W., ed., *W.E.B. Du Bois: A Profile*, New York: Hill and Wang, 1971.

Marable, Manning, *W.E.B. Du Bois: Black Radical Democrat*, Boulder, CO: Paradigm, 2005.

Moon, Henry Lee, ed., *The Emerging Thought of W.E.B. Du Bois: Essays and Editorials from the Crisis*, New York: Simon and Schuster, 1972.

Moore, Jack B., *W.E.B. Du Bois*, Boston: Twayne, 1981.

Moore, Jacqueline M., *Booker T. Washington, W.E.B. Du Bois and the Struggle for Racial Uplift*, Wilmington, DE: SR Books, 2003.

Morgan, Mary Alice, et al., eds., *W.E.B. Du Bois and Race: Essays Celebrating the Centennial Publication of "The Souls of Black Folk,"* Macon, GA: Mercer University Press, 2001.

Posnock, Ross, *Color & Culture: Black Writers and the Making of the Modern Intellectual*, Cambridge, MA: Harvard University Press, 1998.

Provenzo, Eugene F., ed., *Du Bois on Education*, Lanham, MD: Rowman & Littlefield, 2002.

Rabaka, Reiland, *Africana Critical Theory: Reconstructing the Black Radical Tradition, from W.E.B. Du Bois and C.L.R. James to Frantz Fanon and Amilcar Cabral*, Lanham, MD: Lexington, 2009.

Rampersad, Arnold, *The Art and Imagination of W.E.B. Du Bois*, Cambridge, MA: Harvard University Press, 1976.

Rudwick, Elliott M. *W.E.B. Du Bois, Propagandist of the Negro Protest*, New York: Atheneum, 1968.

Smith, Shawn Michelle, *Photography on the Color Line: W.E.B. Du Bois, Race and Visual Culture*, Durham, NC: Duke University Press, 2004.

Sterne, Emma Gelders, *His Was the Voice: The Life of W.E.B. Du Bois*, New York: Crowell-Collier Press, 1971.

Stull, Bradford T. *Amid the Fall, Dreaming of Eden: Du Bois, King, Malcolm X and Emancipatory Composition*, Carbondale: Southern Illinois University Press, 1999.

Watson, Cathryn, and Mullen, Bill V. , eds., *W.E.B. Du Bois on Asia: Crossing the World Color Line*, Jackson: University Press of Mississippi, 2005.

Weinberg, Meyer, ed., *W.E.B. Du Bois: A Reader*, New York: Harper & Row, 1970.

Williams, Yohuru, et al., eds., *"The Souls of Black Folk": Centennial Reflections*, Trenton, NJ: Africa World Press, 2004.

Wolfenstein, E. Victor, *A Gift of the Spirit: Reading "The Souls of Black Folk,"* Ithaca, NY: Cornell University Press, 2007.

Wolters, Raymond, *Du Bois and His Rivals*, Columbia: University of Missouri Press, 2002.

Young, Alford, et al., *The Souls of W.E.B. Du Bois*, Boulder, CO: Paradigm, 2006.

Young, Jason, and Blum, Edward J. *The Souls of W.E.B. Du Bois: New Essays and Reflections*, Macon, GA: Mercer University Press, 2009.

Zamir, Shamoon, ed., *The Cambridge Companion to W.E.B. Du Bois*, New York: Cambridge University Press, 2008.

Zamir, Shamoon, *Dark Voices: W.E.B. Du Bois and American Thought, 1888–1903*, Chicago: University of Chicago Press, 1995.

Zuberi, Tukufu, and Anderson, Elijah, eds., *The Study of African American Problems: W.E.B. Du Bois's Agenda, Then and Now*, Thousand Oaks, CA: Sage, 2000.

Zuckerman, Phil, *Du Bois on Religion*, Walnut Creek, CA: AltaMira, 2000.

Zumwalt, Rosemary Levy, and Willis, William Shedrick, *Franz Boas and W.E.B. Du Bois at Atlanta University, 1906*, Philadelphia: American Philosophical Society, 2008.

INDEX

About the Author

DR. GERALD HORNE holds the John J. and Rebecca Moores Chair of History and African American Studies at the University of Houston. In some two dozen works, he has addressed racism in the contexts of labor, politics, international relations, and war. Professor Horne's books include *The End of Empires: African-Americans and India* (Temple University Press, 2008), *The Final Victim of the Blacklist: John Howard Lawson, Dean of the Hollywood Ten* (University of California Press, 2005), *Black & Brown: Africans and the Mexican Revolution, 1910–1920* (New York University Press, 2005), *Race War! White Supremacy & the Japanese Attack on the British Empire* (New York University Press, 2003), *Race Woman: The Lives of Shirley Graham Du Bois* (New York University Press, 2000), and *Black & Red: W.E.B. Du Bois & the Afro-American Response to the Cold War, 1944–1963* (State University of New York Press, 1985).